A Resurgent Northeast

Celebrating
30 Years of Publishing
in India

Praise for the book

'Ashish Kundra's *A Resurgent Northeast* offers an intricate exposition of the region's history, politics, people and growth brought together by an author who possesses a broad insider's perspective. His detailed account of the efforts, achievements and gaps in the governance and development of the Northeast presents not just the story thus far, but also the opportunities and challenges that lie ahead.'

—**Shashi Tharoor**, author and Member of Parliament

'Ashish Kundra's book is an affectionate and empathetic study of the past, present and possible future of the region known as the "Northeast". The narrative ranges widely over the terrains of history, economics, ecology and sociology. There are incisive portraits of farmers, scientists, officials and entrepreneurs. The author offers a series of constructive suggestions on how best to assure livelihood security and cultural self-respect to the citizens of these states. Gracefully written as well as judiciously argued, the book deserves a wide readership.'

—**Ramachandra Guha**, historian and writer

'The wealth of knowledge, awareness and experience of Northeast India that Ashish Kundra brings to his writing is unique and unparalleled. This book is a moveable feast, a mindscape to carry wherever we go.'

—**Nirupama Rao**, former foreign secretary and ambassador of India.

'Ashish Kundra is a rare thinking bureaucrat, whose arguments about the Northeast must be seriously grappled and engaged with.'

—**Basharat Peer**, author and journalist

A Resurgent Northeast

NARRATIVES OF CHANGE

Ashish Kundra

HarperCollins *Publishers* India

First published in India by HarperCollins *Publishers* 2023
4th Floor, Tower A, Building No. 10, DLF Cyber City,
DLF Phase II, Gurugram, Haryana – 122002
www.harpercollins.co.in

2 4 6 8 10 9 7 5 3 1

P-ISBN: 978-93-5699-056-2
E-ISBN: 978-93-5699-048-7

Typeset in 11.5/15.2 Adobe Garamond at
Manipal Technologies Limited, Manipal

Printed and bound at
Nutech Print Services - India

FSC
www.fsc.org
MIX
Paper from responsible sources
FSC® C143748

This book is printed on FSC® certified paper
which ensures responsible forest management.

For
Ambreen

Contents

Foreword ix
Introduction xiii

1. Nehru's Misplaced Utopia 1
2. The Lost Decades 14
3. Connectivity: The Silver Bullet 23
4. A Bridge to the Far East 33
5. Rivers that Light 47
6. In Search of Shangri La 61
7. Fruit Bowl of India 75
8. Education to Enterprise 89
9. A Sporting Nation 103
10. 'Akha': Hope for Good Health 115
11. The Better Half of the Northeast 129
12. The Governance Challenge 140
13. Change with Continuity 153

Acknowledgements 165
Notes 167
Index 195

Foreword

A COUPLE OF years ago, Ashish Kundra brought up the subject of writing a book on Northeast India. By then, he had finished three stints as a civil servant in the region—two in Mizoram and one in Arunachal Pradesh. Unlike most officers who work in these parts, he demonstrated a genuine affection and empathy for our people. His understanding of the complexity, diversity and challenges of this part of India was not that of an armchair bureaucrat, but someone who travelled to the remotest corners of the state. I encouraged Ashish to write this book, which will serve as an inspiration for other civil servants who get posted in this region—by choice or by chance. *A Resurgent Northeast: Narratives of Change* makes for a brilliant read. It is as much a personal narration by an officer, as it is a beautiful prose of the unfolding dynamics of change.

For most part of independent India's existence, its Northeast has lived in the shadows of the mainland. Geographical isolation, compounded by a deep emotional chasm, left our people alienated from the rest of India. My late father, a former chief minister of Arunachal Pradesh, would often share his angst at the apathy and political neglect handed down by successive regimes in the Central government. The stepmotherly treatment left a whole generation of Northeasterners scarred. Decades of violence in Assam, Manipur, Mizoram and Nagaland created fissures, which took time to heal. The Northeast also faced the brunt of the wars with Bangladesh and China. In fact, Arunachal Pradesh was the theatre of the 1962 war with China. It is only now that we are emerging out of the dark corner that defined our existence. This book, therefore, comes at an opportune time.

Winds of change have swept the mountains and valleys of the eight states that make up this region. Peace prevails in most parts. The last decade has been a transformational period. For the first time, we see a genuine effort by the Central government to bridge the development deficit. During his address at the golden jubilee of North Eastern Council this year, Prime Minister Narendra Modi called the eight states 'Ashta Lakshmi', while spelling out his vision of an eightfold path for their development. Massive doses of infrastructure investments are visible in tangible gains. The quality of this infrastructure—roads, bridges and airports—are comparable now with the best examples in the rest of India. Stalled hydropower projects have gathered momentum and are firmly on track of implementation. Aspirational youth are no longer reticent and are buzzing with a new spirit of enterprise. Connectivity has opened new opportunities for eco-tourism and agri-economy. This is a story that deserves to be shared with the rest of the world.

This book gives a panoramic view of the changing landscape of the Northeast states. It chronicles elements of continuity that persist in the new dynamic of change. Ashish has worked in this region for a long time and has brought forward a unique perspective from the lens of an outsider. For the people of the states where he served, he was always one of them. This book will be of immense value to policymakers and academics across India and abroad, who have an interest in the changes unfolding in this region. The beautiful narration makes it an easy read for any curious reader. For those who live in the Northeast, it offers a peek into the transformation in their neighbouring states, where they are unlikely to have travelled to.

The author has also brought out useful prescriptions on what should be done to make the Act East policy an actionable agenda for the region. While underscoring the immense opportunities in horticulture, tourism and sports, there is a touch of realism. Challenges of capacities in governance and the festering legacy problems in some parts of the region pose real risks.

The effective response by the Indian armed forces during the recent skirmish with the Chinese Army at Yangtse in Arunachal Pradesh mirrors the resolves of the new Northeast. However, it also brings out the fact that this region has a difficult neighbourhood, which necessitates a strong security architecture. The people of the Northeast have a strong nationalistic fervour, which makes them partners of the Indian Army in protection of remote borders.

It was a privilege to read this book, which embodies the rare view of an officer's mind while serving in a challenging terrain. It is a fitting tribute to the unique genius of the people of Northeast India.

Pema Khandu, 2023
Chief Minister, Arunachal Pradesh

Introduction

GABRIEL GARCÍA MÁRQUEZ chose his Nobel Prize acceptance speech to make a statement before the world. Standing before a global audience, he mocked the Western construct that led to 'The solitude of Latin America'. He argued that,

> It is only natural that they insist on measuring us with the yardstick that they use for themselves, forgetting that the ravages of life are not the same for all, and that the quest for identity is just as arduous and bloody as it was for them. The interpretation of our reality through patterns not our own serves only to make us even more unknown, ever less free, ever more solitary.[1]

Marquez's impassioned speech shone the light on a flawed European perception of Latin American reality. Had he been born in India's Northeast, his speech would have followed a similar script, except that he would have pointed a finger at mainland India.

The idea of this book germinated in my head from a dismal self-acknowledgement of my ignorance about the most beautiful part of our country. Twenty years ago, a civil service quirk landed me in Mizoram. Much younger and far less travelled then, for me it was nothing short of a cultural shock. In the crowded Bara Bazaar of Aizawl, I discovered a new reality. Apart from the evident dissimilarity in physical appearances, an air of distinctiveness was palpable. Women dominated the marketplace and even the usually staid civil secretariat wore a feminine look. The egalitarian society stood out in sharp contrast to the class divide, which I was so accustomed to in north India. Drivers, maids, cooks ate at the same table as their wealthy employers. People changed roles seamlessly. A chief minister listening respectfully to the sermon of a church elder on Sunday could be the elder's boss on Monday. The sense of community in Mizoram has no parallel in the mainland. All Mizos, young and old, are members of the all-powerful Young Mizo Association (YMA), which serves as the glue which binds their society. In joy and sorrow, in sickness and health, in victory and defeat, the community rallies behind the individual. Politeness is a highly valued cultural trait, unlike the more familiar Punjabi rambunctiousness. Along the highway, one would find shops without shopkeepers. Neatly packed vegetable bundles with prices affixed on top were left unattended for the convenience of passers-by. This cultural contrast sparked a curiosity in my mind, overlying the burden of guilt of ignorance. I also sensed a mistrust, bordering on disdain, for the people of the plains. The reasons behind that mistrust lies buried in the pages of their lived history. A generation of Mizos had faced the brunt of repression at the hands of the Indian Army, deployed to quell an insurgent movement. Grouping of villages along the roadside to cut off supply lines to insurgents was deployed as a conscious military strategy. A sense of loss and being uprooted from their homes lingers in the minds of Mizo people. A small incident in Silchar, barely a few hours away, was enough to rile the YMA to call for a 'vai' (pejorative phrase for 'the outsider') bandh. The only exception in the written communique was the governor of the state.

After an interregnum of two decades, I got posted to Mizoram again in 2018, just after an enriching two-year tenure in Arunachal Pradesh. This time, I sensed a new vibe. There is a buzz in the region. An aspirational new generation riding on the power of social media is scripting change. Better air connectivity and improved roads have transformed the landscape of opportunity. Aizawl wears a brand-new look. People are warm and friendly. The undercurrent of hostility is a thing of the past. My experience in Arunachal Pradesh, once called the 'Hidden Land', was even more delightful. Entrepreneurial people in a remote hinterland are experimenting with a new kind of agriculture—growing exotic crops like kiwis and blueberries. The highways in the eastern part of the state could delude you into believing that you are driving through a European setting. The rapturous beauty of this pristine land has no parallel, even by Himalayan standards. I made most of my time exploring and learning, criss-crossing the two states, and pushing my own boundaries in this borderland. My love for nature has made me travel across all the states in the Northeast, and I marvel at its remarkable cultural diversity. The Northeast is indeed a unique cultural melting pot.

For far too long have the people of this region remained an enigma for the world. Conflict and ethnic violence spanning over decades had blurred our minds, dissuading even the diehard explorers. A new drama is unfolding in the hills and valleys of the east. The new kids on the block are inheritors of a painful past. They are hungry for development and are in a hurry to make up for lost time. An air of restlessness hangs heavy over the blue mountains. Let us begin by setting a context to the people who inhabit this remote borderland.

'The Northeast', as we refer to in common parlance, is no more than an administrative construct. Apart from capturing its geographical setting, the term does no justice to its profound ethnic diversity. Only those who have lived in these parts of the country would appreciate the enormous differences in language, culture and history. Dutch scholar Willem van Schendel gave the region a more exotic name: 'Zomia'—majestic highlands straddling the Tibetan plateau, Myanmar, parts of China and Southeast Asia.[2] This land has been the crucible of an unusual human migration spanning over centuries, such as the Ahoms, who ruled the Brahmaputra Valley and came from upper Myanmar and western Yunnan. Tribal folklore in the region is replete with multiple narratives describing arduous peregrinations across diverse lands. The Garos of Meghalaya claim ancestry to the Tibetan plateau. The Mizos believe the source of their inception is in the mountains of China. The Khamtis of Arunachal Pradesh draw their lineage from the Tai-Shan people of modern Thailand and Myanmar.[3] Zomia was also the hub of flourishing trade, transacted along the Southern Silk Road. Over millennia, it witnessed a confluence of ideas, culture and commerce. British trade records bear testimony to a thriving trade flow between Tibet, Bhutan and Assam on the one side, and with Burma and China on the other. The Mon-Yul corridor, passing through Tsona Dzong and Tawang, was the shortest route between Tibet and Assam.[4] A Burmese travelogue by H.L. Jenkins, dating back to 1869–70, records that merchants visiting Assam carried back large quantities of opium, which would ultimately reach China.[5] The Indic civilization was alien to the people of this region, who shared greater affinity with residents of China, Thailand, Myanmar and Vietnam. People in the Northeast lived by the dictum of 'Act East', well before such wisdom dawned upon the political leadership of independent India. The historical fact of a distinct ethnicity, coupled with peculiar geography, lies at the heart of understanding the complexity of development in the Northeast.

The Imperial embrace had excluded this region for a significant time. The chance discovery of tea in Assam and the British fascination for the morning brew saw a spurt in European investments. 'Coolies' from the Chhotanagpur–Santhal territory, reckoned ethnically more suited for hardy labour, were brought in to work on the plantations. A large number of them, lured by the abundance of cultivable land, stayed back even after their contracts expired.[6] This was the first wave of non-indigenous migrants who made Assam their home. The non-indigenous population in the Brahmaputra Valley galloped from a mere 6 per cent in 1872 to nearly 25 per cent by the turn of the century.[7] The seeds of discontent around identity, at the heart of current political discourse, were sown in the British tea plantations.

The discovery of oil stoked imperial ambitions and the British gaze shifted towards the hills. There were frequent skirmishes, plunder and killings as the hill tribes swooped down the plains. Residing in inaccessible terrain, these 'runaway fugitives' escaped the tyranny of an intrusive state to reside in 'shatter zones or zones of refuge'.[8]

For the first time, hill tribes came in contact with an alien mode of administration, monetary system and political control, which militated against the tribal way of life revolving around clan, community and forest. Growing British administration in the region was accompanied by the proselytizing influence of Christian missionaries. Colonial administration and the missionaries worked in unison: the former focusing on nuts and bolts of administration, the latter shouldering responsibilities of education, healthcare and spirituality. The Welsh-Calvinists expended their energy in Lushai hills (present-day Mizoram) and Khasi-Jaintia Hills (Meghalaya), while the American Baptists centred around Assam Valley and the Naga Hills. The missionaries endeavoured to 'civilize' the natives through active social engagement. The accusation of Marquez against the Europeans would have resonated in the heart of the Northeast tribals.

True to their grain, British rulers created ingenious instruments of administration that served their enlightened self-interest. The tea plantations had to be protected from the 'savage tribes', even as the missionaries laboured to 'civilize' them. Through an act of cartographic wizardry, they divided the region by conjuring an imaginary 'Inner Line'. An Imperial firmaan dictated that movement beyond the line by British subjects or foreign residents would need a licence.[9] The ostensible logic was an act of benevolence towards the hill tribes. The real rationale was quite the converse: to protect British plantations and extractive industry from the ravaging tribes. The isolation of the hill tribes was then complete. The British administration viewed the hills only as a strategic frontier. So little was their initial interest that they were caught unawares during the Anglo–Burmese hostilities in the nineteenth century. Navigating their way into the hostile territory, they encountered the headhunting Nagas. Ultimately, it was the Nagas who fought alongside the British during the Second World War to stave off a strong Japanese onslaught, supported by Subhas Chandra Bose's Indian National Army. The Battle of Kohima has been called the 'Stalingrad of the East' by war historians.[10] In a way, this 'forgotten battle' underscores the ambivalence of the hill tribes towards British India.

In the shadow of the flickering flame of British Raj, an Imperial dream of resurrecting a Crown colony took shape. The Reid Coupland Plan, backed by Robert Reid, the governor of Assam, and Reginald Coupland, an Oxford historian, advocated that the Mongoloid block bordering India and Burma belonged to neither nation and needed to be converted to a Crown colony to afford a 'protection period of respite' to enable them to 'develop on their own lines without outside influence'.[11] It proposed to combine large parts of what now constitutes India's Northeast with adjoining areas in Burma, converting the territory into a Crown colony.[12] Reid's secretary on tribal affairs, James Mills, cited the examples of

Basutoland, Swaziland and Bechuanaland in Africa as a measure to afford protection against exploitation.[13] The plan remained a figment of fertile academic imagination, born in the hallowed portals of Oxford. Unintentionally, it contributed to a heightened sense of psychological isolation amongst the hill people.

Ultimately, the partition of India created a new entity: India's northeast. Trapped in an effective cul-de-sac, it retained only a tenuous link with the mainland through a 'chicken's neck' corridor. Hastily drawn lines divided people and their lands. The Northeast was bequeathed a difficult neighbourhood: East Pakistan, Burma and China. Road linkages were snapped overnight, as were riverine routes. Meghalaya and Tripura, which had enjoyed unfettered access to the Bengal plains, now stood isolated with a new nation in between. Manipur and Mizoram no longer had access to the Irrawaddy basin.[14] Ninety-nine per cent of the geographical boundary of the new region marks international borders. Yet, boundaries on a map seldom find resonance in the jungles and mountains of the Northeast. People in Mizoram, Manipur and Nagaland still retain ethnic ties with people of Myanmar. No wonder, the coup in Myanmar in 2021 saw a spontaneous expression of solidarity in the Northeast. Chief Minister Zoramthanga went to the extent of giving an assurance on the floor of the state assembly to provide assistance to civilians fleeing the military regime.[15] This magnanimity was replicated for Kuki-Chin refugees fleeing the crackdown by Bangladesh army in 2022. In his days as an insurgent, Zoramthanga had taken refuge in Arakan hills in a 'James Bond type escape' to reach East Pakistan.[16] Perhaps for him, it is an act of reciprocity.

While the rest of India rejoiced in their new-found independence, the people in the Northeast were left with mixed feelings. New borders had ruptured old ties. New Delhi was too distant and too unknown. In the decades that followed, the feeling of isolation was accompanied by a perception of neglect. An understanding of the present-day Northeast would be incomplete without a peep into its past. The narrative of this book starts with an assessment of the vision of India's first prime minister, Jawaharlal Nehru, which became the policy lodestar for times to come. His utopian view of the region gave him the conviction that its people should be allowed to develop according to their own genius. Unlike the British, independent India should abjure from imposing its own sense of civilization on this pristine land. This philosophical approach in a way became an impediment for any modernizing influence. The decades that followed saw an eruption of violent unrest. Students led the charge in Assam while the hills were ablaze with ethnic strife. Nagaland and Mizoram raised a banner of rebellion, claiming that they were wrongfully subsumed in the Indian Union. For people in the mainland, the Northeast became a dark zone of conflict. The Indian state started viewing the volatile situation as a serious threat to internal security with ramifications for external security as well. What followed was a set of iron laws and a deeply militarized territory. Like all conflict zones, the armed forces were viewed as the enemy, representing a hostile Indian state. The tyranny of geography was compounded by a deep emotional chasm. Youngsters trying to escape the abyss—in search of opportunities in the mainland—were left disappointed. Racial slurs such as 'chinki' and being typecast as drug users or easy women added insult to injury. This reinforced the angst against the mainland.

However, something changed at the turn of the century. A new generation that was connected with the world felt exasperated by the lack of development. This more educated and confident generation sought to engage with the rest on an equal footing. The idea of India and an Indian identity is now firmly established in the minds of people. The ideological underpinnings of insurgent movements went adrift, as extortion and corruption took over. New Delhi offered an olive branch, with a generous infusion of resources. 'Act East' became the mantra for connecting the Northeast with a growing Southeast Asian market. The most crucial change, however, has been the dramatic improvement in physical connectivity with the mainland as well as within the region itself. Mobility of people has increased and they are easily travelling out of the region. Sanjoy Hazarika's *Strangers of the Mist* are truly strangers no more.[17]

In the chapters that follow, I have tried to capture the unfolding saga of change in this part of the world. The Northeast is the final frontier that remained aloof in the Indian growth story, which started three decades ago. One can smell the winds of change blowing across the hills and valleys. The new Northeast is set to become a key node of dynamic change. Peace, the underlying condition for development, now prevails in most parts of it. A spirit of enterprise has fired the imagination of its youth. Start-ups are mushrooming in diverse spaces across the Northeast. Farmers in the region are waking up to the immense possibilities of their fertile land. People are now opening up to welcome tourists from around the world. Hydropower potential, which has so far remained trapped in controversy, is finally delivering on its promise. Trade across the borders can become a harbinger of economic change. Hardy youth of the region are winning laurels for the nation in the sporting arena—from football and boxing to weightlifting. Women of the Northeast deserve a special mention, given their unique contribution, which has no parallel elsewhere. Political leadership is under pressure to deliver tangible results.

But some risks remain, which could upset the applecart. The menace of drugs and the burden of cancer are debilitating their society. Normalization of corruption is a disturbing reality. The excessive dependence on the Central government dole is not a sustainable proposition. Vexed boundary issues persist within the region, especially on the borders of Assam. Issues of identity, which were central to the political firmament of the twentieth century, remain unresolved. A slight spark is enough to inflame passions, especially on the issue of 'foreigners'. Technology and the internet boom have reinvented cultural idioms. Young women in Aizawl style themselves along chic Korean designs. The hills of Shillong, Itanagar and Kohima reverberate with catchy K-pop. An evident 'Easternization' of society is underway.

People of the frontier have an air of distinctiveness that sets them apart from the mainland. Their stories often go unnoticed, their voices unheard in the narrative of the mainstream. They are often misunderstood or misjudged. It is precisely for this reason that someone needs to share a slice of their lives with the rest of the world.

This book carries a personal perspective of an outsider who got a unique opportunity to work in two Northeast states—Arunachal Pradesh and Mizoram—across different spans of time. Along the way, I got to admire the strength and fortitude of a remarkable people and their ability to deal with loss and injustice in a spirit of reconciliation. In many ways, their coming to terms holds a parallel to the transition in postapartheid South Africa, where Nelson Mandela gave moral strength to its people to imbibe a spirit of forgiveness. I struck friendships in the Northeast that have endured the test of time. This is the new Northeast, which is a break from its bleak past. I do not claim scholarship or authority on the subject. The complexity and diversity of this region cannot be captured in a single volume. At its heart, this book is my tribute to the amazing grace of a forgotten people of this beautiful land.

1

Nehru's Misplaced Utopia

Stone Walls do not a Prison make.
Nor Iron bars a Cage;
Minds innocent and quiet take
That for an Hermitage.
If I have freedom in my Love,
And in my soul am free,
Angels alone that soar above,
Enjoy such Liberty.[1]

—Richard Lovelace, 'To Althea, from Prison'

A NEW NATION was born on 15 August 1947. The British midwife had ruthlessly undertaken a painful and violent delivery. Millions of people were torn asunder, coming to terms with their new homeland. Old relationships snapped overnight, and new anxieties took over. Freedom ushered in a social upheaval for independent India. The least prepared were the people of Zomia, who found themselves as inhabitants of the nation's eastern frontier. Prime Minister Nehru acknowledged,

> ... those frontier areas were not (so) psychologically prepared (for various changes in India). In fact, they were prepared the other way by British officers or sometimes by missionaries who were there.[2]

Communal fires raged as millions crossed over from East Pakistan into the region. People in the plains of Assam and Tripura found themselves in the eye of the storm. A wave of insecurity swept the Northeast. Fear of 'being a minority in their own state, insecurity from loss of land to outsiders and insecurity of losing ethno-cultural identity'[3] drowned all voices of sanity. Issues of identity, language and land dominated the political discourse. Then chief minister of Assam, Gopinath Bordoloi, shot off a fervent missive to the then home minister, Sardar Patel,

> If Assam is to continue as part of India it must be allowed to exercise the power of restricting the ingress of people not only for avoiding an economic breakdown but also maintaining communal harmony.[4]

Unlike the western borders, movement across borders in India's northeast was unregulated. The Immigrants (Expulsion from Assam) Act, 1950, was promulgated for removal of all immigrants, except displaced persons, whose stay was detrimental to the interest of the general public in India or any scheduled tribe in Assam.[5] The law seemingly drew an unstated distinction between Hindu refugees from Pakistan and illegal Muslim migrants who came searching for jobs.

The architecture of governance for the Northeast had to acknowledge its cultural diversity. The hill tribes feared assimilation and cultural annihilation. Bordoloi resonated this apprehension in a report, stating, 'the sudden disruption of the tribal customs and ways by exposure to the impact of a more complicated and sophisticated manner of life is capable of doing great harm'.[6] The constituent assembly saw a wide-ranging discussion on the subject. K.M. Munshi was not in favour of 'isolated communities or little Republics to be perpetuated forever'.[7] There were Cassandras of doom like Rohini Kumar Chaudhari, who feared that as a result of such isolationism, 'they will combine with Tibet, they will combine with Burma, they will never combine with the rest of India.'[8] Dr Bhimrao Ambedkar nuanced his approach by drawing a distinction between the tribes of the mainland and those of Assam,

> The tribal people in areas other than Assam are more or less Hinduised, more or less assimilated with the civilization and culture of the majority of the people in whose midst they live. With regard to the tribals of Assam, that is not the case. Their laws of inheritance, their laws on marriage ... are quite different from that of Hindus. I think that is the main distinction that influenced us to have a different sort of scheme for Assam from the one we provided for other territories.[9]

In this backdrop, the institutions of autonomous district councils found place in the sixth schedule of the constitution. The councils were accorded autonomy in matters of culture, customary law and land ownership. These political enclaves carved out within states served as pressure valves for venting ambitions. In due course, some of these councils became full-fledged states, leading to a clamour for others to be notified as councils.

In the midst of these tumultuous changes, ethnic discontent simmered across the region. The Nagas leaned upon the Crown-colony plan to assert that they were never part of India. Angami Zapu Phizo, the idealogue of the Naga movement, felt that, 'we shared our house with the British and when they vacated, the whole house has become ours once more'.[10] A prominent obelisk bearing an unequivocal assertion that 'Nagas are not Indians' stands to this day in his village Khonoma. In June 1947, the governor of Assam, Akbar Hydari, thrashed out a nine-point agreement with the Naga National Council, drawing the contours of executive and legislative autonomy. Phizo conducted a plebiscite in May 1951 'to avoid any possible injury that may otherwise be done to the reputation of India, in the event of a plebiscite held under international auspices'.[11] Two years later, Nehru visited Kohima with Burmese Premier U-Nu. A Naga delegation sought time to submit a memorandum, but was refrained from doing so by the deputy commissioner. This riled the Nagas, who walked out of Nehru's public rally. He took this as a personal affront and never returned to the state. Phizo announced the establishment of the 'Naga central government' in 1956. The Naga movement saw the emergence of divergent approaches—a moderate group advocated political resolution, while a more strident militant group insisted upon independence. An overground political leadership competed for influence with the underground struggle. The insurgents sought refuge and arms from China and Pakistan, then referred to as the 'Pindi–Peking axis'. Naga Hills-Tuensang Area was made an autonomous district under the Governor of Assam in 1957, a precursor to full statehood in December 1963. Several rounds of peace talks were held at the highest levels of government, which became a classic game of snakes and ladders. The National Socialist Council of Nagaland's (NSCN) demand for a separate flag and constitution continues unabated even after seven decades of independence. A Framework Agreement signed by Narendra Modi government with the NSCN in August 2015 recognized the 'unique history and position' of Nagas, suggesting 'an enduring inclusive new relationship of peaceful coexistence of two entities' by 'sharing the sovereign power as defined in the competencies' inscribed in the Constitution.[12] The last word on the matter is yet to be written, as the stalemate continues.

On 15 August 1950, as the nation marked its third anniversary of independence, tragedy struck the Northeast. A massive earthquake of 8.6 magnitude shook its remotest corner—the North-East Frontier Agency (NEFA). Fifteen hundred people lost their lives and thousands of villages were inundated in Upper Assam. This cataclysmic event marked a 'significant juncture' in the evolution of Assam.[13] Dibrugarh, its commercial hub, witnessed the greatest devastation. Industrial activity was destroyed and vital communication was snapped. The nation woke up to the existence of its 'Cinderella' province. Assam, which had been on the fringes of national discourse, suddenly caught national attention. Generous humanitarian aid poured in. Pandit Nehru in a letter to all the chief ministers of India wrote, 'The earthquake has not only shaken up the surface of the earth in Upper Assam, but has changed the physical features of that area. It is said that some hills have disappeared and rivers have changed course.'[14] A region, hitherto outside the gaze of government authorities, suddenly became the cynosure of sympathetic attention.

Another storm brewed on the western front of NEFA. Major Bob Khathing, a Tangkhul Naga, along with a motley crew of Assam Rifles, audaciously took formal possession of Tawang, after a fortnight's foot march. This happened just a few months before the Chinese 'Liberation' Army captured Lhasa in September 1951.[15] The residents of Tawang stopped paying taxes to Lhasa and the kingdom became a part of NEFA. Even today, China lays claim to modern-day Arunachal Pradesh (the successor of NEFA), calling it 'Zangnan', referring to it as 'South Tibet'. China's Ministry of Civil Affairs 'standardized' the names of fifteen places in Zangnan in Mandarin. That, of course, met with a strong response from India's Ministry of External Affairs.

Governing an unruly frontier and engaging with a distinctive set of people posed a challenge. In the words of Nehru, 'The frontier breeds a rather different type of people from those who live away from the frontier. My own predilection is for the mountains than for the plains, for the hill folk than the plains people. I would prefer being a nomad in the hills to being a member of the stock exchange.'[16] The conundrum in his mind becomes apparent further, when he goes on to say, 'I find that so far we have approached the tribal people in one of two ways. One might be called the anthropological approach in which we treat them as museum specimens. The other approach is one of ignoring the fact that they are something different and of attempting forcibly to absorb them into normal process of social life. I have no doubt that, if normal factors were to be allowed to operate, unscrupulous people from outside would take possession of tribal lands. We must give them a measure of protection in their areas so that no outsider can take possession of their lands or forests or interfere with them in any way except with their consent and goodwill.'[17] He fretted about the impact of modernity on the cultural fabric of the region and felt that 'The tribal structure of these primitive people is something more than a mere form. It is the very texture of their lives and we break it up at our own peril. It will break, of course, but this must come more through their own agencies, helped by us, than a thing from outside.'[18]

Nehru leaned upon the Oxford-educated anthropologist Verrier Elwin for support. He was appointed Advisor for Tribal Affairs. Elwin had arrived in India 'as an act of reparation'.[19] A poet at heart, Elwin began his affair with India as a missionary, immersing himself in the tribal world of central India, where he worked for over two decades. NEFA became the crucible for testing the ideas of Elwin, which became foundational to Nehru's approach for tribal development across India. His magnum opus, *A Philosophy for NEFA*, became the gospel for development in the Northeast. Nehru lent his heft behind the publication by writing its foreword: 'I agree not only with the broad philosophy and approach of Verrier Elwin, but with his specific proposals as to how we should deal with these fellow countrymen.'[20]

He amplified his own perspective in the second edition of the book by expounding five guiding principles. These came to be called 'Panchsheel' for tribal development:[21]

1. People should develop along the lines of their own genius and we should avoid imposing anything on them. We should try to encourage in every way their own traditional arts and culture.
2. Tribal rights in land and forests should be respected.
3. We should try to train and build a team of their own people to do the work of administration and development. Some technical personnel from outside will no doubt be needed, especially in the beginning. But we should avoid introducing too many outsiders in tribal territory.
4. We should not over-administer these areas or overwhelm them with a multiplicity of schemes. We should rather work through, and not in rivalry to, their own social and cultural institutions.
5. We should judge results, not by statistics or the amount of money spent, but by the quality of human character that is evolved.

Preservation of cultural heritage and protection of customary rights on land and forest were sacrosanct. A light touch administration was advocated. Gopinath Bordoloi and Akbar Hydari envisaged administrative 'integration' of the hills and the plains of Assam. Assamese officers were sent to the hills and tribal people of the hills to the plains of Assam.[22] T.N. Kaul, joint secretary in the Ministry of External Affairs, who was Nehru's confidant, sought to transplant the experience of the USSR in dealing with minorities. He proposed the creation of a separate cadre of officers, largely drawn from defence services, who would dedicate their lives to the tribal cause. That is how the Indian Frontier Administrative Service (IFAS) came into existence, though it was short-lived. Nari Rustomji, who served as Assam's Commissioner of Hills felt that 'the officers of NEFA prior to the constitution of IFAS were, many of them, rough diamonds, lacking in the graces, but they fitted in with the landscape and were content to remain part of it until the end of their service. They came to be known to the tribal people more intimately than the birds of passage of the new cadre.'[23] Rustomji was in sync with Elwin's approach and saw that 'much of the beauty of living still survives in these remote and distant hills, where song and dance are a vital part of everyday living, where people speak and think freely, without fear of restraint. Our workers must ensure, therefore, that the good that is inherent in the institutions of the hill people is not tainted or substituted by practices that may be "modern" or "advanced", but are totally unsuited to their economy and way of thinking.'[24] He rued the scarcity of selfless officers 'marooned in solitary outposts, days and sometimes weeks away from headquarters, the murmur of the trees and the rushing of the hill streams the only solace to their isolation—it is a life which few have been able to bear with patience and equanimity … we move on, training more teachers to carry onward the torch of light, with our agricultural officers spreading in the mountains, the knowledge of terraced cultivation and our engineers building roads and bridle paths to help the hillmen bring the produce to the centres of trade.'[25]

A secret note, prepared by T.N. Kaul for Nehru, acknowledged the good work of missionaries in education and medical care, but cautioned about 'narrow-minded missionary culture, as distinct from Christian culture'. Drawing parallels with the Chinese experience, Kaul argued that the activities of foreign missionaries should be shut forthwith.[26] In NEFA, missionary activity had been negligible and Kaul advocated the establishment of social organizations like Ramakrishna Mission, Gandhi Sewak Sangh and Sarvodaya Samaj 'to send carefully selected workers to go and live among the tribes and make it their life long mission to work among and with them'.[27] Ramakrishna Mission moved into NEFA and established the largest referral hospital in the capital, laying a solid foundation for education in the state.

A committee headed by Elwin concluded in 1960 that 'there is a new sense of integration with India as a whole ... suspicions of the outside world, doubts about the intentions of the government have disappeared or are disappearing rapidly among the tribals'. In the same breath, it also talked of 'unsuitable schemes' foisted from above. The gravest problem highlighted by the committee was tribal poverty, lack of land and poor connectivity which hampered marketing of agricultural produce.[28]

The audacious Chinese incursion through NEFA in 1962 saw a severe critique of Elwin's approach. Some argued that isolationism led to Indian decimation. Rustomji mused, 'The rapid success of the Chinese in moving from the frontier practically up to the Assam plains was for us and more specially for the tribals a traumatic experience and there arose a feeling in some sections of the country that this would not have been possible if our policy vis-à-vis the tribal people had been more realistic and not concentrated so much on "hastening slowly". There was an outcry against Elwin for allegedly misguiding the Prime Minister into believing that there should be no interference in the tribals' way of life.'[29]

Elwin himself in due course refined his thinking, with the wisdom of hindsight. Confessing in his autobiography, *The Tribal World of Verrier Elwin,* he wrote, 'Although in the earlier years, I had thought in terms of *preserving* tribal culture, I came later to think in a less static way.' He concluded, 'whether we like it or not, whether they like it or not, they are going to be civilized.' In this book, he overturned the original Nehruvian Panchsheel, arguing that:

1. Their land should be guaranteed to them and alienation stopped.
2. Their rights in the forest should be respected and a new attitude developed by forest authorities towards them.
3. Problem of indebtedness should be solved without delay, partly by legislation and partly by intensification of the cooperative movement.
4. The problem of industrialization of the tribal areas must be regarded much more seriously and that where they are dispossessed of their land and settled elsewhere, intelligent generous measures be taken to compensate them.
5. The long isolation of the tribes should come to an end, that they should be welcomed everywhere with warm affection and on equal terms and should be given every opportunity of public service.

Cautioning against creating a sense of entitlement, he wrote, 'We must fight the danger of pauperization, the creation of special class called "tribal" which will want to be labelled as backward in order to get material benefits from the government. Unintelligent benevolence can be as great a danger as intelligent exploitation.'[30] His words went unheeded in the years that followed, and a web of patronage was woven under the benign gaze of Raisina Hill.

A region that was the laboratory of his romantic ideal became a theatre of war, which left Nehru heartbroken after 1962. It was a dream turned sour. The Nehru–Elwin approach, in retrospect, comes across as a well-intentioned but failed experiment. The two critical objectives—preservation of tribal culture and protection of tribal rights on land and forests—could not be achieved. Cultural heritage has all but vanished, barring remote hinterlands, where life still revolves around traditional mores. The die is cast and change is irreversible. Christian missionaries were great disruptors of culture. In his report 'New Deal for Tribal India', Elwin himself reflects that,

> The attitude of some missionaries has been completely destructive of the tribal culture. To them everything which is not Christian is "heathen" and some of the finest aspects of tribal life have been abandoned. Dance and song, even the weaving of lovely textiles and the traditional tribal institutions have perished before their intolerance. The tribals have been taught to despise their past and as a result a strong inferiority complex has been created ... the idea that the converts are "saved" and all non-converts "damned" has tended to create a feeling of separateness from the rest of their country.[31]

Rustomji, while reflecting on Elwin's legacy, remarked,

> It was Verrier Elwin's dream that the tribal people should shine bright as a paradise of beauty and loveliness, unspoilt by the raucous dissonance of rock and roll and the fashion displays of *Playboy* and *Vogue*. He rightly opposed the temptation to move too fast. What Elwin did not foresee was that the mere physical isolation of the tribal people would no longer be of much avail in shielding them from alien cultural influences ... television and VCR had not yet come to be accepted as part of the pattern of tribal life. Television has resulted in breakdown of geographical barriers.[32]

Ironically, the tribes of central India, the learning grounds of Elwin, have significantly retained their tribal ethos, much more than those in the Northeast.

Land, the most emotive issue of all, remains an intractable problem even now. Land ownership in the hills follows customary law, and no formal land records have been prepared. Ruling political elites end up claiming vast tracts of land in the name of their kin. Inner line regulations prohibit sale of land to outsiders, and that has afforded a degree of protection. Boundaries between Assam and neighbouring hill states still remain unsettled and become a frequent cause of local skirmishes along the foothills of Mizoram, Nagaland and Arunachal Pradesh.

The policy on forests also had serious infirmities. The tribals who formerly held the forests as sacred were brought at the mercy of the forest department. Traditional rights of the tribals were no longer recognized. From 'rights and privileges', they became 'rights and concessions'.[33] An exploitative relationship between tribals and contractors emerged. Elwin himself remarked that, 'The contractor has become a law unto himself; he has a pull with the officers in the Department: the tribesman, who seldom knows the rules, is at his mercy. The contractor may give him work or he may refuse it; he interprets the rules in his own way. The contract system has operated as an undisguised monopoly in the last ten years.'[34]

Large-scale destruction of forest land followed for decades till the Supreme Court stepped in and banned all felling of trees in a landmark judgment in the 'Godavarman case'.

Gradualism also meant a slower pace of economic development. The leaders of the Northeast had appealed for greater financial autonomy, given the disadvantage of geography imposed by Partition. They argued for retaining 75 per cent of excise duty on tea and petroleum to the producing states.[35] Assam unsuccessfully lobbied for the establishment of a refinery. Crude oil from the state was pumped a distance of 1,500 km to Bihar.[36] In the anxiety to preserve tribal culture, connectivity and economic development of the region became major casualties.

Nehru's radio broadcast to the nation in the aftermath of the Chinese assault had a devastating impact. His words 'my heart goes out to the people of Assam' anguished people of the state who felt abandoned by an ungrateful nation. A sense of alienation vis-à-vis New Delhi seeped in. It may not be judicious to cast the entire blame on Nehru's shoulders. Rustomji, reflecting on that dark hour, felt, 'It is my conviction, however, that it was mainly on account of our not having infringed upon the tribals' right in their land and forest that they have remained loyal to the country, despite the fact that we had failed to protect them during their time of need.'[37] A mixed denouement of Elwin divides the critics. Purists regard Elwin as a tribal messiah, who ensured that their heritage is not trampled by the quick march of civilization. Rustomji described Elwin as the 'Socratic gad-fly that kept the bureaucracy on its toes not by virtue of any administrative powers, for he was not vested with any such, but by virtue of his selfless example and self-evident care and compassion for the tribal people.'[38] Some homegrown sociologists such as G.S. Ghurye were scathing in their assessment. He dismissed Elwin as a 'no changer' who wished to see the 'aborigines' reinstated to their old tribal ways.[39] History has always been a harsh judge of leaders seeking greatness. In 1964, both Nehru and Elwin passed on within a few months of each other, carrying the unfulfilled dreams in their hearts to the other world.

2

The Lost Decades

MY FIRST BRUSH with Mizoram in 2002 instilled mixed feelings about the place. Here was a set of people who were polite and dignified and yet aloof. There was an unmistakable animosity against outsiders. It felt as if I were trespassing upon a sacred grove. The slightest provocation could have grave consequences. A squabble in Bara Bazaar or a fight in the neighbouring district of Silchar was met with a firm reprisal by the Young Mizo Association (YMA). The sense of solidarity in their close-knit community has no parallel in India. The Assamese were viewed with suspicion. The Chakmas, living in the southernmost fringe of the state, were labelled as 'foreigners', even though they had a separate autonomous district council under the Constitution.

The roots of this disaffection lie in the tumultuous events of the 1960s. In 1959, a freak phenomenon of nature, bamboo flowering—'Mautam', led to a proliferation of the rodent population. The flower apparently boosts the virility of rats, who ran amuck in Mizo farms, devouring all crops. Mizoram plunged into a severe famine. Assam dithered in providing timely relief. The seeds of Mizo rebellion against the Indian state were sown in the barren fields of the blue mountains. In 1966, the Mizo National Front (MNF), led by Laldenga, unilaterally 'absolved' Mizoram from 'allegiance to India and its Parliament'. Invoking the Bible, MNF army launched Operation Jericho, assuming complete control of Aizawl. In a sharp reprisal, the Indian Air Force planes bombed Aizawl. The Indian Army, led by an unflinching General Sam Manekshaw, adopted an unusual military tactic—grouping of villages along the roadside. The idea behind the move was to isolate the insurgents and cut off supplies. But it ended up uprooting people from their ancestral lands, which had been their home for centuries. The Indian Army became the symbol of the nation and the target of ire of an anguished people. The psychological impact of military action and the repression that accompanied it scarred a whole generation of Mizos. Violence gripped the hills for two decades till the Peace Accord was signed in 1986 and Mizoram was accorded full statehood. Laldenga became its first chief minister. The Mizo Accord stands out as a unique example of a political resolution to a seemingly intractable challenge. People who have lived through those traumatic times choose not to talk about it even now as it opens up old wounds.

The Northeast, apart from Bengal, is the only part of India that underwent the trauma of Partition twice. On both occasions, there was a massive influx of immigrants. At the time of independence, Sylhet became part of East Pakistan. This led to a cultural assertion by the Assamese, virtually turning their traditional rivalry with the Bengalis into hostility. Politics revolved around the axes of xenophobia, language and identity. The legislature passed a law prescribing Assamese as the official language of the state. This also riled the hill tribes, apart from the Bengalis, who had their own distinctive languages. The creation of Bangladesh in 1971 brought a second rush of Bengali Hindus to Assam and Tripura, severely altering the demography. Tribals, once a majority in Tripura, were reduced to less than a third of the population. A sudden alienation of land, autonomy and culture was a natural consequence.[1] The ascendancy of the left in Tripura was an outcome of a movement to restore tribal rights and language.

In the words of Sanjib Baruah, the identity politics of the Northeast is a result of its treatment as a 'settlement frontier'. He draws a parallel between the Northeast and North-West Frontier Province of Pakistan.[2] The Northeast bore the brunt of sustained immigration in three waves: first at the time of Partition, second during the 1965 Indo–Pakistan war and third during the 1971 war. The 'settlement frontier' logic also applied to the rehabilitation of the Chakmas, who were displaced from the Chittagong Hills tract after construction of the Kaptai Dam. This Buddhist community first crossed the Karnaphuli river into Mizoram, but sensing hostility from the Mizos, they were moved by the Assam government to NEFA. P.N. Luthra, advisor to the governor of Assam, felt that 'settlement of [these] people in NEFA will also help in developing the pockets that are lying unused and unoccupied … Besides, the presence of stretches of vacant land along the border is strategically not desirable.'[3] This was a reflection of the prevailing mainland view of the region.

The North East Areas (Reorganization) Act, 1971, granted statehood to Meghalaya, Manipur and Tripura, and new union territories of Arunachal Pradesh and Mizoram were carved out of Assam. Ethnicity, not language, formed the basis of this reorganization, unlike elsewhere in the country. Sanjib Baruah describes this political process as an effort to create a 'cosmetically federal order'.[4] It was a feeble attempt to contain a rebellion that threatened the very idea of nationhood. Geographically small entities with a limited resource base had limited economic prospects.

In 1972, a restructured Northeast also saw the establishment of the North Eastern Council (NEC), headquartered at Shillong. Balmiki Prasad Singh, a former Union home secretary, described the creation of new states and the birth of the NEC as 'twins born out of a new vision for the North East'.[5] Prime Minister Indira Gandhi, in her inaugural address to the NEC, said, 'In addition to the economic and social problems, the north-eastern region is important to the country, because of its strategic situation. The strength and development of this area are of utmost importance. The primary purpose of the Council is the development of the region. It is not a super government. It is an advisory not a supervisory body.'[6] She underscored the need for a coherent regional perspective, especially in 'sectors such as transport and communications, power, marketing, institutional financing, training, in which a regional approach would be most welcome'.[7] Unfortunately, the NEC never rose to the occasion and became a venting forum for chief ministers and governors of the region, who present a laundry list of demands before central leadership in an annual ritualistic meeting.

Rustomji, the first chief secretary of Meghalaya, felt disappointed by the deep disconnect between the lofty aspiration and murky reality that came with statehood. Efforts to garner funds from the Centre had the sole purpose of spending, with utter disregard to their usefulness for people.[8] The nouveau elite believed in conspicuous consumption and an extravagant lifestyle, far removed from the impoverished reality of the tribal world. Now they had no one but themselves to blame for their travails.

Assam, a shadow of its glorious past, suffered a loss of pride on its truncated status. Sudden influx from across the borders accentuated apprehensions of cultural annihilation. The Chief Election Commissioner, Sham Lal Shakdher, while addressing election officials, kicked up a tempest by highlighting an 'alarming situation in some states, especially in the northeastern region, wherefrom disturbing reports are coming regarding large scale inclusion of foreign nationals in electoral rolls'.[9] Anti-immigrant sentiment reared its ugly head yet again. The All Assam Students Union (AASU) called for a state-wide strike in 1979. It marked the beginning of a six-year-long movement in Assam. Educated elites wove a narrative of economic exploitation by 'outsiders', while being equally complicit in perpetuating it.[10] The army was called in to break an oil blockade that had lasted over eleven months.[11] New Delhi suspected the 'foreign hand' of the Rashtriya Swayamsevak Sangh (RSS) in fomenting trouble. The RSS viewed Bengali Hindus from Bangladesh as refugees, as against Muslim infiltrators who were sought to be deported.[12] Tripura saw the worst outbreak of riots between tribals and non-tribals in 1980, which left 1,300 people dead as per official figures, though unofficial reports suggested the numbers to be nearly 50,000.[13]

A piqued Indira Gandhi upbraided the leaders,

> The agitation in Assam and other parts of the region and the killings in Tripura have caused much disquiet. India is known for traditions of hospitality and goodwill as also our willingness over centuries to assimilate all that is good. The agitators unfortunately have not understood this vital ingredient of our national genius. How much economic loss the Assam agitation has caused to itself and to the nation … it is ironical that there should be scarcity of petroleum products in the north-east.[14]

The 1980s was a gory decade for Assam. Bomb blasts, killings and destruction of public property culminated in the Nellie massacre, which left 1,200 people dead.[15] The panorama of bloodshed forced the hand of Prime Minister Rajiv Gandhi to ink the Assam Accord in 1985, which assured deportment of post-1971 immigrants in the region. It also held out a promise of preservation of cultural and linguistic heritage and protection of tribal land. Fresh elections threw up a new political formation: the Asom Gana Parishad (AGP), which struggled to fulfil the hopes ignited by the Accord.

In the meantime, the Bodos, plain tribals of Assam, decried 'Assamese chauvinism', terming the AGP government as 'deadly anti-tribal and repressive'.[16] Student activists failed miserably as political leaders. A waning AGP saw the rise of the United Liberation Front of Assam (ULFA). A series of extortions and kidnappings followed, bringing industrial activity to a grinding halt. The ULFA projected the Centre as a 'neocolonial power' vis-à-vis Assam. It held a grouse against the Centre for deprivation of Assam's legitimate share in oil and gas resources. Alleging industrial neglect and an unfair allocation of resources for economic development, the ULFA made economic underdevelopment as its central theme for raising arms.[17] Obnoxious sums of money were demanded from tea companies, as high as Rs 10 million in the case of MacNeil.[18] Even state-owned enterprises were not spared. Oil and Natural Gas Corporation (ONGC) officials, civil servants and foreign nationals were abducted with impunity.[19] Operations Bajrang and Rhino, launched by the Indian Army, weakened the ULFA and led to surrenders by some of its leaders, amidst charges of human rights abuse. By 1992, the ULFA ceased to be an awe-inspiring organization, but its sway over the political discourse continued through the 1990s. Violence had shattered the industrial dream of Assam. The Assam Accord, unlike the Mizo Accord, failed to achieve peace in the state. Some cadres of the ULFA, who gave up arms after a generous package, created a new organization: Surrendered ULFA (SULFA). Over a six-year period from 1991 to 1997, there were a series of killings of ULFA cadres by the state-backed SULFA. These 'secret killings of Assam' continued till the turn of the century.

The situation in Nagaland did not improve with statehood. The Shillong Accord of 1975 proposed a phased approach to peace, a precondition being that the Nagas accept the Indian Constitution and surrender arms, while formulating issues for 'final settlement'. The Accord was rejected by a strident underground. The NSCN was formed in 1980, and its ideology was a blend of Baptist Christianity, Maoism and Naga nationalism. Their goal is to establish Nagalim, which would subsume Naga-inhabited areas of other states in Northeast India and northern Burma. Over the years, the NSCN has split into two factions—one led by Issac Muivah (IM) and the other by S.S. Khaplang (K). The Government of the People's Republic of Nagaland (GPRN), a government-in-exile, was established, which reached out to United Nations Human Rights Council in Geneva and the Unrepresented Nations and Peoples Organization in the Hague.[20] This became a rallying force in an intricate web of insurgents spanning across the borders. Its manifesto referred to pouring of financial resources as 'wild money', creating a class of 'reactionary traitors, bureaucrats and Indian vermin'.[21] Naga government servants started paying regular taxes to the underground movement and GPRN. Widespread corruption thrived on an unholy nexus among politicians, bureaucrats, contractors and insurgents, paralysing any meaningful development.

Manipur simmered. The People's Liberation Army of Manipur (PLA) and People's Revolutionary Party of Kangleipak (PREPAK) inflamed passions in Imphal Valley. Manipur was declared a disturbed area in 1980, bringing it under the ambit of the Armed Forces Special Powers Act (AFSPA), along with Assam and Manipur. Smuggling of arms and narcotics across porous borders funded insurgency. Throughout the five decades of the twentieth century post-independence, New Delhi viewed the Northeast from a security lens, to manage what Sanjib Baruah calls 'durable disorder'. With almost the entire region subsumed in a spate of violence, it was a state of contained chaos. Seven of the eight states of the region felt the heat of AFSPA.

The roots of this law, which empowered the army to aid civilian administration, according to Baruah lie in the 'history of imperial policing'.[22] A feeling of neglect and step-motherly approach became embedded in the psyche of an enfeebled people, who had to resort to violence to make themselves heard.

The Central government acknowledged the development deficit of the Northeast and accorded it a 'special category' status in 1968–69. It was put on a pedestal for resource allocation and 90 per cent of Central assistance to the region came in the shape of grants. In 1996, 'New Initiatives for North Eastern Region' stipulated that at least 10 per cent of budget of all Central ministries would be earmarked for development of the region. Finance Minister Yashwant Sinha, during his budget speech of 1998–99, announced the creation of a non-lapsable Central resource pool, 'which will be used for funding specific programmes for economic and social upliftment of the North Eastern States'.[23] The underlying rationale was to use this pot of money for bridging the infrastructure deficit of the Northeast. However, there was a huge chasm between precept and praxis. Zoramthanga, chief minister of Mizoram, minces no words in expressing his disappointment,

> One of the major reasons for infrastructure projects not to take off in the northeast in the past was the non-allocation of Non-Lapsable Central Pool of Resources. Announced with much fanfare, it turned out to be a mirage, and perhaps only a quarter of what was promised was eventually spent.[24]

Generosity in resource allocation did not translate into tangible development. State finances across the Northeast were in shambles, with frequent defaults with the Reserve Bank. In the absence of any growth in industry or agriculture, the only recourse for the educated unemployed were government jobs, government contracts, politics or insurgency. State governments ended up creating posts way beyond their requirements, eating away into resources meant for development expenditure. Government contracts were doled out for petty construction works, overlooking execution ability and quality. Patronage, nepotism and corruption ruled as the Centre turned a Nelson's eye in the interest of peace.

Connectivity remained the Achilles heel of the Northeast. Absence of roads limited the prospects in agriculture. A region blessed with rich water resources ended up importing even half of its fish from outside, mostly from Andhra Pradesh. A Supreme Court judgment in 1996 banned felling of trees, sounding the death knell for a nascent forest-based industry. The Northeast, with a rich reservoir of oil, gas and minerals, is also a resource frontier. Unregulated extraction and practices like rat hole mining in Meghalaya were barred by the green tribunals. The Wanchoo Committee recommended a transport subsidy for industrial units based in the region to overcome the disadvantage of connectivity. A scheme notified by the Government of India in 1971 provided a subsidy for movement of raw materials and finished goods. Thousands of dodgy claims ensured a quick burial for the scheme.[25]

In the first five decades after independence, the Northeast remained to India what Africa is to the world. A laggard in economic development, it also had poor human development indices. The turn of the century brought new tidings. The pages that follow are a narrative of the unfolding change in the new Northeast. It is a story of the resilience of a remarkable people trying to make up for lost time. Northeast 2.0 is buzzing with a new economic dynamism, a large part of which can be termed a 'peace bonus'.

3

Connectivity: The Silver Bullet

PALAK DIL, THE 'swallowing lake' of Mizoram, lies hidden in the forested borderlands of Myanmar. In 2002, an 80-kilometre-long journey on a slushy mud track took me six hours to reach there from Siaha, the district headquarters. A handful of thatched tribal huts surrounded the playfield, with innocent children frolicking around. Curious villagers, surprised at the unexpected intrusion, congregated in the middle. The miracle of life is an accident of birth, I thought to myself. My impressionable mind of thirty years wondered what if I was born to parents who belonged to this village. If caught in sickness, I may not have survived to my teens, the nearest hospital being two days away. If I had chosen to take up farming, reaching the nearest market would have meant carrying a head-load for days. Even if God had generously bestowed me with the genius of Einstein, I still would not have made it beyond primary school. The lake, touted as a tourist's delight, would remain in its splendorous seclusion, since no tourists were reaching any time soon. Siaha itself was a seemingly endless twelve-hour ride from Aizawl on a serpentine road. The hopelessness of an alternate life in these regions that were bereft of any communication was a sobering thought.

In 2016, while serving in Arunachal Pradesh, I went touring to its easternmost parts, abutting Nagaland and Myanmar. This is opium country. People still live in the shadow of fear. Militants had assassinated the local Lok Sabha MP Wangcha Rajkumar a decade ago. After a five-hour drive from Itanagar, the capital of Arunachal Pradesh, I boarded a ferry at Bogibeel Ghat in Dibrugarh, Assam. Men, material, cars and cattle huddled together to travel from one bank of the Brahmaputra river to the other. The surreal experience was straight out of a movie set in Vietnam; only Rambo was missing. This ramshackle contraption of wooden planks, running on noisy diesel sets, was certainly incapable of carrying heavy cargo. A half-finished bridge stood across the river, a monument of neglect. Its foundation stone was laid by former Prime Minister Deve Gowda, amid much fanfare in 1997. My co-passengers on the ferry whispered in a conspiratorial tone, 'Politics derailed the project.' A crucial link of strategic import had suffered and remained unfinished for over two decades. Non-availability of the ferry could mean loss of employment for some, but also potential loss of life for others seeking to reach the hospital at the other end. A dusty drive through marshy terrain led to me to the town of Dibrugarh, a hub of higher education and medical care for people of eastern Assam and Arunachal Pradesh. At the height of its glory, it was a bustling town of commerce. Tea, timber and jute reached global markets through steam navigation, which connected it to Calcutta. The Partition of India, the big quake of 1950 and the 1965 war relegated it to the margins.[1] Dibrugarh became a prisoner of its geography, with scattered remnants of a sublime past. The arduous onward journey to Longding in Arunachal Pradesh, passing through the cocktail-sounding town of Margherita, left me shaken and stirred. The district headquarters was a sight of destitution and opium-induced debility. In the midst of this despair,

I was pleasantly surprised to be greeted by a young and affable deputy commissioner. Exuberantly, he shared his sense of achievement on being able to persuade Airtel to erect a tower in Longding. The town, now a blip on the digital highway, didn't have a bitumen road. People of this border district had access to neither road nor power, though a telecom tower now marked the hilltop.

Let alone these remote parts, travelling from one state capital to another, Guwahati to Itanagar, was a herculean task. The MI-17 chopper of Russian vintage, operated by the state government, transports upto twenty-one passengers from Guwahati for an hour-long ride. Six months in a year, heavy monsoons make the chopper ride uncertain and to some extent unsafe. The alternative is a seven-hour road journey. For the aged, sick and infirm, who wish to visit Guwahati for medical treatment, the only recourse was to be packed like sardines in a rickety overnight Sumo service. There was no civilian airport in Arunachal Pradesh then.

Mechuka is a picture postcard township of Arunachal Pradesh, reminiscent of the rolling hills of Scotland. The only challenge is reaching there: a fourteen-hour-long journey through rugged terrain from the nearest airport in Dibrugarh. Bordering the Tibetan plateau, this Buddhist township was an easy point of access for the Chinese army in 1962. Cut off from rest of India not so long ago, villagers recount stories of active trade with China prior to the war. An unused air force advanced landing ground is situated almost in the heart of the small township. A local leader shuffled his smartphone to show images of the Nyingchi Mainling Airport in Tibet, barely 80 km as the crow flies, which is connected to Lhasa, Chongqing, Guangzhou and Chengdu. It aims to handle quarter of a million passengers and 3,000 tonnes of cargo annually. He was trying to make a point about the abysmal situation on the Indian side.[2] The stark comparison with the northern neighbour is an unstated yet definitive part of the local narrative in the Northeast.

These are not isolated instances, but a sad story of neglect. Silent sentinels of the nation residing along high altitude borders were virtually on their own. Poor connectivity has always been the proverbial Achilles' heel of the Northeast. It stymied economic development and contributed to alienation and discontent. Trade, tourism and horticulture, which could have flourished in these parts, failed to take off. A sense of hopelessness and neglect became embedded in the regional psyche. Even as recent as 2002, only a quarter of the roads of the eight states had been surfaced. Dimapur to Kohima is a bumpy ride on a broken highway.[3]

Manik Sarkar, who was the chief minister of Tripura from 1998 to 2018, minced no words in a meeting with the Union home minister in 2015,

> The primary reason for sustenance of insurgency in northeastern states is underdevelopment and backwardness … Regrettably, the attitude of Union Government in the last 68 years of Independence has also not been very encouraging.[4]

Poor connectivity has a direct bearing on livelihoods and life prospects. Remote geographies and fluid borders challenge access to basic education and healthcare. Schools without teachers and health centres without doctors are common in these parts. Half the year, people struggle with heavy monsoon. Landslides and flash floods cut off already inaccessible areas. Freshly constructed roads get washed out in a single monsoon downpour. Many a time, air force choppers have to be pressed into service for emergency evacuation of stranded people. Apart from the human dimension of poor connectivity, there is also strategic risk in vulnerable borderlands. Movement of troops is slower, tedious and uncertain where roads are bad. Nomads, herders and yak grazers are the civilian sentinels of fuzzy borders, coping with extreme climate zones. Even this hardy lot tends to vacate their hamlets to move down and settle in areas better connected with roads.

The conundrum of connectivity was complicated by the peculiar topography of the Northeast. The Brahmaputra and Barak rivers along with their tributaries posed a colossal challenge. The spine of all road and rail networks had to follow the course of these rivers. The Imperial administration had not deigned it necessary to bridge the tempestuous Brahmaputra.

Something has changed over the last five years. Bogibeel bridge, the second longest rail-cum-road bridge of Asia, was opened in December 2018. Crossing the mighty Brahmaputra is now a breezy affair. On 19 November 2022, Prime Minister Modi inaugurated the Donyi-Polo airport, named after sun and moon gods worshipped by tribal communities. This is the third operational airport in the state after Pasighat and Ziro, commissioned in quick succession. The iconic Bhupen Hazarika Setu, named after Assam's poet laureate, an architectural marvel spanning 9 kilometres over the Lohit river now connects Assam with Arunachal Pradesh. The sleepy town of Roing is abuzz with tourists from Assam, thronging to experience snowfall at Mayudia Pass. The isolation of Arunachal Pradesh has ended.

Borderlands have an implicit remoteness quotient. But Vijayanagar defies even that definition by a degree of kilometres, quite literally so. Surrounded by dense the Namdapha forest, this settlement is a cul-de-sac, surrounded by Myanmar on three sides. Recently, it caught the attention of national media when the chief minister of Arunachal Pradesh decided to trudge 157 kilometres from the nearest township, partly on foot and partly on a four-wheel drive through a marshy terrain. At the end of the two-day journey, he vowed to connect it with a motorable road by March 2022.[5] The area has a peculiar history. Alarming reports of a potential Chinese incursion had forced paranoid authorities to take extraordinary measures in the 1960s. An airstrip was constructed and a hundred soldiers of the Assam Rifles set up a company in this no man's land. Over time, their numbers swelled as their families joined in. A weekly sortie by a Mi-17 chopper is their sole link with civilization. Some youngsters born in Vijayanagar had to walk more than 150 kilometres to see an electric bulb.[6] The isolated village also saw a mob of the indigenous Yobin tribe burn down vestiges of government buildings, protesting against the participation of non-tribals in panchayat polls.[7] Remoteness is no a deterrent for the political economy of ethnic identity.

Rural connectivity for sparsely populated hamlets spread over inhospitable terrain is a difficult and expensive affair. Where government fails to act, people step in happily. All they need is a nudge. Armstrong Pame, a young Naga IAS officer, posted in Manipur as a sub-divisional officer in 2012, was frustrated. 'People would take a circuitous route and waste ten hours on the road to reach district headquarters,' he recalls. He made an impassioned appeal to villagers for making a voluntary effort to repair a shorter route of 65 kilometres, lying in disuse. In an imaginative effort at crowdsourcing, he raised more than Rs 10 million using Facebook as a tool to construct a road that connected the township to Nagaland and Assam. His leadership won him accolades and a sobriquet: 'miracle man'. The 100-kilometre road is known as the 'people's road'. Connectivity had changed the lives of villagers and their economic fortunes. Proud of his accomplishment, Armstrong recalled, 'I visited those villages recently and saw that connectivity had made a huge economic impact and people of those villages who now earn up to Rs 2 lakh by selling ginger to Assam.'[8]

Improvements in rail, road, air, telecom, power and waterway connectivity gained impetus after 'Vision 2020' was unveiled by Prime Minister Manmohan Singh. The primary thrust was on linking the region with the mainland through a national highway network. Thereafter, connectivity of all state capitals within the Northeast was given attention. Roads connecting capitals to all district headquarters and villages were taken up subsequently. One of the most ambitious projects among these was the Trans-Arunachal highway, running parallel to the Tibetan plateau, slicing across the state and linking the Bhutanese border with the Myanmarese end.

In 2014, a new government assumed office at the Centre. At an election rally in Tuensang in Nagaland, Prime Minister Modi said, 'My vision for the Northeast is transformation by transportation.'[9] Improving connectivity was an obvious poll plank in a region with such bad roads. A new corporation was set up to construct national highways in the Northeast. The National Highway and Infrastructure Development Corporation was mandated to supplement the efforts of the Border Roads Organization under the Ministry of Defence, with a focus on quality and speed of execution. Over the next five years, it was able to add 1.5 kilometres of national highways every day, more than twice the average earlier.[10]

Air connectivity has seen huge gains in recent times. Regional connectivity schemes were a welcome move by the Central government. It provided viability gap funding to encourage airlines to venture into unprofitable routes. For the first time in its history, each of the eight states now have at least one functional airport: Pakyong in Sikkim, Umroi in Meghalaya and Itanagar in Arunachal Pradesh being the most recent additions. Ambitious plans are underway to convert Guwahati into an international airport, connecting the Northeast with Southeast Asia, as part of the Act East policy. UDAAN International provides gap funding for international flights connecting Assam with Bhutan, Bangladesh, Singapore and Bangkok.[11] Air connectivity is still inadequate and expensive. An economy class trip from Delhi to Aizawl could be more expensive and time-consuming than a trip to London.

The footprint of Indian Railways never reached beyond the plains of Assam and Tripura. An overnight train now links Itanagar with Guwahati. Indian Railways has drawn up an ambitious plan to connect the capitals of Mizoram, Sikkim, Nagaland and Manipur by 2022.[12] North Eastern Railways has commenced work to connect high altitude border district of Tawang with the rail network, constructing a tunnel cutting across the treacherous Sela Pass. Chief Minister Pema Khandu describes it as a 'befitting reply to China',[13] which has been staking claim over his home district. A trans-Asian railway project will link Agartala and Akhaura in Bangladesh. The 15-kilometre stretch, expected to be completed by June 2023 (according to latest updates),[14] would effectively ensure that the distance between Agartala and Kolkata is reduced by 1,000 kilometres. Chittagong port would once again become easily accessible, opening up new possibilities for trade. There are naysayers nonetheless. Student unions of Meghalaya have been opposing construction of a rail link, expressing fear that there would be a huge influx of outsiders. On the subject of the goods train, they are more accommodating than they are for passengers.[15]

Rivers are the lifeline of the Northeast. Mizoram, for instance, has two rivers on each flank—Karnaphulli, which flows to the Chittagong port in Bangladesh, and Kaladan, which goes up to Sittwe (formerly Akyab) in Myanmar. In the pre-Partition days, these were navigable routes that allowed easy access to goods. Even now, one can't miss the sight of floating bamboos, strung like a cascading wave, sinewing its way along these waters. International boundaries ruptured that link, leaving Mizos the only recourse of passing through the chicken's neck to follow a circuitous land route via Assam to reach Kolkata. Towards the end of nineteenth century, one-third of Assam's trade was with Bengal, transacted along the rivers. Steamers carried 95 per cent of that load. However, post-Partition, this meant passing through East Pakistan, which ran into diplomatic roadblocks. Though the Nehru–Liaquat Pact did partially restore the traffic, the 1965 Indo-Pak war sealed the fate of riverine trade.[16] It has taken seven decades after independence to restore this inland waterway link, through multiple diplomatic negotiations. In 2019, the Indo-Bangladesh Protocol on Inland Water Transit and Trade enabled a cargo laden ship to be ferried from Haldia for Guwahati, passing through Bangladesh's waters.[17] Ironically, along the same links steamer service was started by the British administration to connect Haldia and Guwahati way back in 1847.[18] It is yet to reach the bustling levels of the nineteenth century.

Remoteness breeds a sense of alienation and reinforces the historical experience of neglect. Isolation also creates a deep cultural and emotional divide, which marks the dividing line between us and them. For decades, people in the mainland never got to see the pristine beauty of the region because of poor connectivity. Northeasterners remained trapped in their own cocoon, nursing wounds of the past. Neither could they retain ethnic ties with brethren across new borders, nor could they form a bond with the mainlanders. Racism experienced by students, patients and youngsters seeking jobs in metropolitan cities of the country added insult to injury. The changed paradign of connectivity is bound to have a multiplier effect beyond the obvious economic advantage. Well-travelled youngsters are fired with a new ambition and a spirit of enterprise. They are riding on the digital highway, even though belatedly. More than 70 per cent of youth in the Northeast (barring Assam) are connected on social media.[19] Digital connectivity is building bridges of understanding with the outside world, while acting as a cementing force within.

It is heartening to see plane loads of people flying in and out of the Northeast, ending their enigmatic isolation. Mobility in search of economic opportunity is on the rise. Aspirational rural youth, once rooted to their villages, are now moving to cities. Urban-educated youth are moving to the mainland and overseas looking for business prospects. A survey conducted across university campuses in the Northeast revealed that infrastructure development was a top youth issue. Nearly three-fourth of respondents wanted to settle outside the region.[20]

Sanjoy Hazarika, managing trustee of the Centre for Northeast Studies and Policy Research, sees this as a change of the Northeast becoming a 'migrant producing area' as compared to one which was a 'migrant receiving region'.[21] Of course, connectivity brings with it the curse of civilization. The older generation frowns upon youngsters aping a Western way of life. They fret about the possible loss of culture so zealously guarded over centuries.

4

A Bridge to the Far East

THE VIEW OF the eastern frontier from Raisina Hill changes hue depending on which side of Rajpath you stand. Mandarins of South Block tend to see the neighbourhood from a strategic lens. From those exalted heights, a rose-tinted vision presents Myanmar as an entrepot to the Far East. A land bridge, holding the key to the strategic partnership with the Association of Southeast Asian Nations (ASEAN), it is also the theatre of the unfolding battle of influence between two great Asian powers: China and India. A diplomatic push for deeper trade and economic engagement follows this line of thinking. North Block has a more jaundiced view as it frets over challenges of internal security, checking the influx of drugs and arms across the borders. Safe harbours for insurgent groups give officialdom sleepless nights, who then lends their weight behind border-fencing initiatives with a stern security posture. This dissonance between diplomatic and security establishments reverberates right up to the borders.

A different reality subsists on the ground. People in Aizawl, Imphal and Kohima see Mandalay as neighbour, while New Delhi is distant. Unlike the western border, Partition did not rupture the deep ties of ethnicity that still bind a divided people in the Northeast. It's no wonder that a military coup in Myanmar saw a spontaneous outpouring of sympathy on the streets of India's northeast. Rebecca, a popular Mizo singer rendered an emotional song, in solidarity with the people of Myanmar, which went viral on social media.[1] Villagers gave shelter to refugees who crossed over fearing military reprisal. Political leadership of these states defied the circumspection of Delhi, offering unqualified support to refugees. This is not surprising. It is not uncommon to find Myanmarese women tending to Mizo children in Aizawl. Shops in the capitals sell snacks and cigarettes bearing a distinct imprint of Southeast Asia. Culture, tradition and commerce have bound these communities over centuries.

On the banks of Karnaphulli river lies the impoverished village of Tlabung. In 1871, British forces set sail from Chittagong, in search of the young Mary Winchester, kidnapped by the Lushais. They entered Mizo territory from Tlabung. Today, the village bears no trace of its historical moorings, barring a sole relic bearing the inscription,

> He came to this people in 1865 and worked among them for nine years … He travelled in their unknown land, visiting their chiefs, their villages and their homes, alone and unafraid … The people knew him as Thangliena Tom Lewin and honoured him as Chief.[2]

Lewin's book *A Fly on the Wheel: or How I Helped to Govern India* is still circulated locally by the Chakmas, as a testimonial of their indigenous rights in Mizo land. The Border Security Force (BSF) and Border Guards Bangladesh now stand solemnly on both ends of the river. Each morning, a chain of bamboo rafts moves silently over the river, ferrying goods and people (though illegally) to Rangamati, the headquarters of Chittagong Hill Tracts. Walking around the dusty market, one can see rows of plastic furniture stacked up, bearing an unmistakable stamp of 'Made in Bangladesh'. Trade, in the official sense, is absent, though there is a flourishing commercial exchange across the border.

Longwa, a village of 7,000 Konyak Nagas, lies at the intersection of Nagaland, Arunachal Pradesh and Myanmar. Naga children enrol themselves in Myanmarese schools, while youngsters from the other side come across for menial employment or health treatment. Local residents are clueless of the Act East policy and a dilapidated building stands at the village outskirts for trade promotion. Villagers from Myanmar purchase mobile phones from Mon village (the district headquarters in Nagaland), while opium is commonly smuggled to Nagaland and Arunachal Pradesh.[3] Trade in remote borderlands has a degree of informality intertwined with illegality.

Zokhawthar, the last township of Mizoram, on the banks of the Tiau river, is a marker of India's international border with Myanmar. I visited the township in 2018 in quest of a bustling trading hub. Much to my disappointment, the settlement lacked the veneer of an international bridgehead to the Far East. An overgrown village, shabbier than any other I had seen enroute, only had the local church as its solitary point of interest. Let alone any buzz of economic activity, there was not even a hint of commerce. A precariously balanced rusting iron bridge straddles the shallow waters, barely supporting the movement of a car at a time. The Free Movement Regime introduced a decade ago allowed visa-free access to Indian and Myanmarese citizens up to 16 kilometres on either side of the border. Keen to explore Myanmar, I crossed the bridge on foot. The arches on both sides were laden with symbolism of welcome to another country. The Indian side had a handful of local police and personnel of the Assam Rifles, seemingly doubtful of their own role. The village across the river had a row of shops, selling cheap liquor (including some Thai brands), Chinese home appliances and electronic gadgets. Mizoram, being an alcohol-free state, is a natural market for booze. Further down the road nestled the pristine Rih Dil Lake, a place of pilgrimage for the Mizos. Folklore has it that the souls of all Mizos must pass through the sacred waters before ascending to the gates of heaven. On my way back, a Mizo official nonchalantly driving his official car informed me that he was off to Tahan (some 90 kilometres away) to visit his relatives. A former YMA president had told me proudly in Aizawl that he had even travelled up to Mandalay by road. Of course, all this was before the crackdown by the military junta.

The Land Custom station opened at Zokhawthar in 2015 by the Union commerce minister, with much fanfare, was equipped with a bank branch, a weigh bridge and some other trade infrastructure.[4] Discussions with local customs officials revealed that in the last five years, no formal export consignment left the bridge. Paltry quantities of betelnut were imported formally. This too ceased following a surge in customs duty. Movement of cargo is neither permissible, nor feasible. No plant or animal quarantine facility exists, the nearest functional unit being in Manipur. An outbreak of Porcine Reproductive and Respiratory Syndrome (PRRS) in 2018 owed its origin to illegal imports of infected pigs from Myanmar, leaving thousands of animals dead.[5] The local bank is not authorized to undertake any foreign trade transactions. No custom bonded warehouse exists and the solitary government building lies heavily padlocked. An association of porters sit on their haunches by the bridge as couriers of smuggled cargo. Consignments could range from harmless betelnut to precious gold, arms and Yaba tablets (a dangerous cocktail of methamphetamine and caffeine). Fertilizers, though a controlled commodity, is smuggled across with ease. Private godowns lining the road to Zokhawthar bear testimony to a thriving illicit trade. The magnitude of illegal trade can be gauged from the daily bank deposits at Champhai, the district headquarters, which are reported to be Rs 2.5 crore. A ballpark extrapolation suggests an annual illicit trade volume of Rs 500 crore.[6]

Moreh is India's crucial land link with Myanmar. Manipur's main channel for border trade, it has an Integrated Check Post that was inaugurated by Prime Minister Modi in 2019. Barter trade, hitherto the norm, gave way to formal trade five years ago. However, it has sputtered along, hovering around $20 million annually. Money, however, gets routed through Singapore, in the absence of mutual banking arrangements. Namphalong market across the border bustles with Indian shoppers, looking for Chinese and Thai goods. Exports to Myanmar are minuscule. Bad roads on both sides dissuade the hardiest of traders. From the border to Kalewa, the road was resurfaced a decade ago with Indian assistance—but connectivity with Mandalay, the nearest commercial hub, remains poor. On the Indian side, the 110-kilometre road between Moreh and Imphal is being strengthened with Asian Development Bank's (ADB) funding. Reaching Guwahati, a distance of less than 500 kilometres, takes fourteen hours. Traders also cough up 'informal payments' of almost the same amount as legitimate ones. The trail of extortion includes 'social groups', government officials and underground elements.[7] In 2018, the Indo-Myanmar land border was opened and it was announced that people from both sides would be able to cross over with e-visas at Zokhawthar and Moreh. There hasn't been any visible usage of this until recently.

This bleak reality along the borders strikes a sharp contrast with the lofty vision of Act East envisioned by the foreign office. The roots of this dissonance lie buried in the pages of history. Ambivalent politics in the neighbourhood clouded any prospects of trade. With Bangladesh, the traumatic baggage of Partition saw shifting goalposts of economic diplomacy. Trade with China never came in the realm of possibility, given the history of border tensions with it. A diplomatic freeze with Myanmar followed the military crackdown there on the 8888 Uprising. ASEAN was regarded by Indian leadership as a 'Trojan Horse of United States'[8] during the Cold War period. After 1991, a new pragmatism shaped the economic thought of the Central government. The economies of ASEAN were fully embedded in the manufacturing value chains anchored in China. Prime Minister Narasimha Rao espoused the 'Look East' policy during his Singapore address in 1994. A decade later, Prime Minister Vajpayee, while addressing a business seminar, said, 'Our North-Eastern States can become our economic bridgehead to South-East Asia. Equally, vibrant commercial exchanges with South-East Asia can galvanize growth and development in the North-East.'[9]

Similar sentiments were echoed by Pranab Mukherjee, former minister of external affairs, who asserted that people of the Northeast were poised to benefit from growing relations with Southeast Asia, as globalization can uplift people from poverty and economic backwardness and bring in prosperity.[10] An idea conceived with a strategic eye towards the Far East now engulfed the Northeast. Prime Minister Modi changed the tenor of the engagement, launching the Act East policy ten years further down, during the twelfth ASEAN-India Summit. A confluence of domestic and foreign policy objectives became inevitable. While addressing Advantage Assam Summit in February, 2018, he said,

> We adopted Act East Policy of which the North-east is at its heart ... The Act East Policy requires increased people to people contact, trade ties and other relations with countries on India's east, particularly the ASEAN countries.[11]

Ram Madhav, the former BJP in charge of the Northeast, went a step further to assert that the region will not be the gateway to ASEAN, but a 'hub' or 'pivot' of the Act East policy.[12] From being a fringe player of neighbourhood diplomacy, the Northeast suddenly moved to its centre.

India is viewed by some commentators as a 'reluctant regionalist'.[13] Its eastern overture, therefore, would appear to be a reaction to growing Chinese presence, economically and strategically. The annual political summit with ASEAN Heads of Government shifted focus from diplomatic niceties to bread and butter issues. The Free Trade Agreement signed with ASEAN a decade ago was the marker of shifting sands. Between 2009–10 and 2016–17, trade across all routes of the Northeast and neighbouring countries nearly doubled to touch Rs 1,648 crore, nearly half of which was with Bangladesh.[14] This still remains a fraction of trade transactions across the Petrapole Integrated Check Post (in West Bengal), which crossed Rs 20,000 crore in 2018–19.[15] The bulk of the trade with Myanmar is transacted along the sea lanes, which completely bypasses the Northeast.

A key impediment to formal trade is the poor connectivity across the border. A transnational connectivity corridor linking Myanmar and Thailand would give the Northeast the edge. The 1,400-kilometre trilateral highway from Moreh to Mae Sot in Thailand is under construction and is expected to be commissioned soon.[16] Getting goods across the border is only part of the problem. Circumventing the circuitous route to the mainland bypassing the chicken's neck is crucial for competitiveness. A solution was conceived in 2008, to bring cargo from Kolkata along the sea to the Sittwe port in Myanmar, which has now been commissioned. Cargo would then get ferried along the Kaladan river to a riverine port at Paletwa, and hop across on a 110-kilometre road (yet to be constructed) to reach the Mizoram border. NH-54 would then be the spine to reach Guwahati. The Kaladan Multi-Modal Transit Transport

Project (KMTTP), a seemingly simple proposition, has faced several execution challenges, including road construction in hostile territory that is dominated by the Arakan Army. Seamless movement along that route would require efficient customs management, involving two border crossings and multiple mediums of transportation. The joint statement issued during the visit of Myanmar President U Win Myint in February 2020 was an articulation of a shared resolve to commission the project at the earliest. The operationalization of the India-Myanmar-Thailand trilateral highway was also projected for 2021 and a bus service between Imphal and Mandalay was set to commence.[17] However, recent developments in Myanmar are bound to slow things down.

Indian border trade with Myanmar and Bangladesh fades away in comparison with the flourishing Chinese exchange across Yunnan, its 'bridgehead' to Southeast Asia. Aung San Suu Kyi, the deposed state counsellor for Myanmar, and Chinese President Xi Jinping inked an MOU in 2017 for constructing an expressway and a rail link between Kunming and Yangon. The 700-kilometre segment between the Kunming and Ruili borderpoint on the Chinese side takes less than ten hours to traverse.[18] The journey from Muse (Myanmarese border crossing) to Mandalay can be completed in twelve hours. An identical distance between Guwahati and Zokhawthar takes nearly twenty-three hours. Another sixteen hours ride over a bumpy road to Mandalay renders border trade commercially unviable. The 168-kilometre trade zone at Muse is the epicentre of the $7 billion annual trade across Yunnan. A reciprocal arrangement allows movement of Chinese and Myanmarese trucks inside this zone. An elaborate trade inspection facility houses customs, immigration, police and revenue authorities under one roof, allowing simultaneous inspection of cargo laden trucks. Ancillary facilities such as warehouses and cold storage have been established. The border rice market is a value proposition for farmers, who strike deals on the spot, after inspection sampling and testing.[19] India could take a leaf out of Yunnan's experience for galvanizing trade across the Northeast. This would require a pragmatic fine-tuning of economic and foreign policy.

First, openness to border trade will require a certain degree of realism, which acknowledges the growing regional connectivity corridors linking China. It would be naive to ignore this reality or to shy away from it. Professor Che Zhimin, former deputy director of the Economic and Technological research centre of Yunnan provincial people's government, had argued for subregional cooperation, linking four south-western Chinese provinces—Yunnan, Sichuan, Chongqing, Guizhou—with Myanmar, Bangladesh and Northeast India. These lie at the intersection of three markets—China, Southeast Asia and South Asia. The zone, 'characterized by relative poverty' and 'isolated from world markets', would form the basis of 'rational planning and optimal utilization of resources', becoming the 'land bridge' connecting the Pacific Ocean.[20] This formed the theoretical foundation of the Kunming initiative, which has so far remained a track two dialogue, later mutating into the Bangladesh-China-India-Myanmar (BCIM) forum. The 1,736-kilometre long Stillwell Road, named after an American general, starts from Ledo in Tinsukia district of Assam, traverses through Pangsau Pass in Arunachal Pradesh, before entering Myanmar. Thereafter it runs along the Lake of No Return, cutting across the Patkai range, touching the Myanmarese towns of Myitkina and Bhamo, and joining into Yunnan. Constructed as an alternate supply route by the American Army during the Second World War, the road touches Chinese townships of Longling and Baoshan, culminating in Kunming.[21] The route, lying in desuetude, comes alive only during the annual Pangsau Pass winter festival organized at the border town of Nampong. The revival of this route could have a transformational impact on the economy of eastern Assam and Arunachal Pradesh, with a direct link to a flourishing trade zone at Muse, with a backward linkage right up to Kunming. The Indian government has so far been reluctant to consider opening this route, with overriding security concerns. Recent skirmishes with China on the northern border would throw a spanner in the nascent conversations around this theme.

Second, trade infrastructure planning in India needs an integrated approach. Multiple agencies handle project execution, creating a muddled accountability framework and lukewarm gains. Of the thirty-five Land Customs Stations under the Commissionerate of Customs Shillong, ten are non-functional.[22] Integrated Check Posts at Moreh and Agartala (and one planned at Dawki) are managed by the Land Port Authority of India, under the Ministry of Home Affairs. Security along the porous borders assumes salience as the Northeast falls along the axis of the golden triangle of drug smuggling linking Myanmar and Thailand. Alarming quantities of narcotics flow through the region unchecked. Collusion of police authorities and local politicians makes the task of law enforcement even more complicated. Insurgent groups active in the region, having strong links with counterparts across the border, take shelter in dense forests. Internal security inevitably trumps foreign trade. A compelling case exists to establish a Regional Foreign Trade Authority to harmonize these conflicting goals. This authority, established in partnership with all concerned state governments, could serve as an umbrella organization to handle infrastructure planning and execution, including land acquisition on a turnkey basis. It could be the sole authority for oversight of border management: customs, immigration, trade facilitation and security management.

Third, land transit through Bangladesh could have a remarkable impact on cost competitiveness. The road distance between the capitals of the Northeast states and Kolkata across Bangladesh reduces distance by more than half in some cases, as compared to the existing link through the chicken's neck corridor. It can reduce the road distance between Agartala and Kolkata by four times.[23]

Fourth, creating a strong buy-in of the Northeast states in promoting formal trade is a sine qua non. The Act East policy largely remains a Central government diplomatic initiative with limited participation from the states. Trade must figure high on the policy pyramid of the Northeast states. Ministerial delegations to Bangladesh and Myanmar could possibly also include chief ministers of some states of the Northeast. A regional approach, in the spirit of cooperative federalism, must focus on building behind border capabilities. Transport corridors currently under execution must, therefore, be upgraded to serve as economic corridors. The Greater Mekong Sub-Regional Economic Cooperation Program of China could serve as a useful template for planning economic infrastructure in the Northeast. Exports from the six members of the Greater Mekong Subregion—Cambodia, Lao PDR, Myanmar, Thailand, Vietnam and People's Republic of China (Guangxi and Yunnan province)—amounted to $8.9 trillion, which was 18 per cent of the global export in this period. Of this, 82 per cent was contributed by the two provinces of People's Republic of China. Trade has had a spillover impact on catalyzing gross domestic product.[24] Japan has evinced interest in the region, as a counterbalance to the Chinese Belt and Road Initiative. The joint statement issued on the occasion of the visit of the Japanese Prime Minister Shinzo Abe in 2017 'welcomed the India–Japan cooperation on development of India's North Eastern Region (NER) as a concrete symbol of developing synergies between India's Act East policy and Japan's Free and Open Indo Pacific Strategy.'[25] This was followed by liberal infusion of infrastructure investments to the tune of $610 million, supported by the Japan International Cooperation Agency for the Northeast.

Fifth, the Northeast can serve a transit hub at best in the short term, given its limited export basket. Exports from the Northeast to Bangladesh have an overwhelming share of minerals due to the complementarity of market structures. Meghalaya, with large coal and limestone deposits , feeds into Bangladesh, which has a growing demand for cement production. Trade with Myanmar presents an image of contrasts, where exports across Moreh are largely goods produced outside the Northeast, catering to local demand.[26] Stronger connectivity links with the mainland will certainly help strengthen the position of the Northeast as a transit hub. Even this will require establishment of warehousing, logistics and transportation facilities within the region that are geared to meet the demand. In the medium term, however, a certain degree of value addition at the borders is a desirable goal. Gautam Mukhopadyay, who served as Indian Ambassador to Myanmar (2013–16), articulates, 'We need to create value addition at the borders, using local agricultural produce for exports to Myanmar and beyond. Connectivity without productivity is not a desirable goal.'[27] Unfortunately, industrial strategy in the region is currently driven by each state, overlooking the economies of scale which a collaborative venture could yield.

Sixth, the Act East policy must make economic sense for the people of the region, who are accustomed to the informality at the borders. Transition from barter trade to normal trade has increased the requirement of documentation substantially.[28] Building a trading community in the Northeast would require a strong push for trade facilitation measures and capacity-building. This should include not only familiarization with procedural formalities for becoming an importer or exporter, but also a sound understanding of prevailing customs duty on both sides and handholding support to identify products with strong demand across the border.

Seventh, the governance deficit in the Northeast must be addressed squarely. State government officials lack the training and capacity to unlock the latent economic potential of the region. Mukhopadhyay recalls,

> During the end of my tenure in Myanmar, border trade arrangement suddenly switched over to MFN trade, a unilateral decision by the Ministry of Commerce, without necessary infrastructure and protocols in place. As a result, there was a surge in export of third country goods, leading to creation of vested interest, including insurgent groups of the region. The Integrated Check Post at Moreh, which I visited recently, has a functional immigration set up, but the customs facilitation is still non-functional. The capacity and understanding of local customs officials on the prevailing duty structures is also suspect.[29]

The Assam government has made an interesting beginning by establishing a separate department for Act East policy affairs. Ultimately, gains from foreign trade must see visible improvement in the local context.

Finally, even as the economic, diplomatic and security narrative dominates the Act East discourse, the strength of India's soft power must not be undermined. The Northeast is a civilizational melting pot, which has seen migration of people from Yunnan and East Asia over centuries. Circumstances of history have left them at different ends of the development spectrum, from people who reside in the land of their origin. Yet, there is something fundamental that still binds people separated by geography and time: culture and ethnicity. Sushma Swaraj, former minister of external affairs, had given the mantra of the 3Cs: commerce, culture and connectivity. While focusing on commerce and connectivity, the significance of culture must not be lost. Greater people-to-people interactions and cultural exchanges between the people of Northeast and ASEAN would help build enduring bonds, which will be foundational to commercial linkages that are being sought to be established.

Political developments in Myanmar and the border tensions with China will certainly be an impediment to foreign trade through the Northeast. The Covid-19 pandemic, which brought the whole world to a standstill in 2020, has also altered the approach of people of the Northeast, who are preferring economic self-sufficiency. In spite of these setbacks, there is an inevitability of the region becoming a gateway of regional trade, which it once was. Over the years, realpolitik has defined Indian foreign policy. In due course, a new equilibrium will set in, regardless of the regime in power on either side of the border.

5

Rivers that Light

'For the valleys of the earth have these tilings in common: the waters, the air, the land, the minerals, the forests. In Missouri and in Arkansas, in Brazil and in the Argentine, in China and in India there are just such rivers ... rivers that in the violence of flood menace the land and the people, then sulk in idleness and drought ...'[1]

—David E. Lilienthal, *TVA: Democracy on the March*

RIVERS, WHICH ARE cradles of civilization around the world, assume a sacred character in Indian cultural traditions. The Brahmaputra, the only masculine river of India, is visualized as the fluid embodiment of the mythological son of the Hindu deity Brahma, born out of a holy communion with Amogha. Geographically speaking, the origins of the Brahmaputra can be traced to the glaciers of the Kailasha range in the Tibetan plateau. Yarlung Tsangpo, as it is known in Tibet, is truly the 'Everest of rivers'.[2] Skirting around Mount Namcha Barwa, the highest peak in the Eastern Himalayas, it cuts across the 'Great Bend', before making a majestic entry into Arunachal Pradesh. Siang, which means the river that flows through the heart in the local Adi language, has an unmatched grandeur. Standing on the Ranaghat bridge at Pasighat, one can't help but behold with reverence the teal blue waters roaring with the force of an ocean along white sand beaches. Siang eventually blends into the waters of the Lohit and the Dibang, emerging as the Brahmaputra in the plains of Assam. The braided river, one of the widest in the world, nurtures over 200 million people in India and China. Along with Barak and Teesta, this formidable river trinity criss-crosses the hills and valleys of India's Northeast.

The Brahmaputra is the lifeline of Assam's economy; it sustains the livelihoods of millions of farmers, fishermen, boatmen and tourist operators. It holds an exalted position in the cultural idioms, folklore and songs of Assam. Sanjib Baruah describes the relationship of the region with the river using the poetic expression of Bhupen Hazarika, 'Mother, we are seven sisters who once played in the "sunny sands of the river Luit (Brahmaputra)". Meghalaya went her own way as soon as she was old enough. Arunachal too separated and Mizoram appeared in Assam's gateway as a groom to marry another daughter.'[3]

The Brahmaputra in spate inspires fear. Each monsoon, it flows in fury, leaving a sad tale of death and destruction behind. Bhupen Hazarika captures the despair of people in his poignant verse,

Bistirna paarore
Axonkhya jomore
Hahakar xuniu
Nixobde nirobe
Burha luit tumhi
Burha luit buwa kiyo?
Noitikotar skhalan dekhiu
Manobotar patan dekhiu
Nirlajja alax bhawe buwa kiyo?

> You have heard the cries of millions on your vast shores
> Yet, O' old Luit why do you flow in silence?
> You have seen morality eroding and humanity collapsing
> Yet, why do you flow shamelessly and sluggishly?[4]

A great earthquake struck at the heart of the Brahmaputra in 1950. F. Kingdom Ward wrote about it, '... millions of tons of rocks and sand poured in the main rivers and their tributaries, within a space of weeks, displacing millions of cubic feet of water'.[5] The spectre lives on in the shared experiences of some 2,000 villages whose lands get inundated every year.[6] Reverberations in Tibet cause mayhem in the Northeast. Landslides often form a dam in the river upstream and its outburst causes a deluge in India. In June 2000, a similar episode caused flash floods in Siang, washing off a bridge and leaving thirty people dead and hundreds missing.[7]

The Brahmaputra personifies the collective consciousness of the people of the Northeast. It is a manifestation of the journey of a region through the shifting sands of time, like the chars (riverine islands) that spring up at will in the middle of the river. The Naga poetess Monalisa Changkija speaks in first person as the son of Brahma in her poem 'Mist over Brahmaputra',

> I flow with the currents
> and coherence of Brahma's son,
> sometimes filthy with human inadequacies,
> other times chaste in spiritual serenity. ...
> I will myself to emulate Brahma's son
> to celebrate the sights, scents and sounds
> and the strength in my solitary self,
> and allow time to heal
> these self-destructive tendencies
> that sometimes buzz around my head,
> as they do over Brahma's son.[8]

The initial approach of the Central and state government to address the misery that followed the floods was to stem the tide, literally so. Embankments were constructed along the river to mitigate the impact of the floods. In 1980, the Brahmaputra Board Act was passed by the Parliament, 'epitomizing the nationalization' of the river.[9] The focus then shifted from construction of embankments downstream to hydropower storage dams upstream. Several rounds of investigations and reconnaissance missions inspired the Central government to view the region in a different light. The Northeast came to be known as the future 'powerhouse of the nation', even though its people lived in darkness.

Prime Minister Atal Bihari Vajpayee announced a '50,000 MW hydro-electric initiative' in 2003, most of which was anchored in the Northeast.[10] Five years later, a new government announced a hydropower policy. Those were the heydays of economic liberalization and the private sector was encouraged to take the lead. States were incentivized by allowing a 12 per cent share of free power. Over and above this, 2 per cent of power generated would be monetized for supporting development in the area directly impacted by the hydropower project.[11] Cash-strapped states of the region sensed an opportunity to boost revenues. The Arunachal Pradesh government came out with its own policy. Projects below 100 MW capacity were awarded on a negotiated 'memorandum of agreement' route, while those above this threshold would be awarded on a competitive bidding route.[12] Chief Minister Dorjee Khandu, while addressing the fifty-fifth meeting of the National Development Council, claimed that Arunachal Pradesh would be a power rich state by 2022 and a new power corridor would be created for the region.[13] The journey proved to be far bumpier than he might have envisioned.

In those days of infrastructure boom, ambitious promoters and construction companies without any prior experience waded into unchartered waters. Within a few months, hundreds of projects were allotted. Jairam Ramesh, former Union minister of state for power, cynically called it the 'MOU virus'.[14] Insinuations of political corruption and whispers of a scandal reverberated in the corridors of power. Public perception got muddied and all homilies were meaningless, especially in the absence of any visible outcomes. A maze of regulatory clearances from multiple Central- and state-level agencies made matters more complicated. Around this time, green rights activists became vocal about the rights of indigenous people and environmental risks. Medha Patkar led the Narmada Bachao Andolan against the Sardar Sarovar Project. The World Commission of Dams also cautioned against large projects. The Ministry of Environment, Forest and Climate Change, then under the stewardship of Jairam Ramesh, rolled out the National Environmental Policy. The National Green Tribunal (NGT) Act, 2010, saw an expanding space for anti-dam environmentalists. Much to the chagrin of developers, norms for forest and environmental clearance were tightened. Ramesh admitted,

> I am actually far more ruthless when it comes to forest clearances because while on environment side safeguards are possible, forests are irretrievably destroyed and by building a compensatory plantation, you are not substituting for a forest area. We can find the middle path on environment issues, but in forests, it is very difficult to find a middle path.[15]

Hydropower became a prisoner of conflicting choices: development versus displacement; economic gains versus environmental cost; national goals versus tribal rights. Arunachal Pradesh had no incentive to build multipurpose projects, which involve larger local displacement. These were precisely the projects that would have helped in flood mitigation. Communities agitated around the question: Power for whom? No grand plan existed for an energy-driven industrial development programme. Rural hamlets languished in darkness amidst talks of surpluses.[16] Falling costs of solar power disrupted the energy markets. Multiple contestations and muddled implementation throttled the hydro dream.

In the unfolding drama, each protagonist held a different view. The state felt duty-bound to go ahead with project implementation in the larger national interest. Engineers, citing international experience to bolster their claims, swore by their designs. Residents at the dam location opposed the projects as it entailed displacement from the land of their ancestors. People downstream, for whose misery the storage dams were conceived, raised the red flag of dam safety, fearing a deluge in the eventuality of an earthquake. Geologists cautioned that most of the large dams lie along the faultline of the great quake of 1950. Ecologists worried about loss of precious biodiversity, which is yet to be discovered. Environmentalist Chintan Seth, who has spent considerable time studying the geology of Arunachal Pradesh, paints a larger picture. He draws a parallel between an ecological network with a financial one, each having multiple nodes. If one node falls off the network, another replaces it, he argues. But if a crucial node malfunctions, it could collapse a whole network. The forests of the Northeast, he says, are part of a continuum that leads up to the Southeast Asia and buffers the entire region from ecological hazards and climatic shocks. In a relatively young watershed, which is less than fifteen million years old, he feels, humans have inhabited it for just over 4,000 years.[17]

In a public address at Itanagar in February 2015, Prime Minister Modi proclaimed that, 'Arunachal Pradesh could provide electricity to the entire country.'[18] Chief Minister Pema Khandu tempered this vision with realism of local politics, and felt that, 'There's no point taking up projects at random. Let us focus on 10 feasible and beneficial projects and we will take these up on mission mode.'[19]

The Subansiri is one of the biggest tributaries of the Brahmaputra. It is the dividng line between Assam and Arunachal Pradesh, both physically and metaphorically. The site for the construction of a 2,000 MW hydropower project became the mascot of the anti-dam movement in the Northeast. During my visit as secretary in charge of the power department in 2016, I saw a ghost township and a half-finished dam. Project managers of the National Hydro Electric Power Corporation (NHPC), who had taken over the project sixteen years ago, wore a resigned look. The company was bleeding losses since 2011, when anti-dam activists led by the All Assam Students Union (AASU) and Krishak Mukti Sangram Samiti (KMSS) stalled work. Akhil Gogoi, a self-proclaimed Marxist, led the agitation, labelling the project as 'corporatization of water'.[20] Concerns on dam safety and the livelihoods of fishermen struck an emotive chord with people.[21] Technical experts recommended lowering of the dam's height. The NGT stayed all construction. Meanwhile, the protests acquired political overtones. The Assam government saw this as a bargaining chip for a higher share of free power. The Central government stepped in to break the impasse. In August 2019, the Assam government signed a Memorandum of Agreement with the NHPC, after the NGT gave its go-ahead.[22] Work has now resumed, though the project cost has shot up threefold. It is now scheduled to be commissioned in 2023–24.[23]

The Dibang Valley is home to the Idu Mishmi tribe. It is also the site of one of the largest hydroelectric power projects planned in the country. Prime Minister Manmohan Singh laid the foundation stone of the 2,880 MW project there in January 2008. The Forest Advisory Committee turned it down on two occasions as it involved the submergence of significant forest land. The Cabinet Committee on Investment, mandated to fast track clearances for key infrastructure projects, gave its go-ahead in 2014. The Prime Minister's Office nudged the Ministry of Environment, Forest and Climate Change to 'clear the project expeditiously', and it was done with minor adjustments in the dam's height.[24] It took the NHPC another five years to secure clearance from the Union Cabinet for commencing project construction at an estimated cost of nearly Rs 300 billion.[25]

In its close vicinity lies the ambitious 3,097 MW Etalin hydropower project, whose execution means the diversion of more than a 1,000 hectares of forest land. The Forest Advisory Committee noted that the company responsible for the project had not factored in its environmental impact, including implications for tigers that had been sighted downstream. After further investigations by experts, the committee felt that it would be 'prudent' to get inputs from the Ministry of Power as it may have changed its policy on hydropower projects after 2015.[26] Protests from local communities and environmental groups might have effectively put the project in deep freeze.

The Lohit, another major tributary of the Brahmaputra, saw an eruption of public protests in 2007 following the allotment of the 1,750 MW Demwe hydroelectric project. It took two years of negotiations for the resumption of public hearings.[27] Environmentalists decried its impact on the Kamlang Wildlife Sanctuary and Dibru-Saikhowa National Park. They cautioned against the loss of precious acquatic life downstream, avian life on chapories (river islands) and rare medicinal plants.[28] The NGT stayed the grant for forest clearances, asking for a reconsideration by the Standing Committee of the National Board for Wildlife (NBWL).[29] In the 50th meeting of the Standing Committee of the NBWL, chaired by the Union environment minister, wildlife clearance was accorded in September 2018. In doing so, the board observed that, 'the submergence zone of the dam is a habitat which is available elsewhere within the region and is not critical for the conservation of any known threatened, endangered or critically endangered species' population'.[30] They accepted that some more studies would be required, but construction activity could commence in parallel. The decision dismayed conservationists,[31] but was a shot in the arm for hydropower.

In 2016, while driving up the road to Tawang, I had taken a detour to visit the construction site of the 600 MW hydro project on the Kameng river. The North Eastern Electric Power Corporation Limited (NEEPCO) engineers showed me the intricacies of tunnelling and cascaded development of the run-of-the-river project. The project, cleared in 2004, started full commercial operation in early 2021.[32] The primary purpose of my visit was to assess the local sentiment in Tawang arising out of an unfortunate police firing incident in May that year, which left two monks dead. The immediate provocation for protests was the opposition to public hearings conducted by the NHPC for two hydropower projects, with a combined capacity of 1,400 MW. Lama Lobsang Gyatso, locally referred to as Anna Lama (after the activist Anna Hazare), alluded to the veil of secrecy that shrouded the power projects and expressed fears of submersion of land. Thegtse Rinpoche, who leads the black sect monastery, in a conversation felt that the 'construction activity has a long gestation period and there would be an influx of migrant labour, particularly muslims, which would disturb the demographic balance'. He also mentioned that some land of the Tawang monastery would get submerged. Of course, both of them nursed political ambitions as well. Another project in Tawang was shelved after environmental protests that its submergence area was the nesting ground of black-necked cranes. The cranes, a symbol of peace, are held sacred in Buddhist traditions, which believes that previous incarnations of the Dalai Lama were carried on the backs of these holy birds.[33]

In spite of multiple contestations, Arunachal Pradesh has been able to salvage a somewhat irredeemable situation. It has added a capacity of 710 MW, awaits the commissioning of another 2,000MW and has resuscitated projects of more than 4,000 MW.

Emerging from the Tso Lhamo lake in the Kanchenjunga range, Teesta winds its way down the hills of Sikkim and Darjeeling to enter Bangladesh before blending with the Brahmaputra. According to folklore, a 'furious Teesta once deluged the entire landscape'. Lepcha shamans placate their deities by offering prayers for maintaining environmental balance.[34] The Teesta raged in 1968, causing huge devastation in the Jalpaiguri district of West Bengal. People still carry memories of the hardships that followed.

The erstwhile Central Water and Power Commission drew up a six-stage cascaded hydro development plan over Teesta in 1974. As the plan started taking the shape of projects on ground, Lepchas rose up in revolt under the banner of the Affected Citizens of Teesta (ACT). Gyatso Lepcha, one of the founders, says, 'Teesta is sacred for the Lepchas. Dams choke rivers and during monsoons, when water is released suddenly, there is devastating impact downstream. We have been too greedy in our quest to construct dams. I am not against dams but there must be some correlation with carrying capacity of the rivers.'[35] The 510 MW Teesta-V project was commissioned in 2008. The Ministry of Environment, Forest and Climate Change had stipulated that no other project be taken up in the basin till its carrying capacity is determined.[36] The dam suffered some damages due to a landslide in 2020. Meanwhile, the social impact assessment report was notified by the government for the 520 MW Teesta-IV project. The ACT protested vehemently against the assault on their sacred land in the Dzongu Valley.

The largest project in the basin was the 1,200 MW Teesta-III, for which the Sikkim government invited bids from private developers. Teesta Urja Limited was incorporated in 2005 as a joint venture between Athena Projects Private Limited and the state government.[37] The project was commissioned in February 2017, though the capital cost had shot up nearly threefold.[38] The power tariff set by the regulator was obviously well above the prevailing market rates. Power was sold at half the regulator's price in the open market. Poor planning for power evacuation led to suboptimal production, impacting its viability.[39]

The 500 MW Teesta-VI was allotted to Lanco Teesta Hydro Power Limited. Regulatory hurdles and absence of financial closure delayed implementation substantially.[40] In 2019, the Cabinet Committee of Economic Affairs mandated the NHPC to acquire the project in the interest of commissioning.[41] The Insolvency and Bankruptcy Code was invoked for the first time for the takeover of a private company by a public sector undertaking (PSU). The project is slated to go live by 2024.[42]

In 2017, the Prime Minister inaugurated the 60 MW NEEPCO-run Tuirial Hydro Electric Project in Mizoram. Mizoram thus became the third state in the region to have a power surplus after Sikkim and Tripura.[43]

The upshot of these developments is that nearly 2,000 MW capacity has been added in the Northeast. The Union government also announced a slew of measures in 2019 to boost hydropower. All projects of more than 25 MW capacity were declared as renewable energy projects, now qualifying for hydro purchase obligation, within the existing non-solar renewable obligation. By implication, states would now be required to maintain a mandatory percentage of hydropower in its energy mix. Project developers were also given several incentives.[44] Hydropower has been given a fresh lease of life. And the Northeast will be its biggest beneficiary.

Prime Minister Modi, after visiting Guwahati in 2017 in the backdrop of the Assam floods, established a high-level committee under the Vice Chairman of NITI Aayog, with chief secretaries of all Northeast states as members.[45] The group has recommended the establishment of a North East Water Management Authority (NEWMA), which would be tasked with holistic water resource planning, hydropower, inland water ways, irrigation and flood control. The Central government has proposed to introduce a legislation to create this body.[46]

The geography of the Northeast adds an international dimension to hydropower. The 1,500 MW Tipaimukh multipurpose hydroelectric dam project on the Barak river in Manipur was allotted to NEEPCO in 2003. Its primary purpose was to contain the floods in the Cachar plains of Assam. Bangladesh fears that the project would dry up the Meghana, the Surma and the Kushiara rivers, which provide water in the north-eastern part of the country. The project is a source of strain in bilateral relations between the two countries.[47] Within Manipur, Hmar and Zeliangrong Naga communities associate the barrage site to a sacred place in their cosmology.[48] Concerns are also expressed from time to time about the Chinese intent to divert waters of the Siang northwards, which would reduce the Brahmaputra to a trickle.[49] China commissioned the 510 MW Zangmu in 2014 and had plans for three more dams in their 12th five-year plan. NITI Aayog made a case for a 10,000 MW single-stage storage project on the river in 2017, which would hold enough water, even if China were to divert the waters. This has been vehemently opposed by local tribal communities; and the state government remains non-committal.[50] The fears, so far limited to intelligence inputs, now appear to be closer to reality as China unveiled its strategic 14th five-year plan, which promised to construct a dam three times the size of the Three Gorges project. The local Tibetan government signed an agreement with Power China to execute this project.[51]

The debate between environmentalists and infrastructure aficionados around dam construction continues to rage globally. Klingensmith called dams 'political symbols', which epitomize the conquest of nature, progress and the modern state.[52] Environmentalists believe that large dam projects interfere with nature's equilibrium. Patrick McCully, in his book *Silenced Rivers: The Ecology and Politics of Large Dams*, cautions that, 'Dams also tend to be built in remote areas, which are the last refuge of species that have been displaced by development in other regions.' Calling them 'Temples of Doom', he asserts that the trauma of resettlement is exacerbated for indigenous communities, given their strong spiritual and cultural ties to the land.[53] It would be imprudent to brush aside concerns of environmentalists for protecting biodiversity. In India, a perception remains that, 'only rich countries can afford environmental regulations'.[54] A more structured process needs to be set in place for an Environmental Impact Assessment, which inspires trust and credibility. Pema Khandu accepts that hydropower development must be undertaken in harmony with ecology. In a democracy, he feels, securing people's consent is crucial.[55]

People of the Northeast must not feel that the Central government is foisting projects in their region for the benefit of people elsewhere. Bureaucracy in New Delhi tends to assume that it is easy to displace a small number of people, with a handsome rehabilitation package, in the interest of development. Nari Rustomji observes in his book *Imperilled Frontiers: India's North-Eastern Borderlands* that, 'The tribals' attachment to his land is almost fanatical.' It would be futile to suggest to an Adi of Arunachal Pradesh, whose ancestors have lived along the Siang, to surrender their land and settle in the high mountains of Tawang, which hold no cultural resonance.

For bureaucrats working in the region, Rustomji had a piece of advice, 'Examining the social implications of change requires no less technical and expert know how than performing a surgical operation or the construction of a dam.'[56] It is feared that outsiders would alter demographic balance and destroy tribal culture. A dialogue with deeply democratic tribal communities would give them a sense of ownership in the economic development. Social communication skills, not the strongest forte of government bodies, must, therefore, be strengthened.

6

In Search of Shangri La

IT WAS THE spring of 2016. Well-settled in the coastal town of Daman, I unexpectedly received my transfer orders for terra incognita: Arunachal Pradesh. Googling the place out of curiosity, I stumbled upon diverse imagery—tattooed faces of tribal women wearing hideous-looking nose plugs, Buddhist monks of Tawang draped in ochre-coloured robes, myriad dance forms of different tribes of the state and dramatic landscapes of hills and valleys gushing with pristine waters. It sparked my curiosity as I boarded the plane to Guwahati, its nearest directly connected airport from Delhi. The six-hour journey from there to Itanagar took me through the lush green grasslands of Assam, cutting across the floodplains of the Brahmaputra. The sheer expanse of the floodplains and the magnificence of the river course presented a picture of fertility. My driver casually muttered that not so long ago, this was the hotbed of ULFA activity. The serene setting of paddy fields bore no visible signs of being killing fields in the recent past. Sari-clad girls mirthfully cycling back from school allayed the shadow of fear that crossed my mind. The road wound up along the gentle slopes to Itanagar, already soaked in drizzling darkness. The town surely needs an upgrade, as do the roads—I made a mental note, even though the journey was exhilarating. This sentiment sums up travelling experience in much of the Northeast.

Unlike regular tourist explorations, planned around destinations, the thrill of travel in the Northeast lies in the rapturous joy which the journey beholds. American philosopher George Santayana, way back in 1964, in his essay 'The Philosophy of Travel',[1] wrote about the human motivation to travel,

> The latest type of traveller, and the most notorious, is the tourist. Having often been one myself, I will throw no stones at him; from the tripper off on a holiday, to the eager pilgrim thirsting for facts or beauty, all tourists are dear to Hermes, the god of travel, who is patron also of amiable curiosity and freedom of mind. There is wisdom often in turning from the familiar to the unfamiliar: it keeps the mind agile, it kills prejudice and it fosters humour.

For a 'pilgrim thirsting for beauty', Northeast India offers a delightful rainbow of choices.

Over the next two years, I had the rare privilege to travel to the most unexplored parts of the state, sometimes for work, other times for pleasure. One of my most abiding memories remains the journey to Tawang, known for the seventeenth-century Ganden Namgyal Lhatse monastery. From the moment you cross the foothills of Assam to enter the western part of Arunachal Pradesh, you can smell the tranquil air. The drive along the Kameng river gives a whiff of the rapturous beauty that lies ahead. Bomdila is a quaint township, laden with Buddhist symbolism. Multicoloured flags with printed verses from scriptures flutter in the breeze, wafting a message of peace. Young novice monks naughtily scamper around the town, wearing religious finery, in blissful ignorance to the more austere roles in the offing. The landscape changes dramatically as the road winds down into the Dirang Valley, with apple and kiwi orchards lining the roadside. The journey thereon and up to Sela Pass brings you to a zone of celestial silence at 13,000 feet above the sea. The air is so rarefied and cold that it bites into the bones. The lake nestling at the top is a picture of serenity, with shimmering waters inspiring sacred awe. A small army canteen dishes out hot samosas and tea. This, incidentally, was also the setting for the battle of Nuranang with the Chinese. As per local folklore, a brave Indian soldier held out single-handedly for a while, with the help of two local girls—Nura and Sela. Rifleman Jaswant Singh Rawat was posthumously awarded the Maha Vir Chakra for his gallantry. A war memorial now stands at the place, aptly named 'Jaswant Garh'. The army treats him to be still in service and continues awarding promotions. Bed tea, breakfast and dinner are duly served to his room to keep his memory alive.

Streams, rivers and waterfalls gush along the road to Tawang. Pink rhododendrons adorn the mossy mountains, while yaks and ponies strut around the meadows. The district, which boasts of 108 lakes, is flanked by Bhutan on the one side and Tibet on the other. The town revolves around the monastery, suffused with quietude. The main prayer hall chimes with Tibetan hymns and the fragrance of incense, mixed with that of lamps lit with ghee, fill the air. The monastery has been a big draw for celebrities and public figures from around the world, including Hollywood stars like Richard Gere. Bum La, an hour's drive over a rocky road, is a pilgrimage of sorts. The air exudes a certain mystique, accentuated by the ruggedness of the terrain. It feels as if these mountain ranges have remained frozen in time and only the hardy herders venture in these inhospitable climes. The reclusive road is seeped in history. It was part of the route taken by the young Dalai Lama during his flight from Lhasa in 1959. A few years later, the same rocky road saw the People's Liberation

Army marching down the road. Now an Indian Army outpost stands guard by a heap of stones, a tribute of tourists to mark the friendship between the two countries. Signposts in English and Mandarin greet visitors along the invisible McMahon Line. Driving along the Tibetan border, we reached the meadows of Mago and Tse Chu. According to Tibetan folklore, Bon Lama turned a bamboo grove upside down, which now falls on the Chinese side. Guru Padmasambhava flung his rosary against a rock, which became the font of 108 springs. The 'holy waters' are now inside Indian territory, while the Chinese have planted cameras on their side for viewing the sacred spring. Anecdotal evidence suggests that local Tibetans throw empty bottles tied with strings and helpful neighbours fill them up with holy waters in return.

A journey immersed in such unspoilt beauty left me rejuvenated. It also made me wonder whether such a destination would draw the affluent traveller, accustomed to seven-star luxury. Accommodation is austere. Local cuisine is unique, though an acquired taste. For the explorers, pilgrims and adventure seekers, the Northeast is paradise. Monument chasers, shopaholics and party animals would be disappointed.

There is much on offer across the Northeast. Spiritually inclined travellers could find peace in the Rumtek monastery of Sikkim, offer prayers at the Kamakhya or Solomon temple in Aizawl. Adrenaline rushes in abundance while river rafting in the Siang or hiking up the Gorichen peak. Nature lovers are drawn by authentic forest experiences in the last remaining shelters of wild animals. The fabled one-horned rhino can only be found hiding behind the wild elephant grass of Kaziranga. If you want to spot the elusive red panda, you might have to camp for months in the forests of Namdapha, where it is struggling to save itself from extinction. Pristine waterbodies like the Tsongmo lake of Sikkim to the Loktak lake in Manipur are a draw for migratory birds and people who love spotting them. Music lovers are spellbound by the natural rhythm of the hills. This is truly the land that reverberates with the exquisite sound of music manifested by the talented choirs of Meghalaya, Mizoram and Nagaland. Lahe Lahe, meaning slow living, which became a fashionable proposition during the Covid-19 pandemic, is a way of life in these parts. This is the most culturally diverse region in the country—almost each district has a unique cuisine, dress and dance form. Yet it remains the most undiscovered, least known and most underrated destination of the country. Perhaps, it is a blessing in disguise that it remains hidden in its unspoiled splendour.

The Northeast barely receives eight million domestic tourists and 160,000 foreign tourists a year.[2] Assam, being the gateway of the east, receives the highest footfall, followed by Meghalaya and Sikkim. Nagaland, because of the niggling insurgency, gets much lower numbers.[3] The tourism industry is sensitive to perceptions. Bloodshed, ethnic strife and student unrest defined the region for decades. This dissuaded even the most bohemian of explorers. For the first time in post-independence history, the region has seen sustained peace. Poor connectivity, a hallmark of the Northeast so far, made travel uncertain and expensive. This too has changed now. Accommodation remains a challenge, though homegrown entrepreneurs are making an effort to fill this gap.

Rich forest cover and biodiversity are unique selling propositions of the Northeast, which set it apart from any other part of the country. Ecotourism presents a natural comparative advantage. Sikkim, with some Japanese support, made a pioneering effort to align incentives for conservation and sustainable tourism. Local communities, empowered to manage ecotourism assets, adopted it with great gusto.[4] The state remains a leader in homestays, which are graded into gold, silver and bronze categories.[5] More than 700 homestays were set up under a government-sponsored rural tourism programme. Tourism policy unveiled in 2018 made environmental sustainability and cultural integrity central pillars, with a focus on 'low impact/high value tourists'.[6]

The Lepchas, being protectors of land and water, are very enthusiastic about this environment-friendly approach. A mix of European tourists and young Indian corporates prefer the quiet environs on the fringe of the Dzongu reserve. Imaginative homestay owners have curated experiential holidays, combining cultural expression with immersive forest sights: bird watching, butterfly spotting, angling and trekking. Bhutan, being a neighbouring kingdom, has served as an inspiration to the approach followed by Sikkim. The state has followed a much more modest approach to branding its tourism.

In the other states, the tourism department has arrogated upon itself the responsibility of building infrastructure. In the name of creating accommodation, millions have been spent on badly designed and poorly constructed brick-and-mortar monstrosities. During my tours in Arunachal Pradesh and Mizoram, I was appalled at the ill-maintained tourist lodges. The motivation for deciding the location is usually a greedy landowner, eager to make a quick buck through a contract awarded in lieu of the land donated for the project.

A handful of die-hard conservationists are scripting change, where the state has failed to make an impact. Ramana Athreya, a Pune-based astronomer-turned-conservationist, led a remarkable initiative in Eaglenest sanctuary in Arunachal Pradesh. Rigorous research and documentation over two years revealed more than 700 bird species in a limited zone of 200 square kilometres. The avian rarity comes next only to that found in Amazon rainforests and Central Africa. Roping in the local Bugun tribe, Ramanna started a community-led conservation cum ecotourism initiative in 2006, with a meagre grant of Rs 15 lakh. The bare-bones campsite, on the fringe of the forest, became profitable in the very first year, generating a revenue of Rs 40 lakh. Local communities became partners in the project and several amongst them work as trained bird guides. Marketing biodiversity knowledge was a crucial success factor for attracting the niche community of birders. In Ramana's words, 'Bad facilities surely deter tourists, but good facilities alone don't attract people. Stories do.' Today, despite the basic facility, the sanctuary is on the global map. Ramana advocates the establishment of 'smart townships' on degraded forest land, involving local communities and the forest department. His new fad is 'moth tourism', which he proposes for the lean period. He exuberantly showed me images of a white cloth strung along two bamboo poles in the thick of the sanctuary, with a UV lamp behind. Hundreds of colourful moths congregated there with a vivid display of their wingspans.[7] Citing the example of Kaziranga in Assam, Ramana argues that people associate the one-horned rhino with the state because of its successful branding strategy. In Peru, Bolivia and Ecuador, people take half-hour flights for Amazonia, just for the experience of a real forest.[8] State-backed investments along with community-led conservation cum management could create wonderful results in the Northeast.

Pakke hornbill conservation initiative is a partnership between wildlife scientists and change-making forest officials. Tane Tapi, district conservator of forest, has been posted in the Pakke Tiger Reserve since 2004. Earlier, villagers there used to hunt the rampaging elephants that devoured their crops. Tapi started the 'Ghora Abhe' (village father) society. Roping in the village headmen ('gaon buras') of fourteen villages, he seized sixty-seven illegal arms of villagers between 2007 and 2009. Four cottages were constructed to provide alternate livelihoods, such as local guides, housekeepers etc., for people who gave up farming to save the elephants. Nyishi, the local tribal community, would also kill hornbills for its colourful beak, which they used in their traditional headgear. Gentle persuasion helped them switch over to wooden beaks. Villagers spotting a hornbill nest were rewarded Rs 2,000 for each find and were made their protectors. In the second year, the Hornbill Nest Adoption Program (HNAP) was launched. Any bird lover could contribute money and adopt a nest, to be cared for by hornbill protectors. Tapi says, 'Since 2015, we are organizing Pakke Paga festival annually, where nearly 5,000 tourists participate, including people who adopted the hornbills. Now there is good roosting and tourism also has picked up.'[9]

Institutionally, forest department had practically no role in this unique initiative. Aparajita Dutta, a senior scientist with the Mysore-based National Conservation Foundation and armed with a doctorate in hornbill conservation, mentored the program. She drew inspiration for HNAP from similar initiatives in Thailand. The project receives American and European grants, which are used for micro initiatives at the community level. With a certain degree of pride, she shares that over the last decade Pakke has become a regular draw for a large number of bird photographers and ecologists.[10]

Bano Haralu, a television-journalist-turned-conservationist, led an equally remarkable community-led program for saving the Amur falcons in Nagaland. Recalling the horror she felt during her visit to the 'killing fields of Pangti' near the Doyang Hydro Electric Project, she remembers people carrying 'sack loads of dressed birds' for sale. In 2012, she started engaging local communities and political leaders, explaining the long annual sojourn of these rare winged creatures—from Siberia, through India, and to South Africa. A tenacious woman, she made them give up the abominable practice. She remains bitter about the apathy of the government,

> Pangti is barely four hours from Kaziranga, which is a hotspot for tourists. All that Nagaland government was supposed

> to do was to construct a link road to roosting site, promote homestays and create some amenities. Sadly, they equate tourism with funds. So much money has flowed in the name of conservation, none of which was spent for supporting local communities.[11]

Her exceptional work is captured in the award-winning documentary film *The Pangti Story.*

It is obvious that ecotourism should be accorded foremost priority. Conservation strikes a chord with tribal communities and restores their ruptured affinity with nature. The lead must be taken by state forest departments to align incentives for conservation, ecotourism initiatives and livelihoods. Legislation alone can never be a deterrent for deforestation or poaching. Nor is it practical to expect a sparse battery of guards and officials to safeguard vast forests. Building stakes for communities for conservation is what holds the key.

Nagaland has followed a different trajectory for tourism. Alemtemshi Jamir, a retired chief secretary, reminisces how a bunch of young people wanted to organize a carnival two decades ago. This became the inspiration for the annual Hornbill Festival. S.C. Jamir, former chief minister of Nagaland, was the guiding force behind the initiative. 'Hordes of people spontaneously turned up for the festival, even with sparse infrastructure,' recalls Alemtemshi. The heritage village at Kisama, on the outskirts of Kohima, is now the permanent venue for the festival. An array of thatched huts and traditional morungs (dormitories) styled in traditional architecture that is unique to each tribe of the state, is the hub of winter celebrations, ahead of Christmas. Naga cultural identity and cuisine is showcased with pride, alongside western attractions like rock concerts and fashion shows.[12] In 2019, nearly 2,40,000 people attended the marquee event. Local handicrafts and handlooms are popular takeaways, especially among foreigners. Commodification of culture has ignited a revivalism of the Naga identity in a predominantly Christian society. Puritans frown upon the merrymaking and the consumption of local brew; but the Union Minister of North Eastern Region terms it as the 'torchbearer' of a new cultural journey of the north east.[13]

Inspired by Woodstock of yore, the Ziro Valley in Arunachal Pradesh, home to the enterprising Apatanis, hosts the largest open air music festival. A campsite is set up in the midst of golden-brown paddy fields. The fields are unique, in as much as they also double up as fish ponds. Musicians and music lovers from around the world throng to perform, listen and enjoy. Two elevated bamboo stages called Donyi (sun) and Polo (moon) transform into yin-yang venues for performances during the day and night. Apong, the local rice beer, and Apatani delicacies are a hit with youngsters who loll along the grassy slopes, soaking the music. In 2017, I went to Ziro as a curious traveller and was struck by the presence of African drummers performing on stage, their traditional music resonating with the tribal environs. The festival is acquiring a cult status amongst music lovers. The villagers have embraced the festival happily, opening up their homes for tourists, offering them a peep into their special culture. Folklore has it that Apatani women were endowed with such rare beauty that they would mask it with ugly looking cane nose plugs and large tattoos on their faces. Of course, the practice has died away, though the older women still carry the marks.

Music and dance are a quintessential part of northeastern life. Assamese celebrate Bohag Bihu to mark the onset of spring, ushering in processions that 'transcend caste and creed', uniting a people in celebration.[14] Each tribe of Arunachal Pradesh has its own festival: Mopin of the Galos, Nyokum of the Nyishis, Losar of the Monpas and Solung of the Adis. Nagaland boasts of Mimkut of the Kukis, Sekrenyi of the Angamis, Aoleang of the Konyaks and Tsukheneye of the Chakhesangs. The more homogeous Mizos celebrate Chapchar

Kut, known by its rhythmic bamboo dance. The Manipuri dance Pung Cholom, with its acrobatic drummers whirling in the air with ecstatic beats, is a mesmerizing sight. The Sangai festival of Manipur is a ten-day long winter cultural extravaganza, showcasing diverse cultural heritage. The intersection of culture and rural tourism provides a rare glimpse into the tribal way of life, which is rapidly receding in the past. Namsai's Sangken festival, similar to Holi in the mainland (people spray each other with water), is celebrated all over Southeast Asia—Thailand, Cambodia, Myanmar, Laos, with a different nomenclature. Oken Tayeng, a pioneering entrepreneur, questions, 'Why can't we use soft diplomacy under Act East policy for cultural exchanges in this region.'[15]

A region whose landscape is marked with high mountains, gushing rapids, rugged terrain, is a natural draw for the adventure seeker. The adrenaline rush that makes enthusiasts test their boundaries, is a way of life for the mountain folk. Oken Tayeng has been curating a week-long 'Siang Rush' for the last three years. He invites travel writers, bloggers, instagrammers and other social media influencers for an immersive experience of rafting, trekking, camping, angling and jungle trails. 'Building an unbiased narrative ignites genuine curiosity amongst enthusiasts, which no brand campaign can achieve.' Hiking, mountaineering and rafting camps opportunities are drawing young adventure seekers to Sikkim and Arunachal Pradesh. The Central Government established National Institute of Advanced Mountaineering and Allied Sports in Arunachal Pradesh in 2012, which offers a range of courses in paragliding, mountain terrain biking, white water rafting, scuba diving and mountaineering. The Sikkim government has also set up an institute with a similar menu of courses. The Covid-19 pandemic has sparked a new interest in 'slow travel' and 'trail tourism'. Globetrotters are looking for safe and serene locations to whet their appetite for wanderlust. With the right ingredients in place, the Northeast could become the trendsetter for a new genre of tourism.

Global connoisseurs had first raised a toast to Assam tea in the nineteenth century. The industry now faces stiff competition from new players such as Sri Lanka and Kenya, deeply affecting profitability of tea estates. Plantation owners are now making an effort to create a niche market for tea tourism. In 2018, while travelling to eastern Arunachal Pradesh, I stayed overnight at the Mancotta Bungalow. The 140-year-old colonial property is now a quaint resort, which evokes an old-world charm. Waking up on a winter morning to the delightful sight of a tea garden enveloped in mist is a glorious experience. Walking around the estate, I saw plants of differing vintage, women of the tea tribes carrying bamboo baskets on their backs, diligently picking tea leaves. An educative tour of the factory left me much wiser on the painstaking effort that goes into converting the leaves for a perfect brew. In the evening, I had an invitation for tea at the Victorian era chateau of the cultured and unassuming owner, Manoj Jalan. He showed us around his horse stables, sharing his passion for riding and training racehorses. He rued the declining profitability in tea business, in the face of rising overheads and a fierce global competition. Most estates will soon fold up, he predicts, as the younger generation is diversifying into sunrise industry. He feels tea tourism has potential, but needs a strong government support to grow.

The Wild Mahseer, yet another heritage property in Balipara, and the Chameli Memsaab Bungalow in Jorhat are popular destinations. The latter holds a special appeal for American, Japanese and Koreans travellers. Named after a George Baker film, it offers organic treats and opportunities for golfers next door.[16] The Thengal Manor is an exquisite property owned by the Barooah family of Upper Assam.

Originally designed as a family abode nearly a century ago, this luxurious tea estate bungalow now operates as a high-end resort.

Tea tourism is a growing trend, drawing in well-heeled and affluent tourists in search of solitude, while being pampered with old world hospitality. The Assam tourism department organizes an annual tea festival at Jorhat, combining tea estate experiences with golf and a visit to Nambar forest reserve. Tea tourism is yet to acquire the following that draws global tourists to the vineyards of France, Italy and South Africa, but hold a lot of promise in the coming years.

The exotic locales of the Northeast make it eminently suited for shooting of films. Assam, Arunachal Pradesh and Nagaland have been popular destinations for outdoor shoots. Tourism policy of Assam allows financial incentives for film shoots.[17] In Arunachal Pradesh, Chief Minister Pema Khandu has adopted a more hands-on approach, inviting leading producers and Bollywood actors such as Salman Khan, John Abraham and Nawazuddin Siddiqui to visit the state and to share their experience on digital platforms.

City folks are yearning for 'rustic leisure, the inverse of the seven-star experience', feels Ming Larsing, the urbane owner of Ri Kynjai, a resort overlooking the Umiam lake in Shillong. The attraction of the Northeast lies in its mystique. Cultural ethos, diversity and unspoilt beauty of the nature make it special. The eclectic traveller is drawn to authenticity of experience. Bhutan, right next door, has followed an approach to tourism that keeps cultural integrity and sustainability as non-negotiable principles. Tourism cannot become an instrument of cultural annihilation or natural destruction.

It is ironic that the rich and famous of India who proudly share pictures on social media from exotic destinations of the Far East—Vietnamese cuisine, Balinese art or Cambodian architecture—are ignorant of the treasures that lie closer home. A nebulous picture of the Northeast comes to mind, if ever the conversation veers in that direction. Vacuous expressions of the Lutyens' elite greet you when you begin extolling the beauty of the Northeast. This is a sad testament of the degree of isolation of the region. Part of the problem lies in the absence of a regional branding that could ignite curiosity. The coming years will see a growing trend of people getting closer to nature. The prolonged Covid-19 pandemic hemmed us in the confines of our homes, repeatedly so, igniting the urge to travel once again. To breathe the fresh mountain air, to see the star-spangled skies, to stand in silent surrender before a gushing waterfall are joys one can only find in the Northeast.

In his essay 'Why We Travel', Pico Iyer wrote, 'And if travel is like love, it is, in the end, mostly because it's a heightened state of awareness, in which we are mindful, receptive, undimmed by familiarity and ready to be transformed.' My love affair with the Northeast continues undimmed.

7

Fruit Bowl of India

'The idea of conquering nature is as sensible as if a man should try to cut off his own head so as to isolate his superior faculties ... We have tried to conquer nature by force and by intellect. It now remains for us to try the way of love.'[1]

—Lord Northbourne, *Look to the Land*

SIKKIM, A 300-YEAR-OLD kingdom and trading entrepôt for Tibet, Bhutan and Nepal, became the youngest state of the Indian Union in 1975. By then, the Green Revolution had taken firm roots in the national agrarian landscape. High-yielding seed varieties and chemical fertilizers were the flavour of the season. This went against age-old farm practices in Sikkim and the rest of the region, which were organic by default. In February 2003, Pawan Kumar Chamling, farmer-turned-chief minister, made an audacious resolve in the state legislature: to transform Sikkim into a fully organic state. His statement went beyond a politician's rhetoric and became a personal article of faith. Driven by deep conviction, Chamling invested his political capital in chasing this goal, dismissing sceptics and critics along the way. The state embarked upon what turned out to be a thirteen-year-long epic journey of persistence, persuasion and perseverance. On 31 December 2015, Sikkim became India's first fully organic state. Prime Minister Modi applauded the efforts of the farmers of Sikkim, terming it as an 'example of resolve', expressing hope that this would be a harbinger of nationwide change.[2]

Organic transition experiments in other countries like Australia, New Zealand and the United States of America proceeded incrementally—one farm at a time.[3] Sikkim chose to make a giant leap, covering 50,000 families tilling 75,000 hectare of farmland, all in one go. Chamling the poet-politician mused, 'We have not inherited this earth from our forefathers but have borrowed it from future generations, it is our duty to protect it by living in complete harmony with nature and environment.'[4] With a growing global preference for healthy food, it also made sound economic sense.

Chamling was the chief minister of the state for twenty-five years. He had the political heft to lead Sikkim's organic movement from the front. A bold withdrawal of subsidy on chemical fertilizers was a starting point. In its place, construction of rural composting pits was incentivized. In 2014, sterner measures ensued. Use of chemical fertilizers and pesticides was banned by law. The Sikkim Organic Policy set in motion establishment of 'bio-villages', following the 'one village, one crop' norm.[5] The launch of the Sikkim Organic Mission in 2010 was a turning point. It co-opted officers from agriculture and horticulture departments, creating a parallel structure, devoted to a single cause. Self-sufficiency in food and youth employment became central goals of the mission.[6] A fully funded programme for training and creating rural infrastructure including bio-fertilizer units was rolled out. Farmers were cajoled to go organic, though there were teething troubles. Six agencies were deployed for guiding the process of organic certification at the farm level. Five high value crops and spices were given special attention: ginger, large cardamom, turmeric, buckwheat and cymbidium orchids.

Sikkim is the second largest producer of large cardamom in the world, next only to Nepal. The spice is an essential ingredient of the rich cuisine of South Asia and the Middle East. Ravikant Avasthe, formerly a principal scientist with the Indian Council of Agricultural Research (ICAR), associated with the Organic Mission since its inception, recalls the shift from grain cultivation to more remunerative spices and vegetables: 'Farmers shifted from rice cultivation to large cardamom and acreage under vegetable cultivation grew fifteenfold. Strong political will helped in the alignment of objectives of various wings of government.' A huge administrative effort created a buy-in amongst farmers and consumers alike. 'Local residents, being conscious about the health benefits of organic produce, willingly shell out 15–20 per cent more money.'[7] Sikkim's example, he feels, offers a scalable model for the other Northeast states to follow.

Laxmi Prasad Bista, a thirty-seven-year-old large cardamom farmer from West Sikkim, had humble beginings. Financial stress at home forced him to lease 10 hectares of land for farming. Today, he aggregates the produce of seventeen other farmers and is able to sell it in the local market at Rs 600 per kg, though in the past he has even fetched thrice as much. A neat profit of 30 per cent leaves him with an annual income of over Rs 2 million. Cardamom flourishes the most without pollution. Road construction, ironically, is a cause of worry as fuel emissions are bad for the crop. Siliguiri is the main trading hub for large cardamom. Bista believes holding auctions within the state would eliminate intermediaries and give true value to the farmer. He, unhesitatingly, lauds the role of the state and Central government agencies. The Sikkim government provided water sprinklers, tanks, pipes and seeds—all free of cost. All it took was some courage and a lot of hard work to make it all happen.[8]

Vladimir Nabokov used the symbolism of orchids in his landmark book *Ada* (Ardour) to define the forbidden amorous relationship between Van Veen and his cousin Ada. H.G. Wells in his short story 'The Flowering of the Strange Orchid' lends a mystique to the flower: 'Pride, beauty, and profit blossom together on one delicate green spike, and it may be, even immortality.' Orchids have found their way in the living rooms of the wealthy across the world. World trade in orchids is estimated to be around $150 million. The Netherlands, Thailand, Taiwan and Singapore are the leading exporters. India imports cut flowers worth Rs 340 million annually.[9] The Northeast holds the lion's share of orchid species within the country. In the late nineteenth century, British botanists George King and Robert Pantling documented 449 species of orchids in their book *The Orchids of Sikkim-Himalaya*.[10] In the post-liberalization period, the Sikkim government imported hybrid cymbidium varieties from Holland, New Zealand and Australia. 'Five hundred plants along with a greenhouse were distributed to identified growers,' says Padam Subba, state director for horticulture. Nearly 150 farmers are presently engaged in orchid cultivation and they sell their produce to Mainaam garden, a firm owned by Pawan Kumar Chamling's wife. Nearly a million cut flowers are sold annually to wholesalers in Delhi. Prices at the farm gate are Rs 60–80 per flower spike, which go up threefold in the wholesale market and sevenfold in the retail markets of Delhi. Some farmers prefer selling potted plants directly, each pot of three flowers fetching Rs 3,000. The challenge, Subba says, is the long gestation period of the flowers, nearly five years, during which period farmers need alternate soruces of income.[11]

'Vegetables, much like babies,' says Arjun Chhetri, proprietor of Vartoh Organics, 'need tending not just in growing, but also equal care in transportation.' Chhetri used his ingenuity to bridge the chasm between the farm and the market. An agri-entrepreneur, he supplies seeds to over a hundred farmers with buy-back guarantees. A showroom in Gangtok serves as his base, before goods are dispatched to Siliguri, enroute to Kolkata, where a temporary storage is available in the government-run Sikkim House. Farm-fresh vegetables arrive on the shelves of Spencer's Retail shopping malls in Kolkata, where the Bengali bhadralok shop for veggies. He focuses on niche products like asparagus and pak choi. Organic avocadoes, he says, sell for five times the cost. An astute market observer, he is selling the homegrown yacon, an exotic Peruvian tuber and a cross between apple and watermelon. 'Google it to discover the health benefits,' he says. Chhetri is using heat pump dehydration for vacuum-sealed broccoli, so that it retains its colour and taste. He is now dipping his fingers into the pickling business and vacuum dried chips. With a monthly turnover of Rs 6,00,000, he aims to reach the 2 million mark soon.[12]

The Northeast is blessed with agro-climatic conditions without a parallel in the country. Fertile soil nurtured by perennial rivers and plentiful rainfall give it a distinct advantage. Progressive farmers, with a gentle nudge, have readily embraced cultivation of high-value crops, vegetables, spices and flowers. Kale, quinoa, citrus, red rice, black rice, stevia—all proliferate with ease in these conditions. Nagaland is especially known for growing king chilli, which is the hottest in the world. Most of the Northeast states have a surplus in fruit and vegetable production, opines Dr Dipjyoti Rajkhowa, who heads the ICAR facility in Nagaland. It is just a matter of connecting the dots.

Tamenglong shot to prominence because of the herculean effort made by its people, led by Armstrong Pame, in constructing a 100-kilometre long road. However, it is also the fertile ground for the fabled Tamenglong orange, which now has a distinct geographical indication (GI), much like the Californian Napa wine. The Manipur government has been hosting a festival around harvest season to popularize the fruit. Dr Meghachandra Singh rues over the bad roads that damage large quantities before they even reach Guwahati. A principal scientist with ICAR at Imphal, he boasts of kachai lemon and queen pineapple, which could compete with the finest in the world.[13] A modest beginning has been made for airlifting pineapples and some spices like organic ginger and turmeric to Delhi, though there is a long way to go.[14]

Dambuk, a slumberous township of Arunachal Pradesh, comes alive in December to host the annual Orange Festival. It takes place during the peak fruiting season of the sweet mandarin orange. In 2017, I drove to Dambuk Valley from Itanagar to participate in the festival, a mix of rock music and off-roading. Miles of orange orchards appeared to have been sliced straight out of California. Enterprising women lined up on the road with charming bamboo baskets full of the citrus fruit. It truly was and remains the sweetest and juiciest orange I have ever tasted anywhere in the world. Out of curiosity, I enquired why these were not available elsewhere in the country. Farmers, I was told, sold off their produce for a pittance, mostly smuggled to Bangladesh. One enterprising farmer exported a small consignment to Dubai. A year later, SpiceJet started a sister concern, SpiceFresh, using the underbelly of the aircraft for transporting perishable cargo from Dibrugarh. Ajay Chopra, the former Chief Operating Officer of the company, ventured to Dambuk on an exploratory trip. He says, 'We got the oranges tested in laboratories. It turned out that the sweetness levels of Arunachal mandarins far exceeded Nagpur ornages and Punjab kinnows. A sorting, grading and packaging plant was set up at Digboi, with an investment of Rs 7 million. The oranges reached Big Bazaar and Aditya Birla stores of Delhi, Kolkata, Chennai, Mumbai, fetching twice as much as the Nagpur orange.' Sadly, after a year of operations, the venture was aborted. 'There is too much nepotism and corruption amongst the officials in the field. We got almost zero support from the local bureaucracy, who are averse to transparent practices. The fertile soil of the state with its rich horticultural produce could easily make it a force to reckon with.'[15] In 2022, Arunachal Pradesh Agriculture Marketing Board collaborated with the Central government export agency for dispatching 6 MT of oranges from Dambuk to Dubai.

Eventually, New Delhi woke up to the organic potential of the Northeast. It was too much to expect a small farmer to beat all odds of geography and venture solo in national markets. Mission Organic Value Chain Development (MOVCD), tailor-made for the region, was launched in 2016. Drawing upon Sikkim's experience, it encouraged clustered crop cultivation. Farmer Producer Company (FPC), with at least 150 farmers in a contiguous area, growing a single crop, became the focal point. The FPC became the farmers' interface with the rest of the world. Subsidies are provided for inputs, aggregation, storage, certification, transportation and processing. It also provides a platform for peer learning and sharing. For a buyer from Delhi, it is a one-stop-shop. Okit Palling, the official driving the programme in Arunachal Pradesh, says, 'Farmers tend to listen to a leader who has credible experience to showcase.'[16] So it is with life!

India imports three quarters of its kiwi fruit, costing $34 million. Of the domestic produce, Arunachal Pradesh accounts for more than half, followed by Nagaland, Mizoram and Sikkim.[17] The Ziro Valley, with its salubrious climate and enterprising people, accounts for the bulk of production in Arunachal Pradesh. Gyati Loder heads the 500-member strong 'Subansiri organic kiwi and cardamom FPC', started a couple of years ago. In the business for the last twenty years, he recalls two IAS officers from Ziro who first introduced the plant from New Zealand. The conditions were perfect for the fleshy green fruit. Several farmers joined the kiwi bandwagon, but there was no market to sell the delicate produce. The FPC became a rallying point for farmers. Loder says,

> Last year our company produced a surplus of 350 MT. All big chains such as Reliance and Big Basket buy from us, making immediate online payment on collecting the produce. The Union agriculture secretary visited Ziro and helped us in the establishment of collection centres. Now we have refrigerated vans, which are used by all farmers. Collectively, we set a fixed price for sale, which was Rs 110 per kg last year. We have established a nursery in our district, which we are going to use for selling seeds to other states of the region.

The fresh approach has increased the bargaining power of farmers, introduced efficiencies in production and helped spark interest in buyers from the mainland, minimizing the risk of losses.

Wakro, a small township in the neighbourhood of Dambuk, was once known for its oranges. It abuts an area where poppy cultivation has been practised by farmers for years. The state government has unsuccessfully tried to wean off farmers from the poppy crop. Krisiko Basamlu, a feisty orange grower of Wakro, was grappling with a personal crisis—her mother was diagnosed with cancer in 2007. She was advised organic green tea during recuperation. Basamlu turned adversity into an opportunity and started growing tea in her garden in 2008, with the support of a consultant in Kolkata. Motivating other farmers to join in, she started an organic tea unit in 2011. Last year, she produced 4,000 kg of tea, marketed under the label of Wakro Organic Green Tea. For two years she exported her produce to Canada, but with changing consumer preferences in India, she sells it locally now. Expressing disappointment with the officialdom of the Tea Board of India as well as the local agriculture department, she says that they have misplaced priorities. Instead of linking farmers with a growing concern, they are being given a subsidy for rubber plantation and stevia as alternatives to poppy.[18]

Prince Dhawan, a thirty-year-old computer science graduate from the Indian Institute of Technology (IIT) Delhi who became an administrator, was the deputy commissioner of Lohit, which covers Wakro. The absence of a farmers' database was a big problem for him, so he set out to create one. He geofenced all active farmers on a map for targeted interventions. While working with the FPC, he identified 'anchor farmers', around whom others would readily rally. 'The biggest challenge is to break the credit cycle of farmers. In the absence of land titles, which could serve as collateral, banks are loath to lend and farmers end up falling in the clutches of Assamese moneylenders,' he says. Sensing infirmities in agriculture extension, he hired agriculture graduates, each catering to a group of thirty farmers, for mentoring and support. Finding a market outside the state entails building a story that would fetch a price. The district produces good quality organic turmeric with a high curcumin content, which was information he uploaded on an online platform. It sparked the immediate interest of buyers from as far off as Madhya Pradesh, who placed an order of 10 MT.[19]

Karma Bhutia, a politician-turned-farmer, took up farming as a hobby in East Sikkim. The politician in him did not subside, and he started mobilizing women for farming. A pioneer of the FPC movement in the state, he became a mentor for others. Starting with a modest beginning of just five groups, he has now formed 165 farmers' groups, 90 per cent of the members being women. Using his own farm as a demonstration unit, he motivated others to adopt intercropping practices using an organic approach. He took the lead for transportation and marketing to Gangtok, where the state government had set up an organic supermarket in Lal Bazaar.

However, he worries for the future. With an ageing farming community and recalcitrant youth preferring stable government employment, the prospects of farming are dim.[20]

Palm oil is imported in large quantities in the country, primarily from Malaysia and Indonesia. And so a national mission was launched in 2014–15 to promote large-scale cultivation. Mizoram and Arunachal Pradesh were the first ones to move into this segment, partnering with agro companies like Ruchi Soya, 3F and Godrej Agrovet.[21] Nearly a tenth of coverage under palm oil cultivation lies in the Northeast.[22] Contract farming models were deployed by companies, who would give planting material with buyback guarantees on fruiting. The Lower Dibang Valley district alone has 1,100 hectares land under palm oil cultivation, supported by 3F. The company entered into individual contracts with farmers in an unregulated market. Miuli Dature grows the plant over 200 hectares of land, making him one of its largest producers in the country. He ventured in this space in 2017, and the plant started bearing fruit a couple of years later. But he is anxious about the future as the company has not yet moved to set up a processing unit, as was envisaged earlier. Nor has the floor rate been decided by the state government. For a product that is a crucial ingredient for Indian cooking, prospects are huge. The government must establish a framework to minimize the risk of the farmer against the vicissitudes of market prices.[23]

Samir Bordoloi is an unusual Assamese. He left a flourishing job with Tata Chemicals for his first love—farming. Armed with a degree in agriculture from the Assam Agricultural University, he became a 'plant doctor', visiting farmers with dollops of advice to switch to organic farming. In the first year itself, he managed to link 1,500 farmers to his clinic in Jorhat, with a modest annual subscription of Rs 50. He started providing organic inputs to the farm gate. A turning point in his approach occurred when he got a chance visitor—Peggy, an organic aficionado. He accompanied her to Majuli, the world's largest river island. A quiet conversation made him ponder why he was doing a hard sell for expensive organic manure, instead of chemical fertilizers. Zero-input agriculture with a self-sustaining model would be the way forward. He travelled to Nagaland, Manipur and Arunachal Pradesh to understand indigenous farm technologies of tribal farmers who had no recourse to cow dung. Herbs and extracts of weeds served as substitutes. He used this approach to revive two farms near Dibrugarh with farmers who had earlier enrolled in the old ULFA camps, lured by dreams of an elusive green revolution. Deeply affected during Operation Bajrang and Rhino by the army, they were desperate for a renewal of their farms. Bordoloi also saw young people shying away from agriculture, which became his next area of focus. He started a programme, Parivartan, with 300 schoolchildren in Jorhat, teaching them vermicomposting and organic farming. Young change agents forced their parents to change. Subsequently, he acquired 4 bighas of land next to Lahowal College near Dibrugarh, primarily targeting rural students. He set up an organic farm along with a bamboo house, and started living there. He offered weekly classes for undergraduate students, subsequently enrolling them as interns. Word spread fast. A big industrialist wanting to foray into organic farming made Bordoloi a partner. The largest organic farm in the Northeast, spread over 8 hectares in an industrial area, with 250 cows and a 300 MT vermicompost unit, thus came into being. Bordoloi now got a real chance to put his learning to practice. He then acquired 30 bighas of land near Guwahati to start a learning centre.

According to Bordoloi, there is a 'conspiracy behind food' unleashed by the multinational corporations who sell hybrid seed varieties, decimating local gene pool and crops. He started targeting low-volume high-value crops, modelled on the ULFA camps. He enrols 'green commandos' for a paid three-day training programme. 'Glamorizing farming' with the military outfit of commandos, it became an instant hit. Currently, 426 commandos are spread across Meghalaya, Sikkim, Manipur, Nagaland and Arunachal Pradesh. The 'Farm Connect' programme made him open a store in Guwahati. Urban commandos became a link between farmers and consumers, encouraging people to adopt a farmer. In a win-win proposition, they got organic food at lower price, while the farmer secured higher rates. Digital platforms like Facebook and Instagram are extensively used for targeted outreach. Now, he is expanding into farm plus activities: an organic restaurant and agro-tourism.[24] In recognition of his achievements, he secured the Ashoka Fellowship in 2019 and has bagged several national and state awards. Bordoloi's organization, Society for Promotion of Rural Economy & Agricultural Development, North East (SPREAD-NE), is a pioneering example of private agricultural extension, enlisting youth in agriculture while promoting organic practices.

The Central Agricultural University, Imphal, has seven affiliated colleges in the Northeast and six vocational training centres in the region. Its Vice Chancellor, Dr Premjit Singh, feels that the approach of government departments is 'different', implying a lack of interest in collaboration with academia. Research institutes independently develop rural farm technologies, seed varieties and have an outreach through NGOs. In 2017, they distributed more than 1,00,000 plants to 10,000 families across the region. In his personal capacity, he is also an advisor to the Bhartiya Kisan Sangh, an affiliate of the RSS. He is engaging 5,000 farmers, affiliated with the organization, to establish twenty model fruit villages across the Northeast.[25]

Despite these tremendous gains, the Northeast is yet to transcend the bounds of geography. Sporadic efforts by individual farmers and the FPC are unable to break the glass ceiling. Dr K.M. Bujarbaruah, a well-respected scientist and a former VC of the Assam Agricultural University, feels that a consortium approach to marketing must be adopted. 'Let us say there is a demand for 100 MT organic turmeric. It will be difficult to immediately source good quality turmeric in large quantities.' He argues that states like Arunachal Pradesh have such a low intensity of chemical fertilizer usage that they can easily switch to organic farming. Mizoram and Sikkim have tapped the growing organic market. 'The bio-resources of the Northeast, which include below-the-ground resources, are unique in the country. Bacteria and fungi found in these parts, through genetic manipulation, can transform bio-resource to bio-wealth,' he adds. The states of the Northeast should focus on those crops in which they have a comparative advantage, rather than trying multiple small experiments all over. 'Speciality horticulture' will provide economies of scale and help convert the region into a single market, he says. Medicinal plants found in the Northeast have a strong demand in pharmaceutical companies, but a strong documentation of resources is essential. Bujarbaruah believes that for farmers of the Northeast, digital platforms like the Electronic-National Agricultural Market (E-NAM), initiated by the Central government, provide a useful medium to reach remote customers and secure remunerative prices. His long experience in the region has seen mixed gains. The real value, Bujarbaruah feels, will be realized once agro-processing takes off in the Northeast, which hasn't happened so far. A unified market within the region is a starting point.

The organic revolution of the Northeast is one of the least known facets of the region. As the prolonged impact of the Covid-19 pandemic makes people wiser to the importance of healthy living and healthy eating, the farm practices of the region could serve as an inspiring model for others to emulate. After all, it is but a return to the roots. Albert Howard, the botanist known as the father of organic farming, in his audaciously titled work *An Agricultural Testament,* quotes Henry Wadsworth Longfellow's words from the poem 'The Fiftieth Birthday of Agassiz',

And Nature, the old nurse, took
The child upon her knee,
Saying: 'Here is a story-book
Thy Father has written for thee.'

'Come, wander with me,' she said,
'Into regions yet untrod;
And read what is still unread
In the manuscripts of God.'

8

Education to Enterprise

ONE OF THE most enduring memories of the Covid-19 pandemic etched in our collective conscience will be the moving imagery of millions of migrants, trudging along highways on a painful journey back home. In the shadow of this mosaic is also the story of thousands of youth, students and patients scrambling to reach the eastern frontier. The urban exodus was a sobering reminder of the extent of migration in India. It was also a marker of an aspirational people who define India's new Northeast. Limited employment avenues and low-quality of education in this region drive its youth to look elsewhere. Rural youth in the Northeast move to state capitals for college, while the more affluent ones turn to the mainland. Some venture abroad. At the heart of this movement is a thirst for education and a spirit of enterprise. Migration to the mainland is also a manifestation of the rejection of violence, which sapped the creative potential of an entire generation of Northeasterners.

The journey across Brahmaputra is not an easy choice for a people so rooted in clan and community. In cities, they find comfort in the collective refuge of urban ghettos. Cities rob them of their identity, culture and cuisine. Pork, beef, bamboo shoot and king chilli, part of their daily cuisine, are hard to come by in Indian cities. The convivial feel of their idyllic homes is sorely missed. *Axone,* a 2019 film streaming on Netflix, portrayed the prejudices these youngsters encounter in the mainland. The title of the movie, also pronounced as 'Akhuni', is the name of the fermented soya bean of Nagaland that is used to cook pork across the region. For the unfamiliar nose, the pungent smell is repugnant. The disdain with which mainlanders view this preparation in the movie is symbolic of a cultural condescension experienced every day by the Northeast migrants. Their 'un-Indian' appearance attracts racial discrimination and sexual innuendo. Insensitive mainlanders casually call them 'chinky', a pejorative reference to their Mongoloid features.

Not all educational migrants come with a clear purpose. On one end of the spectrum are those who beat the odds to secure an admission with a goal in mind. Zilpha Modi, aged thirty-two, teaches at the Rajiv Gandhi University in Arunachal Pradesh. In her childhood, she used to walk 11 kilometres to school. An educational pilgrimage took her to Delhi University, before she joined Oxford University. Her more affluent peers, educated in the Catholic schools of Darjeeling or Mussoorie, 'planned summer holidays in Mauritius'. Modi feels that the affirmative action that has helped underprivileged children get admissions needs a review. She says, 'Scheduled Tribe reservation quotas in higher education must have a creamy layer to exclude the wealthy.'[1]

Peer pressure, parental ambitions and prestige value are guiding factors for other students. They end up being lured by commercially driven colleges that have mediocre pedagogy. Those who stay back in the city after their education end up with low-paying jobs such as salespersons in shopping malls, masseurs in spas or waiters in restaurants, where they are hired for their 'exotic orientalism'. Some land call centre jobs due to their fluent English-speaking skills.

Sociologist Duncan Mc Duie-Ra attributes the 'allure of travel, excitement and fulfillment of dreams, very different from their parents' for the strong demand for the airline industry.[2] Air hostesses clad in immaculate uniforms have a glamour quotient. The generous pay package of airline cabin crew jobs makes it a draw for young girls from the Northeast.

Impersonal urban environs can be overwhelming for youngsters. 'Coaching in life skills is crucial for children before they step out of their comfort zones. Resilience to deal with failure and cultural adaptability is a prerequisite for youngsters to work in the mainland,' asserts Mark Stone, a Shillong-based soft skills trainer. Taking instructions from a figure of authority itself is incompatible with flat tribal traditions. In his experience, children belonging to Christian states—Mizoram, Meghalaya and Nagaland—have greater adjustment problems because of different faith and value systems.[3]

Fieldwork by Dolly Kikon, a Naga anthropologist at Melbourne University, traced the journey of young migrants from Nagaland waiting tables at plush restaurants in Mumbai. Parents are desperate to send children away from a conflict-ridden environment. Youngsters are conflicted between the tug of home and the jibes at work.[4] The yearning for home never dies. Kikon says, 'We are like salmon who go back to our spawning grounds. We must know our roots and grow from there.'[5] Hekani Jakhalu was a partner at a law firm in Delhi. She would fret about the working conditions of a large number of Northeasterners employed in shopping malls in the face of racial discrimination and sexual harassment. Fifteen years ago, as a retail boom in Delhi saw a surge in the job market, the Nagaland government opted for a quick fix for the growing unemployment problem at home. Desperate youngsters, trained in basic skills, were pushed to choose these low-paying retail jobs. Hekani quit her job and relocated back home to establish YouthNet, a platform that trains youth for local jobs. The 'Prime Minister's thrust on skilling has helped us in the last couple of years,' she feels.[6]

Much like Hekani, Niranjan Singh returned to Imphal after quitting a flourishing career in international retail in the UK and Dubai. His company, set up a decade ago, trains youth in hospitality, tourism, retail, electrical training, tailoring, accounts and IT literacy. 'In the last five years, law and order has improved and so has the ecosystem. Only half of the trainees are now leaving the state, while the rest work locally,' he says.

In the Northeast, the tenuous link between education, employability and employment snaps at some point. A national leader in primary-level literacy, education in the region collapses beyond secondary school. This is partly attributable to the fact that just over a quarter of secondary school teachers are trained.[7] 'There is a math phobia amongst high school students. A large part of the blame must be apportioned to bad teachers, as the students are second to none,' opines Professor R.P. Vadhera, former pro-VC of Mizoram University.[8] The propensity to avoid maths shows in the lowest enrolment numbers from the region when it comes to engineering courses. The number of engineering colleges are also very low as compared to the rest of India.[9]

Educational opportunities are much greater in Delhi and other metro cities, both for professional courses and the liberal arts. On the other hand, there is a perception of inadequacy of the quality of teaching in local colleges in the Northeast. As commissioner of higher education in Mizoram, I visited a prestigious local college in 2019. The lecturer was using Mizo language as the medium of instruction to teach public administration. That left me flummoxed as the exam conducted by Mizoram University is in English. The lecturer later explained that students who come from rural areas, having done their entire schooling in Mizo, find it difficult to comprehend lessons in English. It is no wonder then that most of them enrol for undergraduate courses in Mizo, even though there would be no jobs for them later. Educated youth aspire for white-collar jobs, and government employment is the only recourse, where openings are too few. College instruction in Mizo in any case rules out employment opportunities outside the state. The Northeast has more than 2.1 million job seekers in the under-thirty age bracket. Educated unemployed, in a region with a history of strife, is a serious political problem.

Then there are those who drop off the education grid—the numbers are worrisome. Nearly three-fourth of children who join school do not finish class ten.[10] There are only two ways to address the unemployment conundrum: bring the jobs to the people or take people to the jobs. Industrial training institutes are an oxymoron in a region with limited industrialization. Along with polytechnics, they churn out youngsters trained on archaic machines. State governments end up roping in partners for training in retail, aviation (cabin crew), hospitality, wellness, banking, call centres, etc., targeting higher secondary school dropouts.[11] These are the youngsters who end up in megalopolises, lured by the promise of fat salaries and a good lifestyle.

There are the inspired few who go back to their roots for skilling and enterprise. Richard Belho is one such unusual Naga. Known as the 'bamboo architect', he runs a training school midway between Kohima and Dimapur, which he calls the 'living school'. A section of the massive structure under construction has his own house overlooking the valley, a poultry farm and a pigsty. His goal is to imbibe skills of resilience, sustainability and adaptability in youngsters. In a state prone to earthquakes and heavy monsoons, concrete should be banned, he feels. Sadly, bamboo has come to be associated with the poor, while concrete has a status symbol attached to it. The green gold grows wild in the Northeast. Northeastern bamboo is far superior to South American or Indonesian bamboo, the former being too weak and the latter too heavy. 'The pandemic is making people look at the future with a different perspective. They had become too dependant on government jobs and easy money, forgetting their relationship with the land. The root of the problem lies in our educational system, which forces students to study twenty years for a colonial job. I work with alcoholics, drug addicts and dropouts. Having fallen off the grid, these misfits of society are more creative.' Childhood was tough for Richard as he saw peers losing lives to drugs and alcohol. They joined the underground, to be shot, killed or to overdose. 'Permanence of the impermanent would bring the community together once again under a thatched roof,' he muses. At any given point in time, he works with nearly 200 youth to train them in sustainable livelihoods and in taking care of the ecosystem. In the lean period, they grow chillies and tomatoes to earn their livelihood.[12]

Sexual exploitation of urban migrants pushed seventeen-year-old Hasina Kharbhih to start the Impulse NGO Network in Meghalaya. She offers a contrarian view of the skilling programme run by the government. 'Skill India turned our rural youth into labourers,' she fumes. She pledged to stem the tide of migration of rural women by leveraging an exclusive source of strength of the region: handlooms. Over the years, she has created a network of 30,000 artisans. Master artisans distribute yarn and oversee production quality. Generous output-based spot payments incentivize women to work. Co-creation and co-branding with twenty to twenty-five designers takes their weaves to the market. The digital platform, Amazon Saheli, helped bridge the locational disadvantage. 'In a post-Covid-19 world, this model is best suited for women, who are truly toiling away on their looms within the confines of their homes,' she says. A Fulbright scholar, Hasina's work has won her many accolades and awards.[13]

The weft of handloom binds the rural Northeast with nearly 2 million handlooms. The region accounts for a fifth of handicraft units in the country.[14] Jesmina Zeliang calls herself a 'cultural entrepreneur'.

She smelt an opportunity during her education in Mumbai. Starting with a single weaver in the '90s, she expanded to more than fifty within a year. 'I realized that we need to transform our designs into something more relevant for people outside the region.' Moving away from bright colours to monochromatic ones, she used pure fibre for soft home furnishing material. Armed with a few samples, she audaciously approached Shyam Ahuja, the 'Dhurrie' king of India, and got her first big break. 'I had a bull run for the next five years,' she recalls. Refusing to put all her eggs in one basket, she tied up with Fabindia to export her merchandise. One consignment ended up with the Conran Shop, the iconic global brand in soft textiles. Great feedback from buyers encouraged her to expand in the export market. 'I dug my own tunnel,' she says. With a bagful of samples, she went on a voyage to the USA, the UK and France. 'I left no stone unturned—from Laura Ashley, Macy to Lehmanns. I came back dejected.' Meanwhile, she got a lucky break with a Dutch scholarship in Rotterdam; she was one amongst forty picked from around the world. 'Ethnic chic' was showcased at the most prestigious exhibition in Paris. Crate & Barrel, the American leaders in home furnishing, gave her an order of $140,000 in 2010 for eri silk cushions, table runners and other merchandise. She developed her consignment in Delhi, using block prints of tribal tattoo designs. Today, her creations reach South Africa, Mexico, Jamaica, Australia and the United States. Now a proprietor of two companies—Heirloom Naga and Cane Concept—she works in a cluster model with women weavers and craftsmen around Dimapur: 'I am a bridge between the maker and the market.' Her textile line fetches an annual turnover of Rs 20 million.[15] A single mother, Jesmina has come a long way from the dusty bylanes of Dimapur.

Jesmina is a role model for Charlee Lalthlennawia in Aizawl. He stumbled upon a course on art history at the National Museum in Delhi, which inspired him to revisit his tribal heritage. Returning to

Aizawl, he researched the puan, the traditional women's wraparound. Limited market appeal of local weaves forced him to improvise. Starting with three weavers, he now works with sixty-four rural women using loin and shuttle looms. Procuring the finest quality natural fibre yarn, he uses contemporary colours to produce home furnishing and clothes, which he supplies to boutiques in Goa and London. Not only does this make economic sense but it also helps empower women, all while preserving the traditional craft.[16]

Sanjukta Dutta is spearheading a revival of the Assamese mekhela chador, infusing modern accents in traditional motifs. The silk yarn is produced by a unique silkworm, found only in a single village of the state. An engineer by training, she found her calling eight years ago, which supports over a hundred artisans preserving a dying tradition.[17] The fabled chador has even reached the Cannes film festival, and several Bolywood stars such as Tabu, Preity Zinta, Karishma Kapoor and Priyanka Chopra have also worn her designs for the ramp.[18]

Handloom and handicraft have been the hallmark of rural traditions of the Northeast. Each tribe boasts of its own unique design and colourful motifs. The challenge for this rural enterprise is on two fronts. Firstly, demand has shrunk. City dwellers have more or less stopped wearing traditional attire, except on the occasional customary occasions. Market outside the region has limited demand for the coarse weave. Secondly, soon, there will be no hands to work the loom. Sualkuchi, once known as the Manchester of Assam, is emptying out. Walking inside the weaving village on the outskirts of Guwahati, I asked a young girl if she would create the pretty designs that her family has been producing for generations. She smartly sidestepped the question and said she would opt for fashion designing instead. The old-fashioned loom, one in each house of the village, is a rickety wooden contraption and requires the weaver to have a perfect hand-eye coordination to get the right design. A few progressive entrepreneurs like Charlee and Jesmina are the saving grace for this sunset enterprise.

Thirty-two-year-old Nixon Bui was born in Daporijo, a nondescript township near the Chinese border. Armed with an MBA from Bengaluru, he secured a job with a Danish company. In Copenhagen, he pursued another MBA course and started a clothing fashion line, inspired by the Northeast's style. He also did a stint with a company making alcoholic beverages. Two years ago, he started the production of Nixonbui Vodka, which is marketed as a premium organic vodka from Greenland. He says, 'I have always been an explorer. My father works for the government in Arunachal Pradesh. I never wanted to follow in his footsteps.' Now he wants to test his entrepreneurial instincts back home.[19]

Educated youth are also turning into agri-preneurs. Tage Rita, daughter of a progressive farmer from Ziro, was born with an indomitable spirit. After securing a degree in agricultural engineering two decades ago, she joined a government job, like most others. Meanwhile, kiwi cultivation had taken firm roots in the valley. She was anguished to see the fruits of her father's labour rotting away in the absence of a market. She quit her secure job and made a bold gambit. Inspired by the Sula Vineyards, she started a winery with a loan of Rs 40 million to launch India's first organic kiwi wine—Naara-Aaba—in 2017. Ironically, its beautifully labelled bottles are imported from China. Over 300 kiwi farmers supply fruit for her winery, which produces 60,000 litres of wine annually. So far, the sales are limited to Arunachal Pradesh, Assam and Meghalaya, though she has global ambitions. 'I left my job to chase a dream. Entrepreneurship in agriculture is not as glamorous as you soil your hands and feet to connect with the earth. But this is where our roots lie,' she says philosophically. [20]

Vijay Byrsat left a plush banking job at Merrill Lynch in New York and returned to Shillong. He ventured on a bike ride across the Northeast and discovered the agricultural diversity of the region. In 2015, he set up the Centre of Learning, Knowledge and Services to train farmers in apiculture. Over the last five years he has trained 8,000 farmers and formed a network of 31,000 farmers across the Northeast. His agri-business revolves around food, beverage and cosmetics. Launched in 2018, Bee Natural is a premium brand for spices and honey. A QR code scan on the label pops up the face of the grower, creating a human connect with a distant buyer. Another venture of his launched in 2017, MADessentials, tapped into the pool of aloe vera farmers who were left in the lurch after an International Fund for Agricultural Development (IFAD) programme folded up. Vijay manufactures aloe vera lip balms, creams, shampoos and face wash, which have a national market. He is currently working on a digital platform to connect farmers with markets across India.[21]

Dasumarlin Majaw completed her masters in biochemistry in 2004, before moving to Gujarat. At the National Innovation Foundation, she learnt how to mobilize farmers. In 2016, she returned to Meghalaya to pursue her first love: coffee. She had fond childhood memories of sipping the hot beverage with her grandmother. With a modest loan of Rs 2.5 million, she launched Smoky Falls Tribe Coffee, linking 800 farmers with the venture. She uses Amazon to sell it across India. Now she has even ventured into value addition in jackfruit, a fruit grown in abundance in the state, large quantities of which (Rs 4 billion) are wasted annually.[22] She makes chocolates and pizzas from jackfruit now.

The 'enterprise bug' has travelled across the Northeast. Hanjabam Shubhra Devi had a similar journey. After completing her masters in food and nutrition from Banasthali Vidyapith in Rajasthan, she sought a government job. But in 1990, she joined as a lecturer in a private college and also started working with an NGO for health, nutrition and women empowerment. In 2015, she took the entrepreneurial plunge to establish Meira Foods. Women empowerment remained her central theme. Pickle has never been a part of Manipuri cuisine, though fermented fish and bamboo shoot are staples. Shubhra started pickling vegetables and fish, blending them with the flaming hot king chilli, a local favourite. It became an instant rage. Last year, her turnover crossed Rs 20 million, four-fifths of which was from sales within the state, the rest was from other parts of India and some from Myanmar as well. Most of her ingredients grow wild: amla, wild apple and bamboo shoots. 'During the Covid-19 lockdown phase, people of the state were discovering the value of going local,' she feels. She sees a sea change in the industrial outlook. People used to look up to only the big players from outside. Policies of the state government and the Startup India scheme of the Union government has helped generate enthusiasm. 'Entrepreneurs are now looked upon as celebrities, like movie stars. I dream that products made in Manipur will be sold nationally.'[23]

Youngsters of the Northeast take to technology with ease, their lack of interest in engineering notwithstanding.[24] This is driving a surge in digital start-ups. Rewaj Chhetri, an exuberant twenty-six-year-old from Sikkim is the founder of NE Taxi. During his engineering studies in Itanagar, he was struck by the vacuum of online travel information. Using his network of college friends, he started a digital cab aggregation company. Chhetri now has a footprint across the Northeast and a growing presence in Bhutan, Nepal and Sri Lanka. He says, 'I want to be the Airbnb of the Northeast and will launch NE Holiday over the next few months, as a composite holiday platform.' His venture earns him Rs 50 million annually.[25]

Sunder Sharma ventured into Edtech in Imphal, starting as a franchise for a Delhi-based company in 2012, providing online lessons for medical entrance exams. Sensing a demand for quality digital content, he established Hillsland Education in 2018, which offers online tutorials in hybrid languages for students of class ten and twelve. Recorded video lessons are loaded on a website and a mobile application called I-Tute. Inspired by the success of the southern giant Byju's, this venture was a great hit with students, who pay a modest fee for the programme. The platform was hugely popular during the Covid-19 pandemic-induced lockdown. He is now expanding his base to Mizoram and Assam.[26]

Dayananda Pibarel Meetei, a twenty-nine-year-old doctor-turned-entrepreneur in Imphal, grew up with a bedridden father and a mother who worked odd jobs. For him, securing an MBBS seat was easy; financing it was tougher. Borrowing money from his extended family, he started earning while learning. A chance encounter with an IT engineer who became a mentor altered his perspective. Thus, Medilan Ambulance Service, an online platform, was born. In 2018, he expanded to home care nursing, adding ventilators, patient beds and other equipment to his ambulance fleet. Within a year, revenue grew from Rs 1,00,000 per month to a million. In 2022, his annual turnover touched Rs 30 million. Startup Manipur, a state-run programme, gave him Rs 3 million subsidy built into a concessional Rs 10 million loan, without any collateral. A competitive process of screening, overseen by the chief minister, picked thirty other candidates. 'We should not wait for anyone to change our lives, but control our own destiny. For me the whole country is a market. Sitting on the eastern fringe, I am looking west,' Meetei shares exuberantly.[27]

Creativity is a genetic dispensation of the people in the Northeast. Three years ago, Sikkim-born Karma Paljor, a former CNN journalist, teamed up with Assam's Tanushree Hazarika for the digital news platform EastMojo. Before relocating to Guwahati, Karma worked in Mumbai, and Tanushree was in Boston. The platform found its mojo, with a monthly viewership touching a million. The duo also curate the annual Brahmaputra Valley Film Festival. Karma feels, 'The Northeast is a storehouse of talent. Each production house in Mumbai has at least five to six youngsters from these states, with a flair for sound, music and videos. Post the Covid-19 pandemic, the demand for digital infotainment is bound to grow.' They aspire to create a state-of-the-art production and post-production facility, catering to film-makers of Bhutan and Bangladesh.[28]

The musical genius of the Shillong Chamber Choir took the country by storm a decade ago. They shot to fame by winning the popular TV show 'India's Got Talent'. A performance before President Barack Obama brought them centre-stage. The versatile choir, nurtured by Neil Nongkynrih, a trained concert pianist himself, innovates with musical medleys. Their repertoire ranges from old Bollywood songs to the Vienna chamber orchestra. Their lead singer William Richmond says, 'Music is like fragrance, bringing a familiar warmth. Our choir is about bringing joy and softness in people's hearts. Church choir traditions of Meghalaya helped, but it was also a lot of hard work.'[29] Sadly, Neil passed away in 2022, but his memory and traditions live on through his music. The quartet of Tetseo sisters from Nagaland is yet another group of musical entrepreneurs. Singing in the Chokri dialect, their songs hearken to Naga legends of love, life, death, war and glory. Their harmonious melody has enthralled audiences in lands as far away as Edinburgh.[30]

State governments have shifted their focus from employment seekers to job creators. Manipur, Meghalaya, Assam and Sikkim are leading the drive. Assam launched a start-up policy in 2017, but soon realized its limitation in ecosystem creation. IIM Calcutta Innovation Park, a company established by the Indian Institute of Management Calcutta, stepped in to help then. With a 360-degree solution—mentors, investors and market—it works on a hub-and-spoke model. In January 2019, the first cohort of fifty joined. Pranjal Konwar, the Chief Operating Officer, shared that a year later twenty-five of them have a stable revenue stream, seven have raised more than Rs 70 million, and ten did business of more than Rs 1 billion. Venture capital (VC) funds are showing a lot of interest, especially in handloom, agro and tourism ventures.[31] The investment vacuum is also being bridged by companies like Imphal Angels, founded in 2018 by Niranjan Singh in Manipur, which provides a digital interface between angel investors and aspiring start-ups.[32]

In 2018, the Central government created a Rs 1 billion VC fund that is managed by the North Eastern Development Finance Institution (NEDFI). The sector agnostic fund has committed Rs 450 million for twenty-one start-ups so far, informs Prashant Talukdar, the fund manager.[33] Mridu Das, a beneficiary of 24 per cent equity infusion in his enterprise Automovill, is a software engineer from Jorhat. He spent more than twelve years between Bengaluru and Chennai in the software industry, meeting a wide several young entrepreneurs. Teaming up with a school friend, he launched a digital platform for car servicing in 2018, bagging contracts for Uber in Bengaluru and Hyderabad. A digital aggregator of service stations, his firm had a turnover of Rs 50 million in 2020.[34]

A mini start-up revolution is taking shape in the Northeast. Nimble-footed entrepreneurs are leveraging technology to break geographical barriers. Women are taking the lead in entrepreneurship. Some of them keep ambitions local, while others are testing boundaries of regional and national markets. There is no dearth of ideas. A key impediment is availability of finance for translating those ideas into action. Banks are hesitant to lend in the absence of collaterals of land ownership documents. But that is not deterring the ambitious young Indians of the eastern frontier. The survival instinct and a hunger for catching up are driving them to take risks and venture into new domains.

9

A Sporting Nation

IT IS UNUSUAL to spot a female-led Bollywood movie, more so a boxing biopic. In 2014, when Bollywood actress Priyanka Chopra donned boxing gloves for the movie *Mary Kom*, she broke a stereotype. The film portrayed the epic story of a village girl from Manipur. A girl with an unconventional life, worthy of narration on the silver screen. In a moment of clairvoyance, her parents had christened her Chungneijang (meaning high, wealthy and agile) upon birth. Tilling paddy fields, her father, though a wrestler himself, had no disposition to encourage his daughter to become a pugilist. Mary's own childhood aspirations were rather modest: get a government job, earn enough money to buy a Pulsar bike 'with my first prize money'.[1] But destiny had other plans. She went on to become a legendary Indian boxer, winning gold medals at the global stage.

Mary Kom's crowning glory is the medal she won at the 2012 London Olympics. It was the first time that women's boxing was introduced as an Olympic sport, and Mary won a bronze medal for it. Her name was etched in history. An Arjuna awardee, she has also been conferred with the highest civilian honours by the Government of India: the Padma Shri and Padma Vibhushan. In 2016, she was nominated to the Upper House of Parliament by the President of India.

In her memoir *Unbreakable: An Autobiography*, Mary shares her story of struggle and sacrifice, which eventually led to her success. Her tribal identity runs across as a central theme in her narrative. She reflects that, 'One of the greatest motivating forces for me has been my desire to assert the identity of my tribe "Kom" within my country and world over.'[2] The accomplishment at the global stage was an act of redemption for all the discrimination she experienced during her early years of training in the mainland. In a candid account, she recalls, 'Because of our oriental looks, people from the Northeast are often mocked in other parts of India.'[3] Mary Kom now runs a private boxing academy, nurturing fresh talent in the sport that brought her laurels. For youngsters in Manipur, she is an iconic role model, whose life they all wish to emulate. Naturally, her academy, replete with modern equipment, is a big draw with the youth of the Northeast.

Manipur has a sporting history without a parallel in the country. Legend has it that modern polo owes its origins to the princely state of Manipur, where it was called sagol kangjei (horse hockey). Club culture is the foundation of sports in the state. Over 1,000 community-run sports clubs across the state, supported by voluntary contributions, are the hubs of athletic activity.[4] It is remarkable that a state that has seen much bloodshed and insurgency is now a fertile playfield for sporting talent.

Today, the craze for football in Manipur matches the fervour of cricket in the rest of India. Despite the odds of remoteness, poor infrastructure and unrest, Manipur emerged out of nowhere to win the Santosh Trophy in 2002. The Bengal bastion was finally breached.

The first crop of footballers were trained at the Tata Football Academy (TFA) in Jamshedpur. The '90s saw the rise of Manipuri footballers like Kiran Khongsai, Gumpe Rime and Khemtang Paite, sparking a soccer movement in the state.[5] 'Kiran made us believe that we can do it. No Manipuri had reached such heights before,' says Renedy Singh, a former captain of the Indian football team.[6] An alumnus of the TFA, Renedy started his professional career with the Mohun Bagan Athletic Club. 'Now, there are several private academies including one backed by corporates like Reliance Industries, who recognize that there is footballing talent to be found in the hills of the Northeast,' he says. Renedy signed up for Mohun Bagan, the leading club of West Bengal, before joining the Indian football team. 'Over the last twenty years, Manipur has been producing footballers in the way Punjab used to once produce hockey stars,' he adds. After his professional footballing, Renedy joined Indian Super League as an assistant coach. Learning the ropes of coaching from Spanish and British coaches, he started his own football academy in Manipur and is now the head coach of Neroca Football club. Renedy underscores that unemployment is a key driver for youth to take up the sport professionally. Many big players can now earn up to Rs 10 million in six months. Most footballers of Manipur come from humble backgrounds, where even schools don't function. 'Sports is a passport to a good life,' feels Renedy.[7]

Close on the heels of Manipur is its neighbouring state of Mizoram. Mizoram's spectacular rise in football is largely attributable to the tenacity of one man: Lalnghinglova Hmar, 'Tetea' to his friends. He took charge of the Mizoram Football Association a decade ago and rejuvenated the sport from amateur level to professional status in a short span of time. A journalist by background, he knew the power of media combined with the local passion for football could work wonders. The Mizoram Premier League (MPL) was launched in 2012 in collaboration with Zonet, the local Mizo cable television—creating a revolution of sorts. Inspired by the Manipur league system, the MPL provides a structure and organization to the game. A pyramidal model, which reaches down to each of the 800 villages, has enthused rural youth to try their skill in the field. With limited recourse for recreation in villages, sports offers a good escape. Intervillage tournaments lead to district-level competition, culminating in the MPL playoffs. Fortuitously, the state government stepped up to invest in quality sports infrastructure with artificial turfs. Each district headquarters boasts of at least one football turf and stadium, which is the sole noticeable structure, apart from the local church. FIFA's grassroots programme also started training in Aizawl. The efforts bore immediate results; and within two years, Mizoram, led by Zico Zoremsanga, lifted the Santosh Trophy in Siliguri.[8]

Robert Rommawia Royte, footballer-turned-sports-entrepreneur, is the owner of the Aizawl Football Club. A key politician of the ruling MNF party, he is now the sports minister of Mizoram. In an exuberant exchange with me, he shared his insights about the game in the state. 'What has really kick-started the football talent in the state is its club culture, which infused a sense of competition and a platform for drawing rural youth. Moreover, football as a sport became a source of employment, with average salaries ranging between Rs 20,000 per month to even ten times more,' he says. A keen footballer himself, who captained his college team, he mobilized resources for his sporting venture through a mix of promoter contribution and sponsorships. Some players who were part of the club are now earning much more in other clubs across the country. He rues over the meagre resources allocated for sports in the state budget, 'Last year, footballers from the state earned an estimated Rs 130 million, while the state government's allocation for sports was just three times as much.' Some footballers such as Jeje Lalpekhlua, who plays for the Chennaiyin Football Club, are said to be earning as much as Rs 20 million. Jeje is the star amongst current Mizo footballers. A member of the Indian football team, he is also the second-highest goal scorer and a leading club player in the Indian Super League.

According to Robert, 'It is imperative that the Central government finances not only infrastructure in the Northeast, but also supports football clubs financially. This will help draw greater rural talent. In fact, the club-based approach is replicable in other sports as well. Drawing youth into sports would help wean them away from social evils like drug abuse and alcoholism, areas of much concern for all of us. A club-centric approach has a sense of community and camaraderie. It helps create viable alternatives for rural youth employment. My own club has engaged 800 footballers.'[9] Royte's Aizawl FC scripted history by winning the national I-League tournament in 2017. He proudly claims to have created 240 sports academies in schools across the state, with an eye to 'catch them young'.[10] It is no surprise that nearly half of the twenty-one-member Indian squad for FIFA under-17 come from the Northeast.[11]

Over 300 Mizo footballers are playing professional football outside the state, assesses Tetea. In spite of a thriving club culture in Meghalaya, Manipur, Mizoram and Tripura, it is far off from global benchmarks. Aggregation of talent across the region would make it a formidable national force. Love for sport drives youngsters to football. Passion and talent alone do not ensure professional success. Mentorship, coaching and infrastructure are crucial ingredients for excellence. Youngsters of the Northeast nurture a sense of pride, not just for individual glory, but also for bringing laurels to their community. 'When Zoramthanga says something, it remains on the margins of national newspapers. When Jeje scores, it hits the headlines,' chuckles Tetea.[12] Sports is a way of reclaiming the lost space in mainstream media, where news of the Northeast is eclipsed by other states. Glory in the sports field provides a reaffirmation of belonging to the nation, through a public recognition of talent.

~

The dearth of quality coaches and infrastructure has been a major impediment. However, on both fronts, much has changed over the last decade. Tata Trust established a Centre of Excellence in Aizawl for coaching budding footballers. One of the finest in the country, it is headed by Mr Colin Toal, a 'no-nonsense Englishman, who brings punctuality and discipline amongst the boys,' chirps Tetea. He adds, 'Sportsmen need good coaches, just like students need good teachers.' Football talent from the Northeast is beginning to catch international attention. In 2020, Ngangom Bala Devi from Manipur had just turned thirty when she was signed up for the Scottish Giants Rangers Football Club.[13] Legendary Sikkimese striker Bhaichung Bhutia was the pioneer amongst male players to represent European football clubs. Now retired, he feels that the region needs a unified league to draw the best sporting talent. Given the richness of talent, the government should ramp up investments to create world-class sports infrastructure.[14] Another Sikkimese, Sunil Chhetri, is the present captain of the Indian football team. He holds the distinction of being the highest international goal scorer. Carrying the legacy of another soccer star from the Northeast, Talimeren Ao, a Naga medical doctor who led the Indian football team in the 1948 London Olympics, Chhetri is leading the national team.

The love for football in the region is now well known, but hockey was an unusual choice for Lalremsiami Hmarzote of Mizoram. Trained by local coaches at the Sports Authority of India (SAI), she was picked up for the National Hockey Academy in Delhi. She was part of the Indian team that won the gold in the Asia Cup in 2017 at Gifu and silver in the Asian games at Jakarta in 2018. 'I miss Mizo food and my people when I go out to play or train in my camps,' says the twenty-year-old player.[15] With formidable striking skills, she has been a top goal scorer for the Indian squad. In 2019, she was picked by the International Hockey Federation as the world's 'rising star of the year'.[16] She became the first female sportsperson from Mizoram to be part of the Olympic squad in the Tokyo Games of 2021, where India finished fourth.

Individual sportsmen and women from the Northeast are brimming with hope and confidence, making a name for themselves in the national and international arenas. A hunger for recognition fires their imagination. Lovlina Borogohain, a twenty-five-year-old pugilist from Golaghat district in Assam, has won two bronze medals in world championships. She has now set her eyes on an Olympic gold. In her village, she used to practise Muay Thai, but was offered a slot for a boxing programme on account of her fitness. Without any background in boxing technique, she found herself on unfamiliar terrain. During international tournaments in Russia, longing for her family would make her break down in tears. Having lost to a Chinese boxer twice in international boxing meets, she has now pledged to beat her in the Olympics. 'I always stop at bronze, I don't know why. Maybe it is psychological. I work hard and never give up mentally,' she says. Back home, girls her age are usually married off. 'My father, who works in a tea garden, made me dream. In the Northeast, people are poor, so we have to work extra hard for success,' she confesses.[17] During the Covid-19 lockdown, Lovlina was busy doing weight training with gas cylinders at home. Union Sports Minister Kiren Rijiju, who himself belongs to the neighbouring state of Arunachal Pradesh, was engaging regularly with sportspeople through video conferencing during the lockdown. She explains her routine and ambition during difficult times, 'Italian coaches train us, drawing a workout plan and a diet chart, which we have to follow. Earlier, I used to train empty stomach, but now the coach insists to do so after breakfast, which makes me more energetic. I am confident of my Olympic dream.' In Tokyo Olympics, she had to contend with a bronze, even as she nurses a golden dream.

Jeremy Lalrinnunga, a twenty -year-old weightlifter from Aizawl, became the first Indian to win a gold at the Youth Olympic Games in 2019. The son of a boxer, he is 'fulfilling his father's dream'.[18] He had joined the Army Sports Institute in Pune earlier, and has now been training at the National Institute of Sports in Patiala. Enthused about Khelo India, the new sports programme launched by the Government of India, he feels it is 'like an international-level tournament'.[19] Incidentally, he has won gold in the first and second editions of the tournament. Sadly, he missed out on an Olympic berth for the Tokyo Games due to a knee injury, though he aims for a medal at the 2024 Olympics in Paris. 'The Northeast can do much better in weightlifting, if infrastructure and facilities are better. The Chinese contingent have much better performance on account of their strong facilities and diet.'[20] Athletes from the Northeast often feel an emotional void when they are unhinged from their families and culture. Young Jeremy faced an emotional breakdown during the Covid-19 pandemic, when he was left stranded in Patiala without any regular calendar of training.[21]

Another young weightlifter aspiring for an Olympic medal is Mirabai Chanu from Manipur. Twenty-eight-year-old Mirabai had set her eyes on archery to begin with but was drawn by the 'intensity of weightlifting'. So strong was her passion for weightlifting that she would trudge 20 kilometres every day from her village to Imphal, cycling or hitchhiking a ride. Following in the footsteps of another legend from Manipur, Kunjarani Devi, Mirabai set a new world record in the World Weightlifting Championships at Anaheim in 2017. She misses life in the village with her family, but says that, 'I have to get that medal at the Olympics. And once I do, I will go home.'[22] She bagged a silver in the Tokyo Olympics and a gold in the 2022 Commonwealth Games.

Success in track and field events has somehow eluded Indian athletes. In 2019, the nineteen-year-old Assamese sprinter Hima Das wowed the nation with the five gold medals she bagged in European track and field events—all in just nineteen days. Nicknamed the 'Dhing Express' after her village in Nagaon district of Assam, she became the toast of a grateful nation. Nursing a back injury, she still harbours an Olympic dream. A farmer's daughter, she catapulted on the global stage inspired by the power of a dream.

A surprising Indian surge on the global cycling scene is being led by youngsters from Manipur. This defies common sense as one would hardly expect cycling to be a natural choice for athletes in the Northeast, given the hilly terrain. But L. Ronaldo Singh secured the top spot in all the four major junior global sprinting events. Of the four-member junior Indian team, three are from Manipur. Named after the Brazilian football star Ronaldo by his parents, he is an ace cyclist who won silver in the Asian Cycling Championship in 2022. His co-cyclist Y. Rojit Singh, also from Manipur, says global exposure has helped. The contrast in his experience of training in Germany were the 'superior food, infrastructure and weather', as compared to India. Like many others, Rojit has a humble rural background. His mother works as an Accredited Social Health Activist (ASHA) worker with the health department in Manipur. 'We find it easier to adjust anywhere we go as we don't have dietary restrictions, which some youngsters from other states face, especially vegetarians,' he says.[23] They are training under a former Air Force officer, R.K. Sharma, who is optimistic about Indian Olympic prospects in 2024. Given that no Indian cyclists has ever participated in the Olympics ever, this is a tall order. Between 2014 and 2021, have seen a budget expansion for the cycling federation—from Rs 10 million to Rs 250 million now. SAI and Honda have chipped in a big way to make this happen. Now the cyclists are trained on modern, technologically advanced cycles.[24]

Dipa Karmakar, a diminutive girl from Tripura, became the first Indian to qualify for a final gymnastic event in fifty-two years. The road to Rio was not an easy one. The twenty-seven-year-old recalls her days of training in Agartala with basic equipment. Her supportive father, a former weightlifting coach, backed her to the hilt. Her exuberance and willpower saw her participate in the Rio Olympics in 2016, where she climbed up to twenty-two notches to reach the fourth position in artistic gymnastics. She has mastered the difficult Produnova vault—a feat applauded even by Nadia Comaneci, the famous Romanian gymnast of yesteryear.[25] Dipa says, 'Everyone used to think gymnastics is for boys and I had to overcome this prejudice early on. I feel proud that I belong to the Northeast. Now I want to get a medal in Tokyo Olympics. Sadly, I couldn't participate in the event. There are so many youngsters in the Northeast, far more talented than me. All they need is good equipment and training to be able to show their true worth.'[26]

The high mountains of Arunachal Pradesh present a formidable spectacle to the untrained eye. Anshu Jamsenpa was born in the Dirang Valley, a stop away from Tawang. During her childhood, she used to 'think deeply' about the purpose of her life, and all she thought of was 'peace'. In 2008, she began her tryst with mountaineering when she enrolled for a fifteen-day programme for training at the National Institute of Mountaineering and Allied Sports in Dirang. Professional mountaineering is an expensive sport, and an attempt to scale the Everest can set you back by Rs 2.5 million. Anshu scaled the Mount Everest for the first time in 2011, and she has audaciously repeated the feat four more times. In 2018, she made history of sorts when she scaled the peak twice within a span of five days, breaking a world record. A mother of two, she was thirty-eight at that time. The first time she had ventured on her Himalayan sojourn, she felt anxious about her children and wrote a diary just for them, in the case she doesn't make it back. 'Now it has become a running joke with people, who ask me whether I have built a home atop the Everest.' Peace, so elusive to mankind in the humdrum of civilization, is to be found in the solitude of pristine Himalayan peaks. She hopes to start an expedition enterprise, but awaits a nod from the state government and the army.[27]

The Government of India has acknowledged the comparative advantage offered by the Northeast in the sporting arena. Under the ambitious Khelo India scheme, eight centres of excellence have been notified across the country—of which four are in the Northeast: Arunachal Pradesh, Mizoram, Manipur and Nagaland. The Union sports minister spelt out his Olympic ambitions thus,

> The Khelo India State Centre of Excellence are being established to strengthen India's pursuit for excellence in Olympics. Our effort is to scale up the best sporting facilities available in each state in India into academies of world-class standard, where athletes from all over the country will want to train in their specific discipline.[28]

A national sports university was set up in Imphal in 2018, which offers undergraduate and postgraduate programmes in sports coaching. Private endowments such as those from the Reliance Foundation are also shifting their focus to the Northeast. Nita Ambani, who heads the foundation, while attending a football event in Meghalaya, said,

> The passion and enthusiasm for sports here in North East is unparalleled, which is why it is a priority region for Reliance Foundation to tap the vast talent pool here. Our endeavor

> is to give North East its due as the region has nurtured and cultivated a sporting culture like no other part of India.[29]

Sports comes naturally to the youth of the Northeast. In the hills and valleys of the region, isolated and neglected for long, there are limited avenues for entertainment. Sports offers an adrenaline rush. Travelling across rural Mizoram, one would feel astonished by the quality of stadiums and badminton halls. Each veng (colony) boasts of local champions. After office, people make a beeline for the badminton court, attired in serious sports gear. The high and mighty gracefully accept defeat at the hands of the humble. Competition and camaraderie go hand in hand. There would hardly be a youngster untouched by sporting fervour. Sports is the only arena where people of the Northeast have broken stereotypes and claimed redemption. Most sporting icons come from humble rural backgrounds. The absence of jobs drives them to sports. Longing for fame and glory stokes their ambitions. Unlike the rest of India, parents happily encourage children to venture full-time into sports, which is a much better proposition than falling prey to drug abuse or insurgency.

Football has set the template for drawing sporting talent in the Northeast. This is easily replicable in other sports like badminton, where, in spite of enormous passion, there are no champions. At least not yet. Contact sports like boxing and individual sports like cycling, weightlifting and gymnastics are a natural fit for the youth of the Northeast. Girls are equally passionate about sports and there is no discrimination in the playfields of the east. The hunger to excel coupled with an innate athletic prowess is a great recipe for success. In all my conversations with sportspersons from the region, I sensed a shared dream of Olympian glory.

10

'Akha': Hope for Good Health

THE ANNUAL MONSOON ritual is a harbinger of massive destruction and human displacement in the Northeast. In Assam, the unrelenting Brahmaputra swells across the floodplains, submerging everything in sight. The hills aren't spared either. Landslides snap all communication, leaving some pockets in complete isolation. The biggest casualty is access to healthcare. The aged, the infirm, the ailing and pregnant women are forced to navigate tumultuous waters and walk several kilometres even for routine check-ups. Sanjoy Hazarika came up with an innovative solution when he started boat clinics in Assam. Fifteen floating clinics, each with two doctors on board, provide year-round healthcare services to the most marginalized and deprived people of the state. A unique public-private partnership with the National Health Mission, the project germinated as a submission to the World Bank Innovation Challenge, titled 'A ship of hope in a valley of flood'. During monsoons, these clinics virtually assume the title and become lifelines for nearly three million people living on the sandbars of the floodplains: the unbiquitous chars and saporis. A 250-member team manages the whole programme, addressing ailments, providing medicines and succour. No wonder the first such floating clinic was named 'Akha', symbolizing human hope afloat.[1]

The geography of the Northeast befuddles policymakers. Rendering healthcare services to sparse populations spread across difficult terrain is not an easy task. Financing primary healthcare facilities in remote border hamlets, with no more than twenty inhabitants, is a complex choice, with limited alternatives. The situation is most glaring in Arunachal Pradesh, which has 90 per cent of its general and district hospitals in urban settlements. Primary healthcare facilities in the Northeast are generally 'poor in quality, inaccessible and unavailable'. The problem is compounded by reluctant doctors and a shortage of skilled medical and paramedical staff.[2] Inhospitable climate, poor housing facilities and remoteness deter even the most spirited ones. Low institutional deliveries in rural areas are a clear pointer of this problem. As against a national average of 75 per cent institutional deliveries in rural India, the numbers for the Northeast, barring Sikkim and Tripura, are abysmally low. In Nagaland, only one in four children are born in a formal medical facility.[3] What is worrisome is that, except for Sikkim, these numbers have deteriorated over time. For every 1,00,000 children born in Assam, 215 mothers die during childbirth. The state has the poorest maternal mortality ratio in the country.[4] Just over a fifth of women receive full antenatal care in India. Even against such a low benchmark, five of the eight Northeast states are at much lower levels. In Nagaland, just over 2 per cent women were covered. The average out-of-pocket expenses for delivery in a public health facility in Manipur is three times the national average.[5] Healthcare in the Northeast is not just inaccessible and inadequate, it is also expensive.

Infant deaths per thousand live births is an important metric to gauge the health of a society. In the last few decades, there has been a considerable improvement in the Northeast. Nagaland, Mizoram and Sikkim now have the lowest infant mortality rates in the country. Infant deaths in Assam, however, are amongst the highest.[6] Immunization levels of most children in this region are far lower than the rest of India. At the national level, more than three-fifths of children received full doses of immunization, while in Arunachal Pradesh and Nagaland, just over a third are fully immunized. Nonetheless, nutrition levels amongst children in the Northeast are much better than the rest of India. Far fewer children under the age of five are underweight, stunted or wasted. This is attributable to the higher intake of protein in the region.[7]

The burden of disease in the Northeast, much like the rest of the country, has shifted from communicable, maternal, neonatal and nutritional diseases to non-communicable diseases, though at a slower rate. The proportion of deaths attributable to HIV/AIDS and tuberculosis are much higher than most of India. Cancer accounts for nearly one-tenth of deaths in the Northeast—the highest in the country. The burden of health problems is captured in one composite index: disability adjusted life years (DALY)—the number of years of life lost on account of ill health. Assam, with a DALY of 1.81, is the highest in the country.[8] In India, nearly three out of ten people are covered by some kind of health insurance scheme. In the Northeast, the coverage is far lower, increasing the health vulnerability. In Assam, the coverage is barely 10 per cent. Some states like Arunachal Pradesh dabbled in cashless treatment for patients, backed by a universal health insurance scheme, with an annual assured coverage of Rs 2,00,000 per family. However, insurance companies raised the red flag when the insurance premium (paid by the state government) fell woefully short of the payouts demanded by hospitals. Ultimately, the scheme had to be scrapped.

In order to benchmark the performance of states across the country, NITI Aayog evolved a composite health index, a function of health outcomes, governance and health service delivery. The formula leaves out non-communicable and infectious diseases and mental health, given the challenges of measurability. States were categorized in larger and smaller groupings and ranked on a scale of 100. Assam, which figured in the larger state grouping, fell at the bottom half, scoring 48.85 as against the best performing state of Kerala, which scored 74.01. In the smaller states grouping, which subsumed the rest of the Northeast, Mizoram was the best performer with a score of 74.97, while Nagaland was at the other end of the spectrum with a score of 38.5.[9]

Healthcare is a multidimensional challenge in the Northeast. Health infrastructure is woefully inadequate and there is a severe shortage of specialist doctors. On the whole, there is a gap of more than 36,000 doctors and a 66 per cent shortfall of trained nurses.[10] More than 50,000 ASHA workers, similar to the 'barefoot doctors', chosen and appointed by the village community, work in villages across the Northeast. Their primary role revolves around mother and child healthcare, including universal immunization. Performance-based remuneration model leaves ASHA workers with limited income support, though some states like Meghalaya and Arunachal Pradesh have topped it up with matching incentives from state budgets. ASHA workers, true to the literal meaning of the acronym, hope, were the frontline warriors during the Covid-19 pandemic. A rural subcentre, catering to a population of 3,000, is the first institutional interface for villagers. However, most of them are beleaguered with infrastructure bottlenecks. In Manipur, four-fifths of the subcentres function without water; in Arunachal Pradesh, nearly half of these are without power; and in Meghalaya, nearly a third are without a road connection. Primary health centres—the first contact point between villagers and medical officers—have their own cup of woes. While there is a 20 per cent surplus of doctors for all states put together, in most remote locations, doctors are unavailable or they manage to get transfers to headquarters. Less than a third of these centres function around the clock in Nagaland. Only three-fifths of them have a labour room in Arunachal Pradesh. Just 6 per cent have operation theatres in Assam. The problem becomes acute at the stage of community health centres, which are supposed to cater to a population of 80,000 and are managed by four specialists: gynecologist, pediatrician, surgeon and physician. In Arunachal Pradesh, as against a requirement of 252 specialists, there are only 4; in Manipur as against 92, there are 3; and in Mizoram and Sikkim there are none. There is scant accommodation for doctors across the Northeast, barring Manipur. In Sikkim and Mizoram there is no accommodation for doctors, while in Arunachal Pradesh barely 4 per cent of centres provide accommodation. It is naive to expect that in areas with such remote geography, specialists would venture for a government job, without even basic accommodation.[11] As a result, women in some cases have to travel a couple of hundred kilometres from eastern Arunachal Pradesh to reach hospitals in Tinsukia or Dibrugarh for deliveries.

District hospitals, mostly housed in old buildings, have deficient infrastructure. Sophisticated medical equipment is either unavailable or defunct. Part of the problem is the 'capital centric' focus for infrastructure planning in all the Northeast states. City hospitals in the capitals are grossly overstaffed, to the detriment of district or subdistrict facilities. Innovative models of public–private partnership are bridging the gaps in healthcare provisioning at all levels. Assam has launched a Chief Minister's Free Diagnostic Services Programme, under which CT scan services (at the district level) , X-ray and laboratory services (at district, subdistrict and community health centre levels) have been entrusted to private players. Ten urban charitable hospitals are ensuring mother and childcare services and OPD check-ups with an annual lumpsum grant of Rs 1.5 million. A public–private partnership arrangement provides an annual grant of Rs 7,50,000 to 150 tea plantation hospitals covering 6,00,000 workers.[12] In Itanagar, the Ramakrishna Mission runs a leading hospital along with a nursing school, supported with government grants. Meghalaya has roped in NGOs like Karuna Trust to manage twenty-two primary and community health centres at the subdistrict level over the last one decade. The NGOs provide doctors and paramedical staff, while the building and other infrastructure is created by the government. State government pays an annual lumpsum amount.[13] Arunachal Pradesh has a similar arrangement with NGOs for managing remote health centres. This model is easily replicable, especially in remote settlements where government provisioning of trained doctors and manpower is difficult to come by.

Gaps in public health delivery have given rise to private health enterprise. In most state capitals, there is a thriving private healthcare industry, ranging from nursing clinics to speciality hospitals. In some cases, serving government doctors run these facilities. Dr N.C. Borah, a neurologist by training, started the Guwahati Neurological Research Centre (GNRC) as a private venture nearly thirty-five years ago. Over time, it expanded to a chain of medical facilities including a 1,200-bed institute of medical sciences which commenced operation in 2014. The GNRC functions on an ultra low-cost model of healthcare, charging very low amounts for diagnostics and patient care. The hospital was constructed using bamboo cladding for better heat insulation and lower costs. A leading centre for trauma care, it provides free services in the first twenty-four hours of an accident or emergency, as road traffic accidents in the region have reached 'epidemic proportions'. Borah feels that, 'a strong PPP model in the region can strengthen the healthcare delivery system, drug distribution, use of technology and pharma supply chain management.'[14]

Dr Palin Khundongbam, a plastic surgeon, is the founder of the 300-bedded Shija Hospital in Imphal. Born to a communist politician father, Palin developed a capitalistic streak. His training ground was the leading government facility the Regional Institute of Medical Sciences (RIMS) in Imphal, which he left twenty-five years ago. Now, they are direct competitors. Shija Hospital has a sprawling campus spread over 12 acres land in Langol. What began as a small clinic, functioning out of a rented premise, is now a regional super speciality hub. With a fleet of 117 doctors and 1,000 caregivers, the hospital caters to neurology, cardiology, kidney transplants and joint replacements. Khundongbam has bigger ambitions. In 2013, he launched Mission Myanmar with the help of the Indian Counsel General in Mandalay, performing free cleft lip surgeries, keyhole surgeries and eye operations at Monywa, the capital of Sagaing province. 'The numbers speak for themselves. Sagaing has a population of 6 million with only seven ophthalmologists, while Manipur with half the population has 40 eye specialists. A kidney transplant in Bangkok for a Myanmarese patient sets him back by Rs 6 million, whereas he can get the same treatment for a tenth of the cost in our hospital,' he says. The Land Border Crossing Agreement signed with Myanmar in 2018 has paved the way for Imphal to aspire to become a hub of medical tourism. 'We met the Union Health Minsiter of Myanmar and agreed on an exchange programme for training doctors and nurses. Before the Covid-19 lockdown, over 2,000 Myanmarese patients were treated in our hospital, and our doctors performed more than 300 operations—surgeries for heart, brain tumour and kidney stone,' claims a proud Khundongbam. This Act East initiative is a purely private venture, not driven by New Delhi. Shija Hospital also caters to patients from the neighbouring states of Mizoram, Nagaland and Tripura.[15] For decades, RIMS was the regional anchor for medical treatment and education. Now Shija 'health city' is envisioning an over 200-acre campus, with an investment of Rs 35 billion.[16]

The private sector boom in the health sector symbolizes an 'accidental liberalization', as a 'pragmatic response to state dysfunction'.[17] Medical science and nursing are preferred professions for youngsters of Manipur, given the growing opportunity for jobs, both in the public and private space. Japan, with an ageing society, has a growing demand for caregivers. Given the strong cultural and historical connect with the Northeast, Japan has expressed a strong interest to hire 15,000 nurses from Manipur.[18]

Navi Mumbai is an unusual choice for the construction of a full-fledged state guest house of a Northeast state. In the heart of an institutional commercial complex rises a seven-storey structure, which doubles up as the official guest house for Arunachal Pradesh. The ground floor has a plush lobby—a sharp contrast to the shabby space on the sixth floor, where families of cancer patients are huddled in dingy surroundings. Next door is the Tata Memorial Advanced Centre for Treatment, Research and Education in Cancer, convenient for families visiting ailing kin. The Northeast has a disproportionately high burden of cancer patients, who travel to Mumbai, Bengaluru, Delhi, Kolkata and Vellore for prolonged treatments. In Mizoram, three persons are afflicted every day by this 'Emperor of All Maladies'.[19,20] High cancer incidence in the Northeast has earned it the epithet 'cancer capital' of the country. Assam accounts for more than a third of total cancer patients in India. However, the per capita numbers are highest in Mizoram and Arunachal Pradesh. The risks of developing cancer amongst residents of the Northeast is abnormally high, ranging from one in five persons to one in sixteen. More than half of the cancer amongst the men of the region and more than a quarter amongst the women has a direct correlation with high tobacco consumption.[21]

The author's wife, Ambreen, in a tea estate in Assam

The Mancotta Bungalow in Dibrugarh, Assam

Ponies grazing in the unruly hills beyond Tawang in Arunachal Pradesh

The highlands beyond Tawang

The meadows of Tawang

The Nuranang Falls, ahead of Tawang.

The Rih Dil Lake in Myanmar, across Mizoram

The Sela Lake in Arunachal Pradesh

Informal trade via the Karnaphully river on the Mizoram-Bangladesh border

A river island in Lohit, Arunachal Pradesh – photo taken from the Bhupen Hazarika Setu

Enroute to Dambuk, Arunachal Pradesh

Bara Bazaar, Aizawl

A handloom machine in Sualkuchi, Assam

A Konyak Morung at Kisama village, Nagaland

A bazaar in Kohima, Nagaland

The border town of Zokhawthar, Mizoram

The bridge in Zokhawthar that connects Mizoram to Myanmar

A sacred grove outside Shillong

Photos from the Tawang festival in Arunachal Pradesh

Cheraw the bamboo dance, Aizawl

Aizawl, Mizoram

Bamboo rafts near Kolasib in Mizoram

The Sangetsar lake, Tawang

The Reiek peak, Mizoram

Yaks slugging it out in the grasslands of Tawang

The author and his wife enroute to Tawang

The Ziro music festival, Arunachal Pradesh

The author savouring a local brew, while dressed in the Monpa attire in Arunachal Pradesh

The Kameng Dam under construction in Arunachal Pradesh

The young Monpas of Tawang

Gangtok, Sikkim

Hoihnu Hauzel

Chardham, Namchi, South Sikkim

Hoihnu Hauzel

The Dalai Lama at Ravangla, South Sikkim

Hoihnu Hauzel

The Chapchar Kut festival, Mizoram

Oken Tayeng

Ima market, Imphal.

Oken Tayeng

Photos from the Hornbill festival, Nagaland

Oken Tayeng

The Sangken festival, Arunachal Pradesh
Oken Tayeng

The Loktak Lake, Manipur
Hoihnu Hauzel

The Manipuri cuisine

Hoihnu Hauzel

Bum La, the border post with China, from the Arunachal Pradesh side

Sonam Chombay

A marker of the Dalai Lama's entry into Arunachal Pradesh from Tibet

Sonam Chombay

A yak in the wild, enroute Tawang

Sonam Chombay

The Sela Pass, Arunachal Pradesh

Young monks inside the Tawang monastery

Sonam Chombay

The Brokpa hut near Yangtse (the theatre of the skirmish with the Chinese Army in 2022)

A lama at the door of Khirmey monastery, Tawang
V.S. Oberoi

A Monpa girl with multi-tasselled Yak hair
V.S. Oberoi

A Tibetan folk dance in Shyo village, Tawang
V.S. Oberoi

The tagline of the Cachar Cancer Hospital and Research Centre is 'There is a CAN in Cancer'. The hospital was established in Silchar in 1996 as a non-profit venture by the citizens of the Barak Valley. Its director, Dr Ravi Kannan, is a surgical oncologist who quit the Adyar Cancer Institute in Chennai in 2006 to relocate to Assam. While his wife was very supportive, their parents were worried and colleagues felt he was embarking on a journey of 'professional hara-kiri'. He attributes the high cancer incidences in the region to the exceptionally high tobacco consumption. Chewing tobacco and areca nut is commonplace, as is consumption of alcohol, both amongst men and women. It is a common sight to see Mizos smoke their traditional Tuibur, an indigenous contraption trapped in a bottle, billowing smoke by burning tobacco and allowing it to travel through a layer of water. Some dietary practices peculiar to the region, such as fermented rice beer (opo or apong), dried smoked fish and meat, are also linked with high cancer incidence.[22] There are variations in the patterns of cancer, explains Dr Kannan. Cancer of the lung and oesophagus is common all over. Stomach cancer is high in the hill states of Sikkim, Mizoram and Arunachal Pradesh, while gall bladder incidence is higher in the plains.

In the last thirteen years, Dr Kannan has seen significant improvement in the medical infrastructure for cancer treatment within the Northeast, but there is a shortage of trained human resources. Skilled practitioners prefer to work in tier I and II cities rather than moving to less developed parts of the country. Local doctors are now moving up the ladder, though they need 'good mentors'. He underscores the importance of community involvement in spreading awareness about a healthy lifestyle, screening for prevention and patient support for the sick. Community organizations are very strong in the Northeast and can easily step in to drive this change. The YMA, for instance, with a hierarchical structure going down to each veng, assumes leadership in a variety of social causes, such as raising a voice for alcohol prohibition. The Silchar facility, treating 4,000 new patients annually, with 25,000 follow-up cases, is largely run on donations. Kannan rues the fact that the switchover to an insurance-driven reimbursement model of the Ayushman Bharat Yojana and Atal Amrit Abhiyan of the Assam government, as opposed to a grant-based approach, has led to the delayed settlement of claims, squeezing the resource base of the philanthropic institution. He says, 'Even if you provide free treatment or free medicine to cancer patients, the chemotherapy cycle takes six months. Poor families need employment support and we provide ad-hoc employment like cleaning, cooking, gardening to people so that their families have some source of sustenance.'[23] Dr Kannan was awarded the Padma Shri in 2020 for his work.

Tata Trusts, the leading philanthropic organization of India, partnered with the Assam government in 2017 to incorporate the Assam Cancer Care Foundation as a special purpose vehicle for cofinancing cancer care infrastructure. The key objective was to establish a state cancer grid, with ten facilities across the state in a three-layered 'distributed care model'. At the top of the pyramid is the State Cancer Institute at Guwahati, to be upgraded to the level of a 500-bed South Asia research centre. At the next level, Dibrugarh, Diphu, Silchar and Barpeta would have cancer care facilities linked with medical colleges. Five centres at the lowest rung would provide diagnostics and cancer daycare services like chemotherapy. The grid also has linkages with two more apex facilities at Guwahati and Silchar. A digital nerve centre established in Guwahati weaves the centres into a common network, providing a framework for seamless consultations and referrals, with an aim to reduce out-of-pocket expenses. The focus is on affordable care, with an ambitious target to cover half of the population. Swasth Assam kiosks have been set up in different medical college hospitals across the state to encourage early stage screening. The initiative was the brainchild of Assam's former health minister, Himanta Biswa Sarma, who is now the chief minister. This hub-and-spoke model of cancer care, is coming up at a cost of roughly Rs 25 billion, according to Lakshman Sethuraman, who heads the project team of Tata Trusts. The trust is engaged in 'catalyzing universal screening' in eight districts of the state and aims to cover 80 per cent of tea garden workers, he explains.[24] Prime Minister Modi inaugurated seven cancer care facilities as part of the statewide network in April 2022.

The porous borderlands of the Northeast contend with the health vulnerability posed by a large inflow of illicit drugs. Lying in the vicinity of the infamous golden triangle spanning over Myanmar, Laos, Thailand and Vietnam, people in isolated pockets of remote fringes are easy prey. Drug smuggling has a debilitating impact on the social fabric of these border states, severely impacting its youth and women. High unemployment, insurgency and political patronage make for a dangerous cocktail for drug abuse and the spread of HIV. Mizoram has the highest HIV prevalence in the country with more than 2 per cent cases, recording nine cases every day. Two-thirds of these cases are sexually transmitted, while more than a quarter are caused by shared needles and syringes. While driving around Aizawl one can spot an unusually large number of billboards on the roadside advocating the use of condoms and cautioning against the risk of AIDS. More than two-fifths of those infected are less than thirty-five years old, reflecting the loss of productive population to the disease. This is closely followed by Manipur and Nagaland.[25] In these three states, HIV incidence is four times the national average. Since 2010, infections have gone up by 65 per cent in Arunachal Pradesh, 37 per cent in Assam, 18 per cent in Mizoram and 10 per cent in Meghalaya, while there have been marginal declines in Nagaland and Tripura.[26]

Heroin, commonly known as 'number 4' in drug circles, finds its way into Manipur via Myanmar through the border town of Moreh and in Mizoram through Zokhawthar. Intravenous use of heroin and sharing of needles make the spread of the blood-borne virus inevitable. In 1989, the first case of HIV infection linked with intravenous drug use was reported in Mizoram. By 1997, the prevalence amongst addicts sprang to epidemic proportions to reach 80 per cent.[27] For Reverend Chingmak, the impact was felt closer to home as two members of his family members fell prey to drugs. 'All evil breeds in the dark, and so does human vice,' he says philosophically. The youth of Nagaland, growing up in an ethos of violence and insurgency, were an easy target for drugs. Chingmak says,

> Homogenous societies respond with denial. HIV was blamed on the needle or on the girl. At some stage pharmaceutical shops were banned from selling needles. Stigma is the core of the problem. Those days an HIV prevalence of 8.1 per cent amongst pregnant mothers in Tuensang was next only to Namakkal in Tamil Nadu.

Chingmak and his wife Phutoli set up the Hope Centre, a rehabilitation home, in Longpang village in Tuensang district, one of the most backward areas in Nagaland. They used 'work therapy' by engaging the youth in cooking, cutting firewood and singing to wean them away from drugs. The Eleutheros Christian Society, coined after the Greek word meaning 'freeing from poverty', was registered in 1997, and started working with 200 youth for drug rehabilitation. They 'tracked' 299 people who had shared needles or had engaged in unprotected sex with a bunch of thirty-three individuals of the first batch. Chingmak opened a dialogue with the church leadership, and a churches alliance for community support was established two decades ago. 'If a pastor from a pulpit says, "Let's pray for an

HIV-positive member," the prayer for healing takes away the stigma associated with the disease,' he says. 'I have myself buried twenty to thirty people as no one from their families was ready to do so for fear of [contracting] HIV.' The intervention of the church helped in expanding the 'circle of concern' and had a significant impact in outreach and testing. The pastor-turned-social worker reckoned that the root of the problem lies in a broken primary health system. The Hope Centre became a community health centre, a unique private–public partnership model where the community appoints doctors, nurses and lab technicians. The project, supported by Tata Trusts, was chosen for a competitive health award by the HCL Foundation, which gave a Rs 50 million grant for scaling the model. Now, five primary health centres run on a similar approach in four eastern districts of Nagaland that have been marked by insurgency and backwardness; their focus is on mother and child health.[28]

Sangthankima stands tall amongst the Mizo community, literally and metaphorically. An alcoholic-turned-evangelist reformer, he presides over the Thutak Nunpuitu Team (TNT), meaning 'the team that lives the truth'—a sprawling facility that serves as a reformation home for nearly 2,000 drug addicts, intellectually disabled persons and as a shelter for orphans. 'God saved me,' he proclaims, 'and wanted me to heal others.' The facility relies on Christian teaching and abjures the use of modern medicine. 'Doctors can heal the worldly body, but only God can heal the soul,' he murmurs philosophically, watching a flight of pigeons swooping down for water in the compound. Nearly two-thirds of the addicts come from border districts. The church doubles up as a volleyball court because 'sports, music and prayer lead to salvation'. The facility is wholly supported by volunteers and donations. Sangthankima aspires to expand his facility to the borderlands of Myanmar, abutting Yunnan province in China. Inspired by the Aizawl set-up, the TNT also has a branch in Tahan, a Mizo-dominated town in Myanmar, which has enrolled over 250 ailing people.[29]

In Churachandpur district of Manipur, a missionary doctor Chinkholal Thangsing, affectionately called 'Lal', started the Touch of Hope Foundation in 1993. Back then, doctors did not want to see or touch HIV patients, but Lal started working for the rehabilitation of drug addicts and HIV patients. His foundation also supported income generation for the widows of patients and school education for their children. He continued serving the people for seven years, until the violence in Manipur peaked and he eventually left for Delhi.

The health narrative of the Northeast resonates with hope. Be it the boat clinics of Sanjoy Hazarika, the Touch of Hope Foundation of Lal or the Hope Centre of Chingkham's. A broken healthcare system and a unique disease burden, bestowed by geography, are being addressed by a mix of public and private initiatives.

11

The Better Half of the Northeast

IMAGES STICK. IMAGES create illusions too. My first impression of the Northeast goes back to two decades, when I was first posted to Mizoram. As a young field officer, I decided to get my feet on the ground on a Saturday morning to acquaint myself with the new environment. Bara Bazaar, the main market of Aizawl, was bustling with women selling imported goods from across the border: blankets, clothes, toys and cosmetics. For an uninitiated Punjabi, it was a cultural shock to see a marketplace completely dominated by women. Men, figuratively speaking, were queued up on the margins of the narrow road, slouching on the wheel of their Maruti 800 taxis, waiting for elusive shoppers. The spectacle in the civil secretariat was no different. Women made up for more than half the staff—from peons and clerical staff to assistants and undersecretaries, while the men took charge of official cars. High fashion consciousness and a strong preference for Western attire were immediately apparent. The bazaar spectacle of Aizawl is a common sight across the region.

Ima Keithel in Imphal is the largest all-women market in Asia. 'Ima', meaning 'mother', has a strong cultural symbolism not just in the marketplace, but in the cultural ethos of Manipur. Wearing colourful phaneks (sarong), nearly 5,000 women squat on their assigned spots every day selling myriad wares: groceries, vegetables, utensils and clothes. The stalls are passed on from mother-in-law to daughter-in-law in a unique inheritance model.[1] The mobility and visibility of women is pervasive across the Northeast—from Shillong to Kohima to Gangtok. Such sights lend themselves to an easy extrapolation that women of the Northeast are far more empowered than those in the mainland. This simplistic assumption merits a deeper enquiry.

Sociologists have romanticized the matrilineal society of Meghalaya to highlight an alternate construct of women empowerment. Ancestral property and the family name get passed on from the mother to the daughter. This customary practice saw the rise of a one-of-its-kind male suffragette movement: Syngkhong Rympei Thymmai (SRT). This would be unthinkable in, say, rural Punjab or Haryana. It would be natural to assume that women genuinely have a dominant social and economic presence in Meghalaya. Patricia Mukhim, the feisty editor of *The Shillong Times*, rejects this view. The title of her book—*Waiting for an Equal World: Gender in the Northeast*—sums up her perspective. It explains that the youngest daughter, khatduh, is not the inheritor but a custodian of ancestral property. She acknowledges that women in Meghalaya have an edge vis-à-vis other women of the Northeast, as they perpetuate the clan and can marry by free choice, without any societal pressure. However, political participation of women is extremely limited. The position of the village headman, Rangbah Shnong, is not open for women candidature. She cites a pejorative khasi phrase for women who dabble in politics: 'crowing hen'.[2] Matriliny, she says is a 'double whammy for women', since abandoned or divorced women (a significant number) have to take care of their children with or without maintenance. Asserting that 'poverty has a feminine face', she points to rising poverty amongst women who no longer have the cushion of the clan in nuclear households. The economic fragility of women running small businesses dependant on tourist inflows became evident during the Covid-19 pandemic.[3] Mukhim even cites National Family Health Survey data that shows almost one in three married women aged 15–49 years experienced spousal violence.

The reality of women in the Northeast can be portrayed in sepia-tinted hues. It is a picture of enormous paradox. Indices of female literacy, work participation rates and mean age of marriage are decidedly better than the rest of India, though there are variations across states.[4] Pernicious practices of dowry and female foeticide are virtually absent. However, there are other disturbing dimensions. In certain pockets of Assam, the superstition around witchcraft still persists. Bodos use the word 'daini' to connote women who are labelled as witches. Cases have also been reported in certain other communities, such as the Rabhas, Mishings and the tea tribes of Assam, in the backdrop of illiteracy and low healthcare. In a large number of cases, the label is ascribed as a 'ploy to grab land and property, sometimes even to settle personal grudges'.[5] The ostensible reason for targeting women is that they bring calamity, but the real reason is economic or non-conformity and not so much superstition, explains Anurita Hazarika, state project director of North East Network.[6] Birubala Rabha has led a crusade against this abominable practice, 'winning admiration, making enemies, scolding, persuading, inspiring, holding out hope'.[7] The Assam Witch Hunting (Prohibition, Prevention and Protection) Act, 2015, was promulgated to make such labelling and stigmatization a criminal offence.

Customary law circumscribes the regulatory framework of property ownership, marriage and divorce. Custom favours men. Barring Meghalaya, the rule of primogeniture leans towards the male child and, generally speaking, women don't have inheritance rights. Traditionally, land was held in the name of the community amongst agrarian hill tribes, which practised jhum cultivation. With the advent of settled cultivation and monetization of private land, patriarchy held sway. Individual generosity apart, institutionally, there is no arrangement for passing on land to daughters. Hoihnu Hauzel, a Delhi-based Manipuri journalist-entrepreneur, cites her own example where her landed parents, after much prodding, have earmarked just an acre of land each for her sister and her, out of a large landholding of over 2,000 acres in Imphal. Men cede space for women only where they don't 'infringe upon their exclusive space', she feels.[8]

There is a growing articulation for change in the age-old customary law, though there is limited traction. Karry Padu, a thirty-year-old Galo girl from Arunachal Pradesh, produced a film with an unusual title, *I Am Property*. The film draws a narrative of complete subjugation of women in the family and clan—a daughter is a 'property' of her father, and after her marriage, she is bought by her husband upon paying a bride price. The practice of levirate marriage obliges a woman to marry her husband's brother in the eventuality of his death. Karry shares the story of her friend's mother, whose brother-in-law claimed her after her husband's death. 'We bought you,' he had asserted. When she refused his overture, her house was burnt down. Karry and her friends had to pitch in to pay off the bride price to settle the matter. Polygamy is common amongst some tribes in Arunachal Pradesh. When a man seeks to bring another woman as his wife, the first wife is required to give an account of her character before an all-male village keba (clan council), which is a traumatic experience. There is no space for women in this 'tight circle of men'. Karry says that regardless of the accomplishments of a woman or the position she might hold as a professional, she has to sit alongside other women to cook for and serve men during family gatherings.

Equality must begin from the home and the clan. But the men 'are too comfortable' with the current situation, and any talk of amending customary law falls on deaf ears. In any case, the legislature hardly has any female voice to stand up for such issues. As a result, a large number of educated women are choosing to stay unmarried because they are unable to reconcile with their inferior position at home. The digital medium affords an opportunity to speak with candour and reach out to a wider audience seeking change, feels Karry. Yet, real change will remain a distant dream till such time women don't get to sit in the driver's seat.[9]

Taw Azu has undertaken academic research on the status of women in the Nyishi community of Arunachal Pradesh. With education, she feels, women have become more mobile and entrepreneurial. They are adapting to the changing times, but men are falling behind. The role of the breadwinner is increasingly shifting to women, but this is unpalatable to the male ego, escalating cases of domestic violence, which are rampant, though mostly unreported. The state has one-third seats reserved for women in the panchayat. But that is also cosmetic, as most decisions are taken by their husbands. She cites the instance of an elected legislator whose husband was the point person for deciding the utilization of the MLA local area development fund. Christianity has spread considerably amongst the Nyishi community, but that has not affected the gender relations. On the contrary, Azu says that she knows several office bearers of the parish who have kept more than one wife, but polygyny is accepted because of their generous donations, which become a form of 'atonement'.[10]

Mizo men have to simply utter '*Ka ma che*' or 'I divorce you' to nullify the marriage as per customary law. Prolonged advocacy by the Mizo Hmeichhe Insuihkhawm Pawl (MHIP) led to the enactment of the Mizo Marriage, Divorce and Inheritance of Property Act, 2014, which blends traditional Mizo practices with the requirements of Christian faith and principles of equality. Alimony in the eventuality of divorce now affords a degree of protection. In matters of inheritance of property as well, the law has introduced progressive measures for entitlements of unmarried daughters, though the scales are still tilted in favour of male progeny.

Women leadership in politics and on the pulpit is non-existent. Across the Northeast, there are hardly any women legislators. The church, which has a dominant role to play in these hill states, is male-dominated. Women civil society organizations, though significant in number, function in the shadow of their male-dominated counterparts. In spite of the large presence of women in the economic sphere, their participation in the political sphere is all but absent. Patriarchy runs deep in the domain of power. Chief Minister of Nagaland Neiphiu Rio famously declared: 'the beautiful darlings who are good for politics but not so good in politics'.[11] Mercy, the lead singer of the Tetseo Sisters, feels that even though Naga girls are doing better than boys in school, they are denied leadership roles in its society. 'Marriageability for a girl is based on her physical attractiveness, feminine manners and household managing abilities.' Sadly, 'her leadership, problem-solving skills and resourcefulness are not much appreciated in spheres where she has to jostle with men for making decisions about the state.'[12]

Men invoked customary law to stymie participation of women in urban local body elections in Nagaland. Naga tribal bodies opposed the 33 per cent reservation for women in these bodies. The Naga Mothers' Association (NMA) challenged the state government's refusal to hold municipal elections. The matter went up to the Supreme Court, which upheld the petition in 2016. The Nagaland government's averments in court were that it would 'upset the peace'. The decision pitted the women against tribal bodies, which threatened that those women who contested would be excommunicated from the tribe. Monalisa Changkija, poetess and founding editor of *Nagaland Page*, compares the refusal of the state intervention to that of Pontius Pilate, the Roman prefect who ordered the crucifixion of Jesus.[13] 'The new Naga woman is very different from our subservient grandmothers, which is truly frightening to the Naga male,' she believes.[14] Rejecting the false narrative of custom, she feels that, 'It is economics that spawn and dictate culture and customs, but also political and martial expediencies.' The core of the issue is ownership and control of land and economic resources.[15] Anthropologist Dolly Kikon attributes the situation as a 'deep nexus of patriarchy, culture and law.' She paints a 'schizophrenic image' of Naga women who are 'nurturing, courageous, sacrificing, moral, hardworking, and docile, carrying baskets on her head, feeding the family, or perpetually serving tea and cooking in the kitchen.' Naga women are thus reduced to a 'token representative ornament in a photo session', surely unsuited for a position at the high table.[16]

The situation in Mizoram is no different. A narrative has been built that 'women are not fit for politics, let men do it,' feels Margaret Zama, an outspoken retired professor of English literature. Men are deemed to be 'wiser' and more 'capable' than women, she laments. She believes that the church, which holds considerable sway over public opinion, has sadly reinforced patriarchy. Biblical teaching is interpreted to suit this narrative. People carry the message heard in the church to their homes. Patriarchy is deeply ingrained in the psyche of even progressive families. The pulpit alone holds the key of reform.[17] Lal Thanhawla, former chief minister of Mizoram, said, 'Women here are not keen on politics as a vocation.' This was vehemently refuted by Lalzirliani, former president of the MHIP, who believed that, 'Our menfolk try to convey the impression that politics is too complex for women.'[18] Low women representation in state legislatures of the Northeast reflects their complete marginalization in politics. In the most recent assembly elections, Nagaland saw no woman candidate elected, while Meghalaya, Arunachal Pradesh and Tripura had barely three women legislators.[19, 20]

The lack of participation of women in politics stands out in sharp contrast to their strident activism in situations of conflict. Consider Meira Paibis, the women vigilante group, started in the 1970s as an informal movement against liquor consumption and sale. Women would go out at night holding out torches in their hands, exposing men indulging in liquor consumption. Kangla Fort, once the royal Meitei palace, became the stage of an unusual protest in Imphal. In July 2004, a dozen 'grannies', between the ages of 45–73, shed their clothes outside the fort, holding banners that said 'Indian army rape us', 'Indian army, kill us'.[21] These Meira Paibis were protesting against the rape and death of twenty-four-year-old Thangjam Manorama at the hands of personnel of the Assam Rifles. She was suspected to be a member of the People's Liberation Army (PLA). At the root of the protest was AFSPA—a law dating back to 1958, which allows sweeping powers to members of the armed forces in a 'disturbed area', in the interest of maintaining 'public order'. Irom Sharmila, called the 'Iron lady' of Manipur, went on a hunger strike for sixteen years from November 2000 to protest for the repeal of this law. She ended her fast and entered the political arena by launching the People's Resurgence and Justice Alliance (PRAJA) in 2016. In spite of her iconic persona, she was handed down a crushing defeat, securing just ninety votes against the sitting chief minister of the state, Okram Ibobi Singh. She moved to Tamil Nadu and married her longtime partner Desmond Coutinho, a British national. Clearly, even a sixteen-year-long fast was not enough for her to secure a victory at the hustings. An 'ordinary human being, with an extraordinary spirit'[22] who sought 'breathing space' was unable to lead the people she stood for.

Women of the Northeast have borne the greatest brunt of prolonged conflict. 'The Last Song', a short story by Temsula Ao, revolves around a village 'singing beauty' named Apenyo. The villagers prepare for a dedication ceremony of a new church building, where Apenyo bursts into her 'solo number' as an 'act of open defiance' against an 'arrogant Indian army' who desecrates the church. She and her mother are gang-raped by soldiers, who also set the church ablaze. Apenyo becomes a symbol of the 'ravaged and ruined children' of Nagaland.[23]

The suffering of women is one of the reasons that they emerged as activists and brokers of peace. The NMA's motto is 'Shed no more blood'. They emerged as the leading mediator for brokering a ceasefire between the Government of India and NSCN(IM) in 1997. Conflict situation led women to 'appropriate whatever public space was available to them in the patriarchal Naga society,' comments Toshimenla Jamir, head of Nagaland University's sociology department.[24] While their activism in peace is welcomed, a foray in electoral politics is 'frowned upon'. In substantive peace talks, there were hardly any women representatives. When asked about their exclusion, the Naga Hoho replied, 'It is too early to include women now. We have to tread carefully because the peace process is very fragile and the Hoho itself as a body has just emerged.'[25] Hoihnu Hauzel feels that women as symbols of protest are not a reflection of their empowerment. Its just that they 'make for better imagery and make greater noise'. Men in protest are likely to be shot and, thus, women are used as a 'convenient tool' to further their own cause. Even the Kangla Fort protest, according to her, was done on the instigation of militants.[26]

On the other hand, women entrepreneurship is certainly a growing trend in the Northeast. In rural areas, handloom is a major part of each household. The Northeast accounts for nearly three-fifths of handloom households in India. More than 1.6 million women are engaged as handloom weavers across the region.[27] In the cities of the Northeast, markets are abuzz with women as small vegetable sellers, salon owners, fashion boutique proprietors and furniture showroom owners. Their mobility allows them flexibility to travel to shop, trade and bargain for their wares, even from Guangzhou. Hoihnu offers a somewhat cynical explanation: 'The extra cash suits men—"Darling, why not?"'[28]

Young women of the region are following their passion, making forays into new ventures. Liter Basar, thirty-five-year-old owner of the Liba Cafe and Pattisserie in Itanagar, baked scrumptious madeleines. She obtained a diploma in patisserie from Le Cordon Bleu in Paris. The Galo girl from a remote corner of the Northeast says, 'I always wanted to shatter the glass ceiling and be a person who in her own capacity brings about a small change.'[29] Tragically, she committed suicide, cutting short her journey and without realizing her dream.

Apart from the inspirational stories of women entrepreneurs in an earlier chapter of this book, there are several changemakers who are altering the rules of the game. A case in point is Lakhimi Baruah, who saw economic hardship firsthand at Golaghat, her hometown in Assam. Turned down for loans after filling complicated forms and queuing up for hours, women would sink into a cycle of penury before her eyes. Three decades ago, she decided to take matters into her own hands and start the Konoklata Mahila Cooperative Bank, with fifty-two promoters to 'popularize thrift and banking habit among women' and instil a spirit of enterprise. After an eight-year-long struggle, her fledgling bank started operations. Today, her all-women bank manages 35,000 accounts and has extended loans of over Rs 350 million to more than 12,000 women.[30]

Women of the Northeast present a picture of contrasts. One part of society allows them the freedom to make choices about work. There are no barriers of entry into the world of work. But when it comes to positions of power, there is a glass ceiling. Top jobs in administration and politics remain an exclusive male preserve. Leadership of tribal bodies, which continue to have a considerable influence, rests with the men. At home, she is shackled to chains of age-old patriarchy and a customary law that relegates her to a secondary position. The façade of empowerment is only skin deep. Behind the smiling pretty faces, they hide stories of their personal daily struggle. In their minds, they remain conflicted—education has raised their aspirations, which are denied by age-old traditions. Much is made about the need for a uniform civil code, but the traditional customary law remains beyond the pale of popular narrative or political debate.

12

The Governance Challenge

INDIA'S NORTHEAST IS an amorphous entity. Yet, this group of eight states has assumed a distinctive political and administrative connotation. The Government of India places the Northeast on a policy pedestal. Like an indulgent schoolmaster, it allows special concessions for a lagging child. Governing an unruly frontier, with a history of neglect and ethnic conflict, is a byzantine task. The Northeast was a late starter in the game of governance. British rulers followed a laissez-faire approach in a hostile territory. Tribal life revolved around the clan and village. Chieftains, aided by the village council, subsumed all political and judicial power. Justice was based on customary law and retribution was quick. Post-independence, its people had to contend with a common political framework and a somewhat alien administrative system.

Framers of the Indian Constitution were conscious of the unique history and ethnic diversity of the region. Special legal provisions were crafted, blending the traditional with the modern. New administrative structures were a mosaic of the old and the new. The hill tribes feared the hegemonic influence of Assam and the minority tribes were apprehensive of neglect by the majority. Culture and identity were non-negotiable. For Nagaland and Mizoram, special provisions under Article 371 of the Constitution stipulate that any law of the Parliament in relation to religious or social practices, customary law, administration of justice using customary law, ownership and transfer of land would apply only if ratified by the state assembly. 'Autonomous district councils', created under the sixth schedule of the Constitution, were instruments of reassurance. Limited legislative, administrative and financial powers were delegated to these councils, some of which have became full-fledged states in due course.

Like most things political, there is a yawning gap between intent and reality. The legal instruments of protection have become entry barriers. People from the rest of India are prohibited from buying land on account of special provisions in the Constitution and inner line regulations. This limits the prospects of serious investors, opens a backdoor for proxy investors and dabbles with local politicians' money.

District councils merely served as a safety valve for thwarted political ambitions. In the process, it ended up creating a parallel hierarchy of administration in the districts. The aspiration of autonomy remained elusive as states hardly ceded real power. Autonomy became a proxy for profligacy. Chief executive members view themselves as chief ministers of their respective councils. Election to office is used for political patronage by doling out petty contracts and jobs. It is a springboard for a higher political orbit. In matters of revenue administration, land allotment and forest management, councils are often on a collision course with the state. The councils have also proved to be 'ineffective at lobbying the state government and shaping the state development budget'. The MLAs elected from those areas often find themselves in an 'adversarial rather than cooperative relationship' with the councils.[1] State governments are wary in parting with limited resources and the councils have no leverage to levy local taxes.

As a young deputy commissioner working in a sixth schedule district of Mizoram, I felt the inherent tension between institutions. Lack of transparency and complaints of corruption were frequently voiced. Two decades down the line, not much has changed. District council areas remain the most underdeveloped in the state. The dismal performance notwithstanding, the clamour for creating new autonomous district councils remains unabated. In Arunachal Pradesh, the state legislature passed a resolution urging the Central government to include the state in the sixth schedule of the constitution to 'protect the tribal rights of indigenous people.'[2] The Government of India has introduced a constitutional amendment bill, which seeks to enhance the powers of the autonomous councils, including direct devolution of grants from the Finance Commission and enhanced scope of delegated functions.[3] Greater autonomy, unless backed by greater accountability, will end up in a drain of resources.

Traditional tribal village institutions have been sanctified by law in some states. For instance, the Lushai Hill District (village council) Act, 1953; Nagaland Village and Area Council Act, 1978; Manipur State Hill People's Regulation Act 1947; and Manipur Village Authorities (in Hill Areas) Act, 1956, envisage a statutory role for village councils. Provisions of the 73rd Constitutional Amendment, which mandate the establishment of elected village panchayats, do not apply to Nagaland, Mizoram and Meghalaya. Village councils assume the role envisaged for panchayats and discharge a mix of administrative, quasi-judicial and developmental functions. Gaon burhas (village headman), distinctive in attire by their ceremonial red coats, are the point persons of the deputy commissioner, transcending the blurred boundaries of the customary and the official. Increasingly, village councils also shoulder responsibilities of management of community forests, allocation of jhum sites and identification of beneficiaries for government schemes. The nature of these councils ranges from direct democracies, 'little republics' or monarchical structures to chieftainships. In Arunachal Pradesh, panchayati raj institutions set up under the 73rd Constitutional Amendment coexist with tribal councils.[4] Nagaland village development boards, with one-fourth women members, oversee development functions, while the village council remains an exclusive male preserve. The Communitization of Public Institutions and Services Act, 2002, seeks a 'third way of governance', wherein village communities become owner of government institutions and assets, with powers to manage employees.[5] They play a significant role in elementary education, healthcare, power, water supply and rural tourism. Novel institutional arrangements in the Northeast have stoked competitive political struggle and 'threaten the legitimacy of traditional institutions'.[6]

Multiplicity of structures has created cross currents in governance, most glaringly so in the case of land management. In hill states, land ownership follows uncodified customary law. Land is a sacred totem of tribal identity. Each tribe has its own land ownership pattern—in some cases held in the name of the chief, in other cases in the name of the clan, while a few recognize individual ownership. None of the hill states have carried out cadastral surveys. There are no formal land records. This vagueness lends itself to manipulation and elite capture. Individuals make outlandish claims of ownership of mountains and patches of rivers as personal property. In Mizoram and the Jaintia hills of Meghalaya, land allotment is under the control of the state, which has displaced traditional tribal bodies for issuance of temporary or permanent land certificates.[7] In Aizawl, there are several instances of duplicate certificates for the same piece of land. Privatization of land ownership has created a landed elite in a hitherto classless society. Fuzzy land ownership is also an impediment for its monetization. Banks are reluctant to lend in the absence of collateral land ownership documents. Interestingly, during acquisition of land by the government, a host of 'landowners' come forward to make exaggerated claims of compensation. In the absence of any price benchmarks, the award of acquisition tends to be arbitrary and politically driven. The Arunachal Pradesh Land Settlement and Records Amendment Act, 2018, confers de facto rights, empowering people to lease their land for commercial ventures to non-residents for a period of thirty-three years. Of course, unless backed by a cadastral survey and land titling exercise, the legislation would remain infructuous.

The 'special category states' of the Northeast are also eligible for more generous funding, giving it a unique character in the matrix of economic planning. Tax revenue raised internally by the Northeast states is the lowest in the country, necessitating disproportionately high central transfers.[8] A 'dependency syndrome' has come to define the relationship between the Centre and these states. Low economic activity and limited private investment constrict the resource generation capacity of these states. The Northeast accounts for one-fourth of India's forest cover. This is a positive externality, but also a fiscal disability. Forest land cannot be put to productive use—ruling out its monetization. In such a scenario, the only recourse for white collar employment is government service. This creates political pressure for carving new administrative divisions and subdivisions, creating more jobs where none are required. Governments across the Northeast are flabby and oversized beyond the requirements of its sparse population. The advantage of a generous resource allocation from the Centre is frittered away through the high cost of running the government itself.

Ubiquitous petitioners, hovering around minister's offices in the civil secretariat of state capitals, carrying neatly typed representations for petty contracts in their pockets, are a manifestation of this dependency syndrome. A convenient arrangement follows. Generous offers from a landowner to 'donate' a piece of his land becomes a tacit quid pro quo for a construction contract. Thousands of poorly constructed, half-finished tourist lodges built in complete wilderness are a sad testimony of this rot. Political leaders now realize the futility of this economic trap and are desperate to promote entrepreneurship. A different funding regime for the Northeast will continue in the foreseeable future, but there is a need to infuse a sense of competition amongst the states. Complacency of assured fund transfers, dissociated from any agenda of governance reform, could be counterproductive. Entrepreneurship and investments in private eco-friendly verticals are inescapable for a sustainable future.

The prism of national security filters the view of the Northeast from Raisina Hill. The Chinese incursion of 1962 and the spate of immigrants following the creation of Bangladesh left an enduring imprint. The wave of ethnic conflicts that swept the region bloodied this imagery. Conflict became so endemic that political leaders of small states started using it as a bargaining chip for additional funds. For instance, a 'peace bonus' of Rs 2.4 billion was sanctioned for Mizoram in 2000–01.[9] Zoramthanga, the chief minister of the state during that period, claimed that, 'Every rupee you give me gets spent on development. Whereas, of every rupee you give Nagaland and Manipur, 50 percent goes to the underground, including half of the police director-general's salary.'[10] In June 2020, R.N. Ravi, then governor of Nagaland, wrote a scathing letter to its Chief Minister, asserting that the state was being run by over half a dozen 'armed gangs' who were challenging the legitimacy of a constitutionally elected state government. The 'taxes' levied by these parallel governments and the cost escalation of development projects were attributed to a portion being siphoned off to insurgent outfits. In response, the NSCN(IM) issued a terse statement,

> Taxes have been the sources of sustenance that has brought the Naga political movement this far ... NSCN did not and does not commit extortion at any point of time but levies legitimate taxes from the people.[11]

Nagaland governor's candour hit the proverbial nail on its head. For decades, insurgency has bred criminality and leakage of development funds. Insurgency is now confined to limited pockets of the Northeast, most pronounced in Nagaland and Manipur; but political corruption is endemic. Political leaders used to seek funds to 'fight insurgency'. Even where insurgency had abated, political compulsions and not economic logic guided the demand for development funds.[12]

Ukhrul, the hometown of NSCN(IM)'s leader Thuingaleng Muivah, is an 'illustrative case of parallel governance system at its most acute'.[13] On 14 August 2015, a day marked as 'Naga Independence Day', Muivah spoke as the Ato Kilonser (prime minister) of the unrecognized GPRN, unfurling the blue flag, featuring a rainbow in the sky.[14] A multiplicity of underground factions have seen the levying of multiple illegal taxes by these organizations. Some of the entrepreneurs end up paying tax seven times while government employees cough up to a quarter of their salary for the Naga underground.[15] The parallel governance structure has the same formalistic hierarchy as the civil administration of the state. The GPRN has a Tatar Hoho, apex legislative body, and twenty-six administrative regions have a chief administrative officer, counterpart of the deputy commissioner. Ukhrul has a 'town command', a parallel police station with a reputation for summary punishment and efficiency. The Kilo Kilonser, self-proclaimed home minister, claimed that state employees, MLAs and MPs have to pay loyalty to them—with them being the 'people's government'. Uncooperative civil servants are transferred out or even forced to flee.[16] Camp Hebron, the official headquarter of the NSCN(IM), bears an unmistakable stamp of authority with all the symbolic appendages of the state.

The Government of India mooted a good governance index to assess the performance of states across ten sectors. The Northeast and hill states were clubbed as one unit for ranking. Within the Northeast, Tripura and Mizoram are at the top, while Arunachal Pradesh and Nagaland are at the lowest rung.[17] In a way, this matches exactly with anecdotal references to levels of corruption in the Northeast. My experience of working in Mizoram and Arunachal Pradesh was a study in contrast. As chief electoral officer, I saw Mizo politicians approach the Election Commission for a reduction in the cap on permissible spending by candidates during elections.[18] Campaigning is a muted affair, overseen by the Mizoram People's Forum (MPF), a church-led body. The MPF entered into an agreement with all political parties of the state, prescribing dos and donts.[19] Enforcing the model code of conduct during elections was a breezy affair for the election machinery, as the MPF itself became a voluntary watchdog. In contrast, corruption was endemic in Arunachal Pradesh, with complicity between contractors, bureaucrats and politicians. It was rumoured that in some small constituencies, candidates gifted SUVs to families of their voters in return for an assurance to vote. As finance commissioner, it was a nightmare to instil a culture of transparent spending, even though I had the full support of the chief minister. Pema Khandu, as Arunachal Pradesh's chief minister, has demonstrated a firm resolve in reigning in the political leaders and backing governance reforms to the hilt. But change is painful and slow to come by.

E-governance as a tool for fostering transparency has grown enormously in mainland India. Challenges of digital connectivity have hampered its penetration in the Northeast so far. A public financial management system enables a trickling down of funds of Centrally sponsored schemes right up to the last beneficiary. Seven states of the region are now part of this platform, used for direct benefit transfers, a major innovation in administration of beneficiary-oriented schemes. In the last few years, the Central government has given it a relentless push in several schemes of rural livelihoods, disbursal of old-age pensions and honorarium to anganwadi workers. A concerted effort on digital governance would help curb corruption and bring in greater transparency. The Central government is now insisting on geotagging all assets on a Geographical Information System (GIS) framework to ensure that money is paid only for completed projects. This is particularly relevant in remote areas where physical monitoring of each project is not an easy proposition.

All-India service forms the core of state bureaucracy, supported by locally recruited state civil service. Invariably, those allocated a cadre in the Northeast become despondent, given its harsh topography, inaccessibility and popular imagery of violence. Most of the time, officers try and find avenues of Central deputation. Only a handful of them immerse themselves in the sociocultural ethos to appreciate the underlying complexity of this region. The situation in Mizoram and Arunachal Pradesh is even more precarious as officers allocated to erstwhile union territory cadres get posted there. These 'suitcase officers', with one leg in Delhi, rarely step out of the state headquarters when in station. Ruing the lack of 'institutional memory' and absence of 'continuity', Pema Khandu has asked for a separate cadre for the state.[20] Bureaucracy across the region functions in silos with no institutional interface or sharing of best practices amongst states. Revival of the erstwhile Indian Frontier Administrative Service could serve as the binding tissue of civil service across the region.

Fragmented economic planning by small states, with a low resource base, invariably leads to suboptimal outcomes. The NEC, established with the intent of fostering a regional approach to planning and investment, has failed to live up to expectations. Its annual meetings are a ritualistic exercise, with daylong proceedings marked by lengthy speeches by all chief ministers and governors. Prime Minister Modi, while addressing its sixty-fifth plenary session, suggested, 'There is a need to re-orient and upgrade the North Eastern Council.' He mooted its development as 'a state-of-the-art resource centre for the North Eastern states with the necessary resources, knowledge and skills.' The Centre would help the states to 'properly plan and execute projects, promote research and innovations and provide strategic policy vision for the region.' The council was advised to focus 'on issues in emerging areas of livelihood, entrepreneurship, venture funds, start-ups and skill development. All this will help in generating jobs.'[21] A remodelled NEC could take a leaf out of the successful transition of the erstwhile Planning Commission to NITI Aayog, now a policy think tank leading national policy debate. The NEC could also assume the role of a regional project management body for key infrastructure projects of hydropower, roads, airports and inland waterways. It could fill the gap in local capacities to formulate and design new projects by providing specialist support. The Ministry of Development of North Eastern Region in New Delhi is too distant to take the lead, which makes the reinvention of the NEC an urgent imperative.

The need for regional planning can be illustrated in agriculture and allied sectors. More than two-thirds of people living in the Northeast are engaged in subsistence farming, most of whom use outmoded farming practices. It is ironic that a region endowed with a wealth of riverine resource imports fish from other parts of the country. Manipur imports more than three-fourths of its requirement from Andhra Pradesh.[22] Even Arunachal Pradesh gets its stock of fish from the distant states in south India. Assam's story is similar—it imports three-fourths of its milk, 98 per cent of its meat and 94 per cent of its eggs from outside the region.[23] This is a glaring pointer to the extent of underdevelopment of allied sectors of animal husbandry and fisheries, which could boost farm incomes. Each state government has embarked upon its own path of agriculture or horticulture development, often without any forward linkages. Small produce from these states finds no buyers in the market outside. Aggregated produce, especially in high-value crops, would enhance the bargaining power of the farmers. The Northeast itself must emerge as an integrated market with three regional hubs: Guwahati, Agartala and Imphal. This needs integrated planning for cold chains, warehouses, aggregation and collection centres and regional market hubs. The NEC could take the lead in nudging the states in this direction.

The Northeast has an unusually large number of civil society organizations, registered associations and youth bodies, which function as informal pressure groups. Civil society organizations like the YMA have a powerful voice, given its universal membership approach. Such bodies mostly articulate their position on issues surrounding ethnic identity. On the positive side, they partner with the government pro bono in providing remarkable support for disaster relief and rehabilitation. The YMA also immerses itself in a range of social activities: blood donation camps, forest conservation efforts, grassroots campaigns against drug abuse and so on. Yet, the sheer number of its membership often makes it transgress the 'apolitical' charter. During my tenure in Mizoram, I felt the YMA stepping into vigilante activism by enforcing liquor prohibition and checking and seizing cars entering the state borders. On certain issues of political import, it assumes the mantle of a parallel government and the state is forced into a dialogue with the YMA leadership. Ahead of the 2018 assembly elections, the YMA brought the election machinery to a standstill by demanding the removal of the Chief Electoral Officer. A bandh call by the YMA is a diktat for all Mizos—even the law-and-order machinery appears helpless to enforce order. The only body that is deemed to have the power to reason with the

YMA in a crisis situation is the church. A delicate balance is required to harness the potential of a strong civil society in emerging as a partner for development rather than as a disruptor.

A culture of economic blockade and political bandhs plagued the Northeast for long. Such a manifestation of protest, where a section of civil society resorts to blocking off all supplies by staging prolonged sit-ins or strikes, owes its origins to the Assam students' agitation. The contagion spread across other states of the region. Communities wanting to make a point centred around an ethnic issue or a political demand routinized such protests. This put off potential investors and sullied the image of the region for a long time. Manipur was said to be 'topping the list' of such incidents, leading to the disruption of all traffic and essential supplies along critical national highways. Short of violence, this appeared to be the most 'viable option' of registering protest. Between 2004 and 2007, the state was estimated to have lost Rs 5 billion annually on account of economic blockades. In 2011, the Sadar Hills District Demand Committee (SHDCC) blocked the two national highways for ninety-one days till the government ceded ground and accepted their demand for the creation of a new district.[24] Political tolerance has gone down for such protests; but in close-knit societies, coercive action on dissent is usually counterproductive.

During my first stint in Mizoram two decades ago, the Mizo Zirlai Pawl (MZP) would routinely call for a vai bandh, targeting only outsiders. The trigger could range from a minor scuffle in the market or an incident of rape of a Mizo girl in Silchar. In twenty years, there has been a significant change in the animosity against outsiders. The younger generation has no memories of the trauma of the past, though some elements keep stoking the fires of identity. In Meghalaya, student bodies such as the Khasi Students' Union, Jaintia Students' Union and Garo Students' Union assume the role of saviours of ethnicity, taking up causes well beyond campus issues.

There has been a steadfast demand for the introduction of inner line regulations, regulation of trade by non-tribals and issuance of work permits to migrant labour. These have often resulted in a direct confrontation with the state, and also runs counter to the pro-investment pitch made by the state government. Demands for job reservation quotas for locals tend to dampen the pitch for investors who are reluctant to compromise on the availability of skilled manpower.[25] Insecurity runs deep. Lack of opportunity compounds it. A protest by the Khasi Students' Union against Bengalis saw threatening posters saying, 'Khasiland for khasis; foreigners go away.'[26] Xenophobia scares away tourists and investors alike.

Nepotism and corruption in recruitment for government jobs has been a bone of contention for student bodies. With growing education and limited avenues for employment, this becomes a thorn in the flesh. To paraphrase Charles Dickens, there is nothing so finely perceived and so finely felt as injustice. Growing awareness and public pressure are forcing change. Following a recruitment 'scam' in Arunachal Pradesh in 2020, its livid chief minister invoked drastic action against concerned officials. In the next recruitment drive, the staff selection board allowed the downloading of optical marked reader answer sheets for comparison with the answer key to assure transparency. Sadly, the same institution saw another scandal in 2022, over a leaked examination paper for recruitment of assistant engineers in the state, leading to public furore and protests. So much so that the Central Bureau of Investigation was called in to ensure a fair inquiry.

The transformation of the Northeast is critically dependent on serious governance reforms. The restoration of faith in institutions of the state and a push for transparency are vital for change. Civil service lies at the heart of governance structures in the Northeast. No reform would be successful without a serious overhaul of bureaucratic machinery in this region.

13

Change with Continuity

INDIA'S NORTHEAST HAS witnessed nothing short of an upheaval over the last seven decades. Winds of change have swept its entire landscape—disrupting traditional polity, economy and culture. Enigmatic people emerged from the shadows to engage with ambivalent mainlanders. The interface commenced on a note of mistrust and hostility. The mainland appeared distant and indifferent to the people of the frontier. Perceptions of injustice and a feeling of prolonged neglect deepened the emotional chasm. Racial prejudice experienced in the mainland added to the angst. The tyranny of geography added to the sense of isolation. A bonfire of ethnicities and a plethora of armed struggles muddied the waters. The mainlanders saw the Northeast as an alien, unsafe and unknown land.

But in the last two decades, there has been a perceptible shift. Improved connectivity and technology are helping build bridges of understanding. A generational shift is now giving shape to a fresh dialogue with a 'new India'. A region deeply steeped in tradition has been sucked into a gale of modernizing influences. The millennials are self-assured and aspirational. The older generation has also moved on, though embers of a traumatic past still smoulder in their hearts.

In the twenty-first century, race has 'become a palimpsest, a parchment written by successive generations where nothing is ever *entirely* erased'.[1] The political firmament in the Northeast has always revolved around the axis of identity. At a macro level, this assumed the shape of dichotomies: hills versus valleys, insiders versus outsiders, inheritors versus intruders. That was not all. The complexity of the jigsaw reveals itself only with a finer lens. Within a state, multiple identities are competing for political influence and economic dominance. A clarion call for Naga unity might hold relevance outside the state, but sounds hollow within. People identify themselves as Konyaks, Tangkhuls, Aos, Angamis and so on. Ironically, the institution of democracy has deepened the sense of tribalism. District boundaries are determined more along tribal affiliation than on administrative logic. Minority tribes claim injustice at the hands of the majority, creating a clamour for autonomy within the state. This is evident in the case of the Hmars of Mizoram, the eastern tribes of Nagaland and the Bodos of Assam. The issue of religious minorities such as the Chakmas and the Brus in Mizoram is even more complex.

The story in the plains is incomplete without Bangladesh in the picture. In Assam, the question of who is an Axomiya still haunts intellectual and political discourse. Himanta Biswa Sarma, the influential chief minister of the state, draws a distinction between the Muslims of Indian origin and the Bangladeshi Muslims: 'They call it Miya culture, Miya poetry … Miya language … We have to protect the composite Indian culture and more particularly Assamese culture …'[2] The reappropriation of Miya, once a pejorative connotation, and the rise of revolutionary Miya poetry are a rejection of the Bengali-origin Muslim tag.[3] Politics in Tripura pits the hill tribes against the Bangladeshi migrants. Porous borders and politics of patronage have vitiated the narrative. The enactment of the Citizenship Ammendment Law saw a wave of protests across the Northeast, stoked by fears of a fresh influx of migrants of Bangladesh's religious minorities. Pradyot Deb Barman, scion of Manikya dynasty, argued, 'When the state acceded to merge with the Union of India (in 1947) we were promised that the culture, language and ethnicity of Tripura will be protected. Then why is it being disregarded?'[4]

Tremors in the neighbourhood bring reverberations of seismic proportions in these borderlands. The unexpected military coup in Myanmar has created a piquant situation in the Northeast. Firstly, the Act East policy and the projected gains for the Northeast precariously hinge upon a conducive economic climate in Myanmar. Soon after the coup, foreign trade across Moreh came to a grinding halt. The Chin National Army, the armed wing fighting for a federal union in Myanmar, has sought asylum in Mizoram for their family members, apprehending a crackdown by the military junta. Mizoram and Manipur already have an estimated 20,000 Chin refugees who fled Sagaing province following a military crackdown.

It has taken more than five decades for people of the Northeast to reconcile to the idea of nationhood. It has taken much longer for New Delhi to shape a policy that strikes the right chord. For the first time since independence, substantial parts of the Northeast are experiencing sustained peace. In some cases, there has been a reconciliation of sorts, while in others there is a sense of fatigue. Even the great Naga warriors hope for an honourable settlement. Peace is fragile as long as fundamental fault lines remain. Yet, a sense of renewed hope reverberates in the region.[5]

Assam, the gateway to the region, was the epicentre of violence. The stranglehold of the ULFA, the National Democratic Front of Boroland (NDFB) and the United National Liberation Fund (UNLF), which created an atmosphere of fear, has all but vanished. This flowed from astute statecraft and an enhanced security collaboration with Bangladesh and Bhutan.[6] The tripartite Bodoland Accord, signed in 2020, has finally brought the three-decade old insurgency to closure. The establishment of a Bodoland territorial region envisages expanded legislative, executive and financial powers to the expanded district council under the Sixth Schedule.[7]

A famine and Assam's indifference at the time gave birth to the Mizo insurgency in the '60s. A brutal army crackdown and deployment of unusual military tactics saw a forcible regrouping of villages along the roadside to cut off the insurgents. In Mizo consciousness, Rambuai (years of trouble) evoke painful memories of untold brutality and loss. 'People remain silent about it, hoping it would go away. It is too painful to recall. A lot of people expect the Indian government to apologize,' says Lalhlimpuii Pachuau, a sociologist. The younger people are curious about their history and are conflicted about their identity, she feels.[8] The Mizoram Accord, signed in 1986, has been a model template of peace in the Northeast. The church played a significant role in nudging the MNF to sign the agreement. Mizos have moved on, in a spirit of reconciliation and forgiveness. The present chief minister, Zoramthanga, is leading an MNF government for a third term. He was a former military leader of the group, which waged a war against the state.

The bumpy road to Kohima is a dusty reminder of the difficult political journey of the people of Nagaland. Much has altered since 14 August 1947, when Phizo famously unfurled the flag of rebellion. Staunch idealism gave way to rank opportunism and expediency. The formation of the state of Nagaland saw a fragmentation of political space into the overground, underground and middle ground. Saner voices for peace were muzzled by the barrel of the gun. God was invoked by the underground with emotional appeals like 'Nagaland for Christ.' Even the underground became a divided lot with multiple factions claiming dominance. The 1997 ceasefire agreement signed by the Government of India with the NSCN(IM) marked a turning point. Instances of violence and kidnapping came down significantly. But 'extortion became legalized' and people had 'nowhere to run', laments microfinance entrepreneur Neichute Doulo. The spirit of enterprise was stifled by the culture of violence in the state. Doulo feels that even now several Nagas believe that the struggle is morally justified, even though independence is out of question. But people hate the underground, which has been 'used to good effect, as a drama by bankers and politicians in the state'. Much like how Covid-19 became a pretext for inaction, the underground has become a convenient alibi for the underdevelopment in the state. 'Flag or no flag, separate constitution or none, people are now waiting for a new dawn.'[9]

The framework agreement signed between the NSCN(IM) and the Government of India, at the residence of Prime Minister Modi in August 2015, raised much expectations. Public posturing and a reiteration of earlier positions of negotiation obfuscate the extent of real progress. Intelligence agencies are working overtime to bring all the factions on the table to arrive at a settlement. With the NSCN(K) Chief Niki Sumi joining the talks, there is greater optimism amongst negotiators.[10] Yet, the history of failed negotiations in the past infuses a sense of cynicism. S.C. Jamir, the veteran of Naga politics, points to a series of agreements in the past: the Akbar Hydari Agreement, the 16 Point Agreement and the more recent one of 2015. 'The Government of India should be strong enough to implement what has been agreed. There would be tremendous support from the people, who don't want to carry the baggage anymore. If there is any further delay, unseen forces may derail the process,' he feels. Bitter on the current state of governance, the former chief minister candidly expressed that, 'Governance has totally collapsed in the last two decades. There are too many prime ministers, commanders-in-chief and multiple governments run the state. Parallel regimes are directing businesses to pay taxes, which is nothing short of extortion.'[11] The forum for Naga reconciliation is playing the role of bringing multiple factions together. Akum Longchari, the scholarly founder of *The Morung Express*, a leading daily of Nagaland, strikes a cautionary note,

> There is a growing feeling that there could be an agreement but no solution. Conditions may have changed and so have generations, but the original question remains, irrespective of what form it takes in articulation. Peace, in order to be sustainable in the long run, must address core issues of sovereignty and what it means for the Nagas. The process being followed is designed not to transform but to manage. The more you try to manage, the more it slips out of your hands. There has been a breach of trust in the past at multiple levels. We need to see if the larger population of the state reconciles with the agreement and whether it fulfils the aspiration of the majority. The Naga imbroglio has been about justice, and not so much about identity. Mizoram went through a process of reconciliation and nation-building, but Nagaland has always remained in a perpetual fire-fighting mode.[12]

Monalisa Changkija sums up by saying, 'Nagas have a great fighting spirit, but they don't know which battles to fight.'[13]

Armed struggles and violent uprisings were pitted against the extraordinary might of state power. The AFSPA was enacted in 1958 to deal with the Naga rebellion against independent India.[14] Over time, its ambit was expanded to cover the entire Northeast. In Manipur, the legislation has been in force for more than four decades. Civil society and human rights activists have protested the sweeping powers accorded by law to even non-commissioned armed personnel to shoot on mere suspicion, without fear of any recrimination. The law gets armed only when an area is declared a 'disturbed area' by the state or the Central government, thereby implying that civil administration on its own is inadequate to deal with the local security situation. The public outrage in Manipur following the brutal killing of Manorama led Prime Minister Manmohan Singh to set up the Justice Jeevan Reddy Committee, with a mandate to suggest how to make the legislation 'more humane'. The committee immersed itself into a series of public consultations and concluded that it was a 'symbol of hatred and oppression'.[15] Sanjoy Hazarika, a member of the committee, describes at length the dissonance in views expressed by the security establishment on the one hand and the state governments and civil society on the other. Security forces deem the protection accorded under the law as necessary to avoid opening a 'can of worms' subsequently. Those seeking its removal argued that it was a 'bad law which had been misused/abused', citing instances of human rights violations. The committee recommended the repeal of the law, suggesting the insertion of appropriate amendments in the Unlawful Activities (Prevention) Act, 1967, to provide necessary safeguards to curb terrorism. In the words of Hazarika, the committee tried to 'defang AFSPA' to ensure that the 'bond of impunity and immunity from prosecution for the security forces was challenged'.[16] In the absence of political consensus for its repeal, the recommendations of the committee went into deep freeze. The shadow of AFSPA still looms large over Manipur, Nagaland and parts of Assam and Arunachal Pradesh, though instances of reported misuse have come down.

Technology is becoming a big cultural disruptor in the Northeast. The utopian isolation envisioned by Verrier Elwin is antediluvian in the age of social media. Youngsters are befriending strangers from around the world with ease. A silent social and cultural revolution is stirring up the Northeast. Lalnunpuia, the young director of Zonet, a popular Mizo cable television service, feels that sports and music on social media has 'broken down barriers'. But social media is a double-edged sword. For some, the content is a vindication of their own culture, while for others it breeds a self-deprecating feeling of 'primitiveness'. He explains that Mizoram was a late starter in the digital world, 'Jio was introduced in 2012, and our society made a leap from television to digital media without experiencing the age of cinema.' His five-year-old daughter is glued to YouTube, and converses only in English. This, in a society where Mizo is the universal lingua franca, is a tectonic shift. He foresees that over the next couple of years, he might have to generate 'interesting content' to teach Mizo culture to his daughter, who currently finds it 'boring'.[17] Old-timers like S.C. Jamir are disapproving of it,

> People have indulged too much in fake Western culture, to the extent of forgetting their own language. I am disappointed to see so many boys and girls aping the West, assuming it is a superior culture. We are not living as Nagas or Khasis or Mizos. The obsession with fashion shows and beauty contests has created an artificial world in young minds. Momentarily, a girl might bag the beauty crown in Kohima or Dimapur, which makes her delusional. When she returns home to a life of penury, her dreams stand shattered. This is affecting youngsters psychologically. Applause in a beauty contest stands in stark contrast to the sad reality of her abode. How will she keep up? Either she has to abdicate the crown or resolve to means, which are not in conformity with our culture or religion.[18]

Cultural conformity runs across the social ethos of the Northeast. Any departure is met with stern disapproval of elders, and people feel extremely wary of social ostracism. In Mizoram, the cultural mores are defined by the church, family and the YMA. This hems in the horizon of free will and individual choices. Lalrinngheti Sangsiama, a young barrister of law trained in the United Kingdom, sees two sides. On the one hand, there is a strong sense of community that binds people together. On the other, religion 'blocks our sense of viewing the world'. The ritual of churchgoing is a social compulsion, and absentees are frowned upon. The youth find this compulsion stifling. The institution of the YMA is a unique social organization without any parallel. It is premised on the Mizo principle of 'tlawmngaihna', selfless service—similar to Africa's ubuntu. Every Mizo is expected to contribute voluntarily for social causes in the community. There is an underlying moral compulsion to do so, which is 'killing the youth'. A culture of 'model citizenship', where the community takes salience over individual, creates a pressure on the youth.[19] This pressure also permeates the personal. Marrying outside the tribe is generally frowned upon—more so if one ends up marrying a non-Mizo. Hill tribes of the Northeast are struggling to retain racial and cultural purity. Young people of the region feel conflicted about the multiple layers of identity. Tribe, clan, village, state, region, religion and nation have created a complex identity matrix.

A hitherto classless society has started embracing the Western class construct, which separates the elite from the masses. A handful of political and bureaucratic families form the upper crust of society. Their sons and daughters jostle with the wards of the rich and powerful from around the country. Invariably, they would be educated in convents or the elite boarding schools of Mussoorie, Sanawar or Shimla. The wealthy are uninhibited in flaunting their designer labels. This club of the nouveau rich is far removed from the impoverished reality of rural hinterland. The aspiration of the rural youth is to migrate to the capital and gain the means to live the lifestyle of the rich. They are no longer interested in farming or weaving, instead they seek a government job.

The monetization of land has created vested interests for short-term gains, with scant regard for consequences. The wealthy have a propensity to demonstrate their riches through opulent buildings and private farmhouses. The urge to rapidly climb up the development ladder has led to a surge in public investments for construction. Ecological and geological risks are often given a convenient burial. A region falling in the highest seismic risk zone in the country should abjure from mindless construction of high-rise concrete structures. The devastation in Uttarakhand should serve as a red flag for the Northeast. This raises serious questions around the model of economic development and basic concerns around sustainability.

Forests hold a sacred place in the tribal cultural construct. Nearly two-thirds of land in the Northeast is classified as forest land.[20] Over time, there has been a gradual but consistent decline in forest cover. This is partly on account of the practice of shifting cultivation, but more recently on account of development construction. Environmentalists caution against the push for construction of big dam projects, citing underlying ecological fragility and the risk to biodiversity. The challenge for governments is the absence of any substantial revenue generating economic activity, which constricts their ability of resource generation. This, in turn, forces the states to be perpetually dependant on the Central government, leaving little room for political flexibility to set the developmental agenda. Elected governments, in their quest for resources, start exploring avenues of exploitation of mineral wealth and hydropower. Policies are tailored to suit the interests of investors, mostly with an utter disregard to environmental considerations.

In the eye-opening documentary film *Broken Landscape: Confronting India's Water-Energy Choke Point*, Michael T. Miller portrays the deep nexus of politicians and the coal-mining lobby that led to the proliferation of rat hole mining in Meghalaya. Its impact on the pollution of the river downstream and the death of fish by water 'plague' forced the National Green Tribunal to step in and ban this practice. The mine owners were typically influential local residents. The miners, mostly migrant Assamese and Nepalese labour, disregarded the risks of a hazardous profession for the sake of livelihood. The ban gave rise to a grey market of mining. Mines 'poisoned the land'—now forcing even local villagers to enter this hazardous profession, many a time at the risk of their lives. Environmental activist Brian Daly says,

> The whole valley has become acidic, like a desert. Mining has robbed the poor villagers of their farmlands. The toxic cocktail unleashed by coal and limestone mining and the cement plants has turned the rivers either orange-yellow or a sickly blue.[21]

In his book *Unruly Hills: A Political Ecology of India's Northeast*, Swedish social anthropologist Bengt G. Karlsson uses the metaphor of a single tree atop Shillong Peak, which stands as a 'lone reminder' of the forest that once covered the peak. He draws a contrast between the wet desert and the sacred forest on the outskirts of Shillong. The former 'stands as a warning of nature rendered barren, a kind of dystopia with the environment', while the latter shines as an emblem of a 'green future based on indigenous wisdom and respectful engagement with nature'.[22] Modern development has broken the environmental compact which bound tribal societies with nature.

Change is the iron law of nature. An accelerated pace of change in the Northeast in the twenty-first century has disrupted the traditional way of life. Were Elwin to descend from heaven, he would hardly recognize the pristine hills that he so passionately fought to preserve. The older generation maintains a tenuous link with a fading past, while the youngsters are trying to chart a new one. The tension between the aspirations of the youth and the traditions of the old is palpable. People are fiercely protective about land and cultural identity. Those who find it difficult to adjust to the pressures of conformity relocate outside the state or overseas. This brings us back to the original Nehruvian dilemma—which model of development, for whom and at what pace? There are no easy solutions. People of the Northeast will hopefully make wise choices, and not tread on an unsustainable path of development like the rest of us. For then they run the risk of losing everything that makes them so special.

Acknowledgements

THIS BOOK HAS been a labour of love for me. I would like to give my deepest gratitude to my biggest motivator for this project—my wife, Ambreen, who nudged, encouraged and prodded me to pick up the pen and start writing. My father, who was also a civil servant, was an inspiration for taking up academic pursuits while in service and my mother has been the silent force behind my interest in books. Thanks also to my daughter Ananya, on the threshold of her professional life, who also felt that I had the potential to write a book.

For this book, I interviewed nearly a hundred people in Delhi and across the Northeast. I owe a debt of gratitude to many of them, who facilitated human connections, even where I didn't know the individuals personally. Oken Tayeng, a friend in Arunachal, opened doors to several connections in Meghalaya and Nagaland. Hekani Jakhalu graciously introduced me to several people in Nagaland and Sikkim. Hoihnu Hauzel, a journalist and a friend, opened a world of new contacts for me in Manipur. Imkongla Jamir, a younger service colleague, introduced me to her circle of friends in Nagaland. In Mizoram, my personal assistant, Lalhlimpuii, was very helpful in making sure I met the right people in the state to gain fresh insights. Pema Khandu, chief minister of Arunachal Pradesh, was extremely encouraging and supportive for this project and motivated me through his constant support. I am grateful to S.C. Jamir, a stalwart of Indian politics, for being generous with his time and giving me a statesman's view of the unfolding scenario in Nagaland. Pu Zoramthanga, chief minister of Mizoram, was equally candid in his conversation and his sense of history helped build perspective. My younger colleagues in service—Prince Dhawan, Sonam Chombay and Himanshu Gupta—rallied around me with support and encouragement. The people of the Northeast, who shared their stories and the story of the region, agreeing in friendship and trust to have candid conversations with me—thank you.

I have drawn upon the wisdom of several scholars who have written extensively about various aspects of the Northeast, following decades of academic research. Reading their work helped me gain better historical insights into complex issues of this diverse region. I also referenced manuscripts and records at the Nehru Memorial Museum and Library in New Delhi. To the custodian of these records, my gratitude.

The HarperCollins India team merits a special mention. Thank you to Krishan Chopra, who helped give a structure to the book in its nascent stage. Ananya Borgohain, who went through the initial chapters and guided me to add a contemporary flavour to it. Finally, Tanima Saha and Suchismita Ukil, who laboured over the entire manuscript, giving some pertinent and insightful feedback.

My friends, S. Prasanna Rajan and Mini Kapoor, both remarkable writers themselves, encouraged me to finish the book. Mini, even graciously, went over large parts of the manuscript with dollops of generous feedback. Ultimately, what started as an amateur adventure in writing has taken the shape of a book, thanks to friends, family and well wishers.

Notes

INTRODUCTION

1. https://www.nobelprize.org/prizes/literature/1982/marquez/lecture/
2. Van Schendel, Willem, 'Geographies of Knowing, Geographies of Ignorance: Jumping Scale in Southeast Asia', *Environment and Planning D: Society and Space* (20 June 2002), pp. 647–668.
3. Bhattacharya, Swapna, 'The Khamtis of Arunachal Pradesh', in *The Southern Silk Road*, ed. Lipi Ghosh (New Delhi: Manohar, 2019), p. 71.
4. Pommaret, Francoise, 'Ancient Trade Partners: Bhutan, Cooch Bihar and Assam (18th and 19th Centuries)', *Journal Asiatique*, vol. 287 (1999), pp. 285–303.
5. Jenkins, H.L., 'Notes on a Trip across Patkoi Range, from Assam to the Hookong Valley', *The Journal of the Royal Geographical Society of London*, vol. 41 (1871), p. 37.
6. Sharma, Jayeeta, '"Lazy" Natives, Coolie Labour and the Assam Tea Industry', *Modern Asian Studies*, vol. 43, no. 6 (2009), pp. 1287–1324. Cambridge University Press.
7. Guha, Amalendu, *Planter-Raj to Swaraj Freedom Struggle and Electoral Politics in Assam 1826-1947* (New Delhi: Indian Council for Historical Research, 1977), p. 39.

8. Scott, J.C., *The Art of Not Being Governed: An Anarchist History of Upland Southeast Asia* (New Haven and London: Yale University Press, 2009).
9. Mackenzie, Alexander, *History of the Relations of the Government with the Hill Tracts of the North-East Frontier of Bengal* (Calcutta: Home Department Press, 1884).
10. Kire, Easterine, *Walking the Roadless Road: Exploring the Tribes of Nagaland* (New Delhi: Aleph Book Company, 2019), pp. 224–225.
11. Reid, R., 'Assam', *Journal of the Royal Society of Arts*, vol. XCII (April, 1944), p. 27.
12. Chan, Chai-fong, 'British Colonial Policy in the Naga Hills: With Special Focus on Control Area Policy', *The Komaba Journal of Area Studies*, no. 3 (University of Tokyo, 1999), pp. 167–187.

    https://www.jstage.jst.go.jp/article/jjasas1989/2001/13/2001_13_76/_pdf/-char/ja
13. https://www.thehindu.com/books/books-reviews/the-secret-british-plan-that-fell-through/article6002139.ece
14. Van Schendel, Willem, 'Afterword-Contested, Vertical Fragmenting: De-partitioning "North-East India" Studies', in *Geographies of Difference: Exploration in Northeast India Studies,* ed. Mélanie Vandenhelsken, et al., (London and New York: Routledge, 2018), pp. 272–288.
15. https://scroll.in/article/989166/why-mizo-groups-are-organising-events-to-show-solidarity-for-coup-protestors-in-myanmar
16. https://economictimes.indiatimes.com/news/elections/assembly-elections/mizoram-assembly-elections/zoramthanga-from-being-an-insurgent-to-becoming-mizoram-cm/articleshow/67109534.cms?from=mdr
17. Title of a book written by Sanjoy Hazarika.

NEHRU'S MISPLACED UTOPIA

1. Excerpt from the poem 'To Althea, from Prison' by Richard Lovelace, as inscribed by hand on a personal notebook of Gopinath Bardoloi, Nehru Memorial and Museum Library (NMML), New Delhi.

2. Singh, B.P, *The Problem of Change: A Study of North-East India* (New Delhi: Oxford University Press, 1987).
3. Madhab, Jayanta, 'Social Conflicts in the North East: An Economic Interpretation', *Contemporary India: A North-East Special,* vol. 1, no. 4 (October–December 2000), p. 184.
4. Bordoloi to Patel, 5 May 1948, Sardar Patel's correspondence, vol. IV, document 85, pp. 119–120, in *Gopinath Bordoloi, 'The Assam Problem' and Nehru's Centre* by Nirode K. Barooah (Guwahati: Bhabani Publishers, 2010), p. 319.
5. Nag, Sajal, 'Nehru and the North East', NMML Occasional Paper, 2015, New Series 75, p. 10.
6. Rao, B. Shiva, *The Framing of India's Constitution: A Study* (New Delhi: Indian Institute of Public Administration, 1976), vol. III, pp. 770–779.
7. Constituent Assembly Debates 1949, pp. 997–998.
8. Savyasaachi, *Tribal Forest-dwellers and Self-rule: The Constituent Assembly Debates on the Fifth and Sixth Schedules* (New Delhi: Indian Institute of Social Science, 1998) p. 127.
9. Verghese, B.G., *India's Northeast Resurgent: Ethnicity, Insurgency, Governance, Development* (New Delhi: Konark Publishers, 1996), p. 34.
10. Means, Gordon P. and Ingunn N. Means, 'Nagaland: The Agony of Ending Guerrilla War', *Pacific Affairs,* vol. 39, no. 3 /4 (Autumn 1966), p. 290.
11. Naga Independence: A Memorandum to the Honourable Prime Minister, Government of India, Kohima, Naga National Council, 1951, p. 2.
12. https://www.asianage.com/opinion/columnists/071119/naga-peace-process-back-on-track-again.html
13. Guyot-Réchard, Bérénice, 'Reordering Border Space: Relief, Rehabilitation and Nation-Building in North-Eastern India after the 1950 Assam Earthquake', *Modern Asian Studies,* vol. 49, no. 4 (July 2015), pp. 931–962.
14. Nehru, Jawaharlal, *Letters to the Chief Ministers, 1947-1964,* vol. II: 1950-1952, (New Delhi: Oxford University Press, 1986), p. 179.

15. Rustomji, Nari, *Enchanted Frontiers: Sikkim, Bhutan and India's North-Eastern Borderlands* (New Delhi: Oxford University Press, 1971), p. 126.
16. 'Speech at the Opening of the Scheduled Tribes and Scheduled Areas Conference, New Delhi, 7 June 1952' in *Jawaharlal Nehru Selected Speeches: Volume Two: 1949-1953* (New Delhi: Publication Division, 2017), pp. 576–583.
17. Ibid., p. 582.
18. Nehru, Jawaharlal, 'Note on the North-East Frontier Agency,' 28 August 1955. Elwin Papers, NMML.
19. Elwin, Verrier, *The Tribal World of Verrier Elwin* (New York: Oxford University Press, 1964) p. 36.
20. Jawaharlal Nehru, foreword to *A Philosophy for NEFA*, by Verrier Elwin (Shillong, 1957).
21. Ibid.
22. Rustomji, Nari, *Enchanted Frontiers: Sikkim, Bhutan and India's North-Eastern Borderlands* (New Delhi: Oxford University Press, 1971), p. 123.
23. Ibid., p. 132.
24. Ibid., p. 137.
25. Rustomji, Nari, 'Birth of a new policy for the Tribal Areas', speeches and writings by him, 2 March 1949, NMML Manuscripts.
26. Kaul, T.N., 'A brief note on NEFA, Manipur state, Naga Hill district (Kohima) and Lushai Hills (Aijal)', 21 April 1953, p. 4. Verrier Elwin subject file 8, NMML Manuscripts.
27. Kaul, T.N., 'A brief note on each tribal area', 29 April 1953, p. 4. Verrier Elwin subject file 8, NMML Manuscripts.
28. 'Needs of Tribal People–Elwin Committees Report', 16 October 1960, Press Information Bureau, Government of India. Verrier Elwin subject file 89, NMML Manuscripts.
29. Rustomji, Nari, 'Jawaharlal Nehru and the Tribes: Romance and Compassion'. In *Jawaharlal Nehru, Tribes and Tribal Policy* by K.S. Singh (Calcutta: Anthropological Survey of India, 1989), p. 30.

30. Elwin, Verrier, *The Tribal World of Verrier Elwin* (New York: Oxford University Press, 1964), p. 302.
31. Elwin, Verrier, *A New Deal for Tribal India* (New Delhi: Ministry of Home Affairs, 1963), p. 116.
32. Rustomji, Nari, 'Verrier Elwin Memorial Lecture', in speeches and writings by Nari Rustomji, 29, NMML Manuscripts.
33. Ibid., p. 53.
34. Ibid., p. 54.
35. Misra, Udayon, 'Ethnicity, Territoriality and Autonomy in India's North-East'. In *Challenges of Development in North-East India*, ed. David R. Syiemlieh, et al. (New Delhi: Regency Publications, 2006), p. 4.
36. Ibid., p. 6.
37. Rustomji, Nari, 'Jawaharlal Nehru and the Tribes: Romance and Compassion'. In *Jawaharlal Nehru, Tribes and Tribal Policy* by K.S. Singh (Calcutta: Anthropological Survey of India, 1989), p. 30.
38. Nari Rustomji's speeches and writings, NMML Manuscripts.
39. Guha, R., 'Savaging the Civilized: Verrier Elwin and the Tribal Question in Late Colonial India', *Economic and Political Weekly*, vol. 31, no. 35/37 special number (September 1996) pp. 2375–89.

THE LOST DECADES

1. Saqib Khan, 'A "Reading" without History: Questioning a Flawed Reading of Left Politics in Tripura', *Economic & Political Weekly*, vol. 53, no. 7 (17 February 2018).
2. https://scroll.in/article/990541/interview-sanjib-baruah-on-assam-elections-identity-politics-and-the-cash-transfer-state?utm_source=rss&utm_medium=news360
3. https://indianexpress.com/article/explained/how-chakmas-and-hajongs-settled-in-north-east-why-arunachal-worries-about-citizenship-4851866/

4. Baruah, Sanjib, *Durable Disorder: Understanding the Politics of Northeast India* (New Delhi: Oxford University Press, 2005), p. 191.
5. Singh, B.P., *The Problem of Change: A Study of North-East India* (New Delhi: Oxford University Press, 1987), p. 117.
6. Indira Gandhi's speech at the inauguration of the North-Eastern Council, Shillong, 7 November 1972. In *Indira Gandhi: Selected Speeches and Writings: 1972-1977* (New Delhi: Publication Division, 1984), p. 1.
7. Ibid., p. 2.
8. Rustomji, Nari, *Imperilled Frontiers: India's North-Eastern Borderlands* (New Delhi: Oxford University Press, 1983), p. 84.
9. Cited in Verghese, B.G., *India's Northeast Resurgent: Ethnicity, Insurgency, Governance, Development* (New Delhi: Konark Publishers, 1996), p. 42.
10. Sinha, A.C., 'Managing Social Consequences of Smallness'. In *Northeast Region: Problems and Prospects of Development*, ed. B.L. Abbi (Chandigarh: Centre for Research in Rural and Industrial Development, 1984), p. 122.
11. Baruah, Sanjib, *India Against Itself: Assam and the Politics of Nationality* (Philadelphia: University of Pennysylvania Press, 2001), pp. 125–128.
12. Pisharoty, Sangeeta Barooah, *Assam: The Accord, the Discord* (Gurugram: Penguin Random House India, 2019), pp. 54–57.
13. https://indianexpress.com/article/north-east-india/tripura/tripura-insurgency-riot-displaced-families-homes-settlement-northeast-india-5314370/
14. Indira Gandhi's speech at the meeting of the North-Eastern Council, Shillong, 22 December 1980. In *Indira Gandhi: Selected Speeches and Writings: 1980-1981* (New Delhi: Publication Division, 1985), pp. 136–140.
15. Verghese, B.G., *India's Northeast Resurgent: Ethnicity, Insurgency, Governance, Development* (New Delhi: Konark Publishers, 1996), p. 44.
16. Ibid., p. 52.

17. Baruah, Sanjib, *India Against Itself: Assam and the Politics of Nationality* (Philadelphia: University of Pennysylvania Press, 2001), pp. 150–151.
18. Baruah, Sanjib, *Durable Disorder: Understanding the Politics of Northeast India* (New Delhi: Oxford University Press, 2005), pp. 154–55.
19. Ibid., p. 155.
20. Kire, Easterine, *Walking the Roadless Road: Exploring the Tribes of Nagaland* (New Delhi: Aleph Book Company, 2019), pp. 248–253.
21. Verghese, B.G., *India's Northeast Resurgent: Ethnicity, Insurgency, Governance, Development* (New Delhi: Konark Publishers, 1996), pp. 97–98.
22. Baruah, Sanjib, *In the Name of the Nation: India and Its Northeast* (California: Stanford University Press, 2020), p. 170.
23. Development of North Eastern Region, Union Budget 1998-99, Ministry of Finance, Government of India, https://www.indiabudget.gov.in/budget_archive/ub1998-99/bs/bs16.htm
24. Interview with the author on 31 January 2020.
25. https://cag.gov.in/uploads/download_audit_report/2010/Union_Performance_Civil_National_Library_3_2010_chapter_3_0.pdf

CONNECTIVITY: THE SILVER BULLET

1. Saikia, Arupjyoti, *The Unquiet River: A Biography of the Brahmaputra* (Noida: Oxford University Press, 2019), pp. 186–190.
2. https://economictimes.indiatimes.com/news/politics-and-nation/tibets-second-largest-airport-terminal-opened-close-to-india/articleshow/57497353.cms?from=mdr
3. Basic Road Statistics of India, 2001-02. Ministry of Shipping, Road Transport and Highways, Government of India. Quoted from Basic Statistics of NER 2006, NEC Shillong.
4. https://economictimes.indiatimes.com/news/politics-and-nation/tripura-cm-manik-sarkar-flays-successive-central-governments-for-ne-backwardness/articleshow/48034695.cms?from=mdr

5. https://economictimes.indiatimes.com/news/india/pema-khandu-becomes-first-cm-to-reach-remote-vijaynagar-the-last-administrative-headquarters-near-myanmar-border/articleshow/81726247.cms?from=mdr
6. https://www.thehindu.com/life-and-style/travel/in-lockdown-land/article31215884.ece
7. https://scroll.in/latest/981212/arunachal-pradesh-24-arrested-after-protestors-burn-government-offices-over-voter-rights
8. Phone interaction with the author on 2 April 2020.
9. https://www.outlookindia.com/website/story/electricity-for-all-vision-for-the-northeast-is-transformation-by-transportation/308647
10. https://theprint.in/india/governance/modi-govt-built-1-5-km-of-highway-per-day-in-northeast-up-from-0-6-km-per-day-by-upa/322472/
11. https://economictimes.indiatimes.com/industry/transportation/airlines-/-aviation/chief-minister-sarbananda-sonowal-flags-off-guwahati-bangkok-flight/articleshow/71240238.cms
12. https://timesofindia.indiatimes.com/india/modi-govt-changed-emotional-disconnect-with-northeast-president-kovind/articleshow/73799758.cms
13. https://economictimes.indiatimes.com/news/politics-and-nation/railway-reaching-to-tawang-will-be-befitting-reply-to-china-arunachal-pradesh-chief-minister-pema-khandu/articleshow/71235746.cms
14. https://timesofindia.indiatimes.com/city/agartala/agartala-akhaura-rail-link-in-september-2021/articleshow/74001708.cms
15. https://www.thehindu.com/news/national/other-states/meghalaya-shows-signs-of-relenting-on-rail-link-to-shillong/article32554390.ece
16. Saikia, Arupjyoti, *The Unquiet River: A Biography of the Brahmaputra* (Noida: Oxford University Press, 2019), pp. 185–190.
17. https://journalsofindia.com/protocol-on-inland-water-transit-and-trade/
18. 'Steam Communication between Calcutta and Guwahati, Assam', *Orunodoi,* vol. 2, no. 9 (1847), p. 69 in Neog, *Orunodoi* (1983). In

The Unquiet River: A Biography of the Brahmaputra by Arupjyoti Saikia (Noida: Oxford University Press, 2019), p. 172.

19. 'Social Media for Youth and Civic Engagement in India', UNDP India (2019).
20. https://www.thehinducentre.com/multimedia/archive/02670/Policy_Report_No_1_2670863a.pdf
21. Hazarika, Sanjoy, *Strangers No More: New Narratives from India's Northeast* (New Delhi: Aleph Book Company, 2018), p. 296.

A BRIDGE TO THE FAR EAST

1. https://www.youtube.com/watch?v=1Cnrh4AIqD4
2. Inscription on a statue at Tlabung, captured during a field visit in August 2018.
3. Bhattacharya, Rajeev, 'Reality on the Indo-Myanmar border', in *India and Myanmar Borderlands: Ethnicity, Security and Connectivity*, ed. Pahi Saikia and Anasua Basu Ray Chaudhury (New Delhi: Routledge, 2020), pp. 65–69.
4. https://indianexpress.com/article/india/india-others/mos-nirmala-sitharaman-opens-zokhawthar-land-customs-station-near-indo-myanmar-border/ Indian Express, March 25, 2015
5. https://www.telegraphindia.com/states/north-east/over-2900-pigs-dead-in-mizoram/cid/1450343 Telegraph, 23rd May 2018
6. Seshadri, V.S., 'Transforming Connectivity Corridors between India and Myanmar into Development Corridors', Research and Information Systems for Developing Countries (2014).
7. Taneja, Nisha, et al., 'India Myanmar Border Trade', working paper 378, Indian Council for Research in International Economic Relations, June 2019, https://icrier.org/pdf/Working_Paper_378.pdf
8. Isabelle, Sait-Mezard, 'The Look East Policy: An Economic Perspective', p. 25, in Haokip, T. *India's Look East Policy and the Northeast* by Thongkholal Haokip (New Delhi: Sage Publications, 2015) p. 16.
9. https://archivepmo.nic.in/abv/speech-details.php?nodeid=9277

10. Cited in 'Looking "East" through India's North East' by Namrata Goswami, Institute of Defence Studies and Analyses, New Delhi, Occasional Paper no. 2 (June 2009).
11. https://www.narendramodi.in/text-of-pm-s-address-at-the-inaugural-session-of-advantage-assam-global-investors-summit-2018-in-guwahati-assam-538784
12. https://openthemagazine.com/columns/guest-column/north-east-india-the-centre-of-gravity-in-act-east-policy/
13. A term coined by K.S. Rana. Uberoi, Patricia, 'The BCIM Forum: Is It Sustainable', in *Look East to Act East Policy: Implications for India's Northeast*, ed. Gurudas Das and C. Joshua Thomas (New York: Routledge, 2017), p. 76.
14. 'Harnessing the Potential for Cross Border Trade between North East India and its Neighbouring Countries', CUTS International and FICCI (2017), https://www.cuts-citee.org/pdf/Harnessing_the_Potential_for_Cross-border_Trade_between_North_East_India_and_its_Neighbouring_Countries.pdf
15. http://www.lpai.gov.in/content/innerpage/icp-petrapole.php
16. https://www.thehindubusinessline.com/economy/logistics/trilateral-highway-with-myanmar-thailand-to-be-ready-in-about-2-years/article25624095.ece
17. https://mea.gov.in/incoming-visit-detail.htm?32435/IndiaMyanmar+Joint+Statement+during+the+State+Visit+of+the+President+of+Myanmar+to+India+February+2629+2020
18. Ishida, Masami, 'GMS Economic Corridors under the Belt and Road Initiative', *Journal of Asian Economic Integration*, Sage Journals, vol. 1, issue 2 (December 2019), https://journals.sagepub.com/doi/full/10.1177/2631684619894102
19. Seshadri, V.S., 'Transforming Connectivity Corridors between India and Myanmar into Development Corridors', Research and Information Systems for Developing Countries (2014), pp. 46–49.
20. Che, Zhimin, 'Proposition on Formation of Sub Regional Cooperation Zone of China, India, Myanmar and Bangladesh', Presentation at

IGNCA-ICS conference on Regional Development in India and China: With Focus on Southwest China and Northeast India, November 1998. Delhi, Institute of Chinese Studies, Mimeo, cited in 'The BCIM Forum: Is It Sustainable' by Patricia Uberoi, in *Look East to Act East Policy: Implications for India's Northeast*, ed. Gurudas Das and C. Joshua Thomas (New York: Routledge, 2017), pp. 77–79.

21. Majihi, Prithibi, 'Keynote Address', in *Reopening of the Stilwell Road-Prospects and Problems*, ed. D. Nath (Kolkata: Anamika Publishers and Distributors, 2003).
22. http://shillongcustoms.gov.in/english/about-us/brief-history-of-shillong-customs-commissionerate/
23. Das, Gurudas, *Security and Development in India's Northeast* (New Delhi: Oxford University Press, 2012).
24. The Greater Mekong Sub Region 2030 and Beyond. March 2021, Asian Development Bank, pp. 15–76.
25. https://www.mea.gov.in/bilateral-documents.htm?dtl/28946/IndiaJapan+Joint+Statement+during+visit+of+Prime+Minister+of+Japan+to+India+September+14+2017
26. Das, Gurudas, 'Trade between the North-Eastern Region', in *Border Trade: North-East India and Neighbouring Countries*, ed. Gurudas Das and R.K. Purkayastha (New Delhi: Akanksha Publishing House, 2000), pp. 32–37.
27. Interview with the author on 19 March 2020.
28. Taneja, Nisha, et al., 'India's Act East Policy: Facilitating India-Myanmar Border Trade', ICRIER (July 2019), https://icrier.org/pdf/India_Myanmar_Border_Trade.pdf
29. Interface with the author on 19 March 2020.

RIVERS THAT LIGHT

1. Lilienthal, David E., *TVA: Democracy on the March,* in *One Valley and a Thousand: Dams Nationalism, and Development* by Daniel Klingensmith (New Delhi: Oxford University Press, 2007), p. 41.

2. https://himalaya.yale.edu/news/ruth-gamble-pure-one-yarlung-tsangpo-river-through-history
3. Baruah, Sanjib, *Durable Disorder: Understanding the Politics of Northeast India* (New Delhi: Oxford University Press, 2005), p. 133.
4. Joy, K.J., et al., 'Understanding Water Conflicts in Northeast India', in *Water Conflicts in Northeast India* by K.J. Joy, et al. (Routledge, 2018), p. 1.
5. Kingdon-ward, F., 'Aftermath of the Great Assam Earthquake of 1950', *The Geographical Journal*, vol. 121, no. 3 (September 1955), pp. 290–303.
6. Das, P.J., 'Water and Climate Induced Vulnerability in Northeast India: Concerns for Environmental Security and Sustainability', WATCH Programme Research Report 1 (2009). Aaranyak, Guwahati, Assam.
7. Ibid.
8. Changkija, Monalisa, *Cogitating for a Better Deal* (Dimapur: Heritage Publishing House, 2014), pp. 53–54.
9. Saikia, Arupjyoti, *The Unquiet River: A Biography of the Brahmaputra* (Noida: Oxford University Press, 2019), p. 485.
10. Central Electricity Authority, 2015.
11. http://www.ielrc.org/content/e0820.pdf
12. http://finance.arunachal.gov.in/wp-content/uploads/2019/01/HydroPowerPolicy2008.pdf
13. http://164.100.161.239/plans/planrel/55ndc/arunachal_55ndc.pdf
14. https://www.india-seminar.com/2010/605/605_amita_baviskar.htm
15. https://economictimes.indiatimes.com/opinion/interviews/jairam-ramesh-for-95-of-industry-i-am-dr-yes-for-5-i-am-mr-no/articleshow/7153763.cms?from=mdr
16. Rao, V.V.K., 'Hydropower in the Northeast: Potential and Harnessing Analysis', Background paper no. 6 (September 2006), p. 29, input to the World Bank Study, 'Development and Growth in Northeast India: The Natural Resources, Water, and Environment Nexus'.
17. Interaction with the author on 13 April 2021.

18. https://www.narendramodi.in/pm-in-arunachal-pradesh-7276
19. https://arunachaltimes.in/index.php/2020/02/12/seminar-on-hydropower-development/
20. https://india.blogs.nytimes.com/2013/09/24/a-conversation-with-environmental-activist-akhil-gogoi/
21. https://www.downtoearth.org.in/news/assams-dam-crisis-1978
22. https://energy.economictimes.indiatimes.com/news/renewable/nhpc-to-resume-construction-on-lower-subansiri-project/70813274
23. https://www.deccanherald.com/business/business-news/subansiri-project-resumes-after-8-yrs-angers-agitators-768988.html
24. https://indianexpress.com/article/india/india-others/6-years-2-rejections-later-indias-largest-hydro-project-cleared/
25. https://pib.gov.in/PressReleasePage.aspx?PRID=1579129
26. https://www.thehindu.com/sci-tech/energy-and-environment/decision-on-power-project-deferred/article31568655.ece
27. Ete, Mibi, 'Hydro-dollar dreams. Emergent local politics of large dams and small communities', in *Geographies of Difference: Explorations of Northeast India Studies*, ed. by Melanie Vandenhelsken, et al. (New York: Routledge, 2018), p. 110.
28. https://www.downtoearth.org.in/news/environment-ministry-to-clear-controversial-demwe-hydroelectric-project-35883
29. http://www.indiaenvironmentportal.org.in/files/Demwe%20Lower%20Hydro%20Electric%20Project%20forest%20clearance%20NGT%20Judgement.pdf
30. https://parivesh.nic.in/writereaddata/Order%20and%20Release/Minutes%20of%2050%20Meeting%20of%20the%20Standing%20Committee%20of%20National%20Board%20for%20Wildlife.pdf
31. https://www.thehindu.com/news/national/arunachal-pradesh-mega-dam-clearance-shocks-greens/article25063272.ece
32. https://www.financialexpress.com/industry/ntpc-kameng-projects-4th-150-mw-unit-commercially-operational/2193266/
33. https://wwf.panda.org/wwf_news/?75440/Buddah-birds-Protecting-the-black-necked-cranes-of-Shangri-la

34. Arora, Vibha, 'They are All Set to Dam(n) Our Future: Contested Development through Hydel Power in Democratic Sikkim', *Sociological Bulletin*, vol. 58, no. 1, January–April 2009, pp. 94–114.
35. Phone interaction with the author on 5 April 2020.
36. http://www.actsikkim.com/docs/CCS_I_Introductory_Volume.pdf
37. https://cag.gov.in/sites/default/files/audit_report_files/Chapter_3_Economic_Sector_PSUs_Sikkim_Report_No_3_of_2016.pdf
38. http://www.sserc.in/power-generators/teesta-urja-limited-teesta-iii-hydropower-project
39. https://economictimes.indiatimes.com/industry/energy/power/teesta-iii-a-failed-ppp-project-alleges-aipef/articleshow/59308055.cms?from=mdr
40. http://www.lancogroup.com/pdf/IRP/teesta/10_LancoTeestaTeaser.pdf
41. https://energy.economictimes.indiatimes.com/news/renewable/govt-nod-to-nhpc-acquiring-lancos-teesta-hydro-power-project/68303207
42. https://energy.economictimes.indiatimes.com/news/renewable/nhpc-takes-over-lanco-teesta-hydro-power-limited/71513656
43. https://timesofindia.indiatimes.com/city/guwahati/pm-modi-to-inaugurate-tuirial-dam-today-in-mizoram/articleshow/62092978.cms
44. https://powermin.nic.in/sites/default/files/webform/notices/Measures_to_Promote_Hydro_Power_Sector.pdf
45. https://pib.gov.in/newsite/PrintRelease.aspx?relid=171377
46. https://timesofindia.indiatimes.com/india/center-to-set-up-an-exclusive-authority-to-manage-water-resources-of-north-east-india/articleshow/74519269.cms
47. Islam, Md Saidul and Md Nazrul Islam, '"Environmentalism of the poor": the Tipaimukh Dam, ecological disasters and environmental resistance beyond borders', *Bandung: Journal of Global South*, vol. 3, no. 27 (30 June 2016).
48. Arora, Vibha and Ngamjahao Kipgen, '"We can live without power, but we can't live without our land": Indigenous Hmar oppose the Tipaimukh Dam in Manipur', *Sociological Bulletin*, vol. 61, no. 1, January–April 2012, pp. 109–128.

49. https://www.telegraphindia.com/states/north-east/assam-concern-over-china-hydropower-dams/cid/1751052
50. https://economictimes.indiatimes.com/news/politics-and-nation/siff-opposes-10000-mw-power-project-over-siang-river-in-arunachal-pradesh/articleshow/61120523.cms
51. https://www.ndtv.com/india-news/chinas-plans-for-mega-dam-in-tibet-on-brahmaputra-river-raises-concern-in-india-2410971
52. Klingensmith, Daniel, *One Valley and a Thousand: Dams Nationalism, and Development* (New Delhi: Oxford University Press, 2007).
53. McCully, Peter, *Silenced Rivers: The Ecology and Politics of Large Dams* (London and New York: Zed Books, 2007), pp. 37–70.
54. Baruah, Sanjib, 'Whose River Is It Anyway? Political Economy of Hydropower in the Eastern Himalayas', *Economic & Political Weekly*, vol. xlvii, no. 29 (21 July 2012), p. 44.
55. Interaction with the author on 27 April 2020.
56. Rustomji, Nari, *Imperilled Frontiers: India's North-Eastern Borderlands* (New Delhi: Oxford University Press, 1983), pp. 49, 143.

IN SEARCH OF SHANGRI LA

1. Santanayana, George, 'The Philosophy of Travel', *The Virginia Quarterly Review*, vol. 40, no. 1 (Winter 1964).
2. https://economictimes.indiatimes.com/news/politics-and-nation/centre-wants-to-double-tourist-growth-in-northeast-in-3-years/articleshow/61948703.cms?from=mdr
3. Report of Working Group II: Sustainable Tourism in Indian Himalayan Region, NITI Aayog, August 2018, https://niti.gov.in/writereaddata/files/document_publication/Doc2.pdf
4. Sikkim Eco Tourism Policy, 2011.
5. Sikkim Registration of Home Stay Establishment Rules, 2013, notified in the Government Gazette on 5 December 2013.
6. State Tourism Policy, 2018, Government of Sikkim.

7. Presentation made at Dream Change Arunachal Conclave. Interaction with Professor Ramana Athreya in 2017 at Itanagar.
8. Interaction with the author on 6 April 2020.
9. Interaction with the author on 4 April 2020.
10. Interaction with the author on 6 April 2020.
11. Interaction with the author on 31 March 2020.
12. Interaction with the author on 29 March 2020.
13. https://www.thehindubusinessline.com/news/variety/hornbill-festival-239-lakh-people-witness-nagalands-annual-cultural-function/article30247394.ece
14. Baruah, Sanjib, *Durable Disorder: Understanding the Politics of Northeast India* (New Delhi: Oxford University Press, 2005), pp. 129–130.
15. Interaction with the author on 31 March 2020.
16. https://www.telegraphindia.com/culture/travel/tea-planters-punch/cid/1695757
17. https://tourism.assam.gov.in/sites/default/files/swf_utility_folder/departments/tourismdept_webcomindia_org_oid_5/do_u_want_2_know/Tourism%20Policy%20of%20assam%202017.pdf

FRUIT BOWL OF INDIA

1. Northbourne, Lord, *Look to the Land*, cited in 'Lord Northbourne, the man who invented organic farming, a biography', by John Paull, *Journal of Organic Systems*, vol. 9, no. 1 (2014), pp. 37–38.
2. https://www.pmindia.gov.in/en/news_updates/pm-inaugurates-sikkim-organic-festival-2016-addresses-plenary-session-of-national-conference-on-sustainable-agriculture-and-farmers-welfare/
3. Paull, John, 'Four New Strategies to Grow the Organic Agricultural Sector', *AGROFOR International Journal*, vol. 2, no. 3 (2017), p. 65.
4. Rai, Jiwan, *Remember the Name Sikkim: India's First Organic State* (Gurugram: Penguin Random House India, 2019), p. 52.

5. http://scstsenvis.nic.in/WriteReadData/links/Sikkim%20Organic%20Policy%202015-401740061.pdf
6. http://ofai.s3.amazonaws.com/Sikkim_Policy%20vision%20n%20mission.pdf
7. Interaction with the author on 11 April 2020.
8. Interaction with the author on 8 April 2020.
9. https://nrcorchids.nic.in/images/vision-2050.pdf
10. https://www.kew.org/read-and-watch/sikkim-himalayas-orchids
11. Interaction with the author on 22 April 2020.
12. Interation with the author on 11 April 2020.
13. Interaction with the author on 11 April 2020.
14. https://nenow.in/north-east-news/manipur-tripartite-agreement-signed-export-organic-ginger-turmeric.html
15. Interaction with the author on 8 April 2020.
16. Interaction with the author on 12 April 2020.
17. Mani, Gayanendra, et al., 'Kiwi value chain in Arunachal Pradesh: issues and prospects', *Agricultural Economics Research Review*, vol. 31, no. 1 (2018), pp. 123–130.
18. Interaction with the author on 13 April 2020.
19. Interaction with the author on 12 April 2020.
20. Interaction with the author on 12 April 2020.
21. https://economictimes.indiatimes.com/news/economy/agriculture/palm-oil-producers-look-to-expand-acreage-capacities-in-north-east/articleshow/60320139.cms?from=mdr
22. http://www.nfsm.gov.in/ReadyReckoner/Oilseeds/BriefNote_OS2018.pdf
23. Interaction with the author on 14 April 2020.
24. Interaction with the author on 23 April 2020.
25. Interaction with the author on 11 April 2020.

EDUCATION TO ENTERPRISE

1. Interaction with the author on 2 May 2020.
2. McDuie-Ra, Duncan, *Northeast Migrants in Delhi: Race, Refuge and Retail* (Amsterdam: Amsterdam University Press, 2012), monograph number 9, p. 55.
3. Interaction with the author on 10 May 2020.
4. Kikon, Dolly, 'Dreams and Desserts: Indigenous Migration, Services and Mobility in India', *International Journal of Communications*, vol. 12 (2018), pp. 4143–4157.
5. Interaction with the author on 2 May 2020.
6. Interaction with the author on 20 March 2020.
7. Zaidi, S.M.I.A, 'Access to Secondary Education in North-Eastern States', Occassional Paper, National University of Educational Planning and Infrastructure, New Delhi (2013).
8. Interaction with the author on 3 May 2020.
9. Tiwari, Rajiv, 'Engineering Education in North East India: A Survey', Conference: National Symposium on Engineering Education, NSEE-2005, 25–26 February 2005 at the Indian Institute of Science Bangalore.
10. EPWRF desktop compilation from NSSO data.
11. Khuntia, P.A., 'Skill Development of Youth in North East India: Way Forward', NLI Research Studies Series, no. 124 (2017).
12. Interaction with the author on 29 April 2020.
13. Interaction with the author on 28 April 2020.
14. Khuntia, P.A., 'Skill Development of Youth in North East India: Way Forward', NLI Research Studies Series, no. 124 (2017).
15. Interaction with the author on 29 April 2020.
16. Interaction with the author on 17 May 2020.
17. Email response to the author on 20 May 2020.
18. https://nenow.in/north-east-news/assam-fashion-designer-sanjukta-duttas-ensemble-flaunted-at-cannes.html
19. Interaction with the author on 10 May 2020.

20. Interaction with the author on 16 May 2020.
21. Interaction with the author on 16 May 2020.
22. Interaction with the author on 12 May 2020.
23. Interaction with the author on 17 May 2020.
24. 'Education in India', NSS Report no. 575, A-23, Ministry of Statistics and Programme Implementation, Government of India (March 2016).
25. Interaction with the author on 28 April 2020.
26. Interaction with the author on 11 May 2020.
27. Interaction with the author on 12 May 2020.
28. Interaction with the author on 15 and 16 May 2020.
29. Interaction with the author on 9 May 2020.
30. https://www.thehindu.com/features/metroplus/in-conversation-with-the-tetseo-sisters/article8341843.ece
31. Interaction with the author on 21 May 2020.
32. Interaction with the author on 11 May 2020.
33. Interaction with the author on 16 May 2020.
34. Interaction with the author on 20 May 2020.

A SPORTING NATION

1. Mary Kom, M.C., *Unbreakable: An Autobiography* (Noida: HarperCollins Publishers, 2013), p. 43.
2. Ibid., p. 53.
3. Ibid., p. 91.
4. https://www.hindustantimes.com/more-lifestyle/it-takes-a-village-a-look-at-how-manipur-is-getting-it-so-right-with-sports/story-VN0ktbLqCqxwTW6Zg0zVUO.html
5. Bandyopadhyay, Kausik, *Sport, Culture and Nation: Perspectives from Indian football and South Asian Cricket* (New Delhi: Sage Publishing, 2015).
6. Interaction with the author on 26 May 2020.
7. Interaction with author on 26 May 2020.

8. Sinha, Neel, *Goals of Glory: The Amazing Story of Aizawl Football Club and Its Coach* (New Delhi: Pan Macmillan, 2018), pp. 64–79.
9. Interaction with the author on 30 January 2020.
10. Interaction with the author on 31 January 2020.
11. https://www.thequint.com/sports/football/northeast-dominant-force-fifa-u-17-world-cup
12. Interaction with the author on 26 May 2020.
13. https://www.thebetterindia.com/225406/first-indian-women-football-legend-ngangom-bala-devi-rangers-fc-inspiring-nor41/
14. Interaction with the author on 26 May 2020.
15. Interaction with the author on 24 May 2020.
16. https://scroll.in/field/952780/hockey-indias-lalremsiami-bags-fih-womens-rising-star-of-the-year-award
17. Interaction with the author on 24 May 2020.
18. https://www.thehindu.com/sport/other-sports/i-am-fulfilling-my-fathers-dream-says-youth-olympic-games-champion-jeremy-lalrinnunga/article30425134.ece
19. https://www.thehindu.com/sport/other-sports/i-am-fulfilling-my-fathers-dream-says-youth-olympic-games-champion-jeremy-lalrinnunga/article30425134.ece
20. Interaction with the author on 26 May 2020.
21. https://www.newindianexpress.com/sport/other/2020/jul/02/mental-balm-for-top-weightlifters-2164235.html
22. https://www.thehindu.com/society/the-iron-women-of-manipur-who-live-and-breathe-olympian-dreams/article30711797.ece
23. Interaction with the author on 26 May 2020.
24. https://indianexpress.com/article/sports/sport-others/uci-union-cycliste-internationale-cycling-breaking-the-cycle-5934350/
25. https://www.youtube.com/watch?v=Vi_il_XjT8c
26. Interaction with the author on 11 July 2020.
27. Interaction with the author on 12 July 2020.
28. https://pib.gov.in/PressReleasePage.aspx?PRID=1632031

29. https://www.indiatoday.in/education-today/news/story/reliance-foundation-s-nita-ambani-wants-inclusive-growth-of-sports-in-education-1354510-2018-10-03

'AKHA': HOPE FOR GOOD HEALTH

1. https://www.livemint.com/mint-lounge/features/ferrying-hope-on-the-brahmaputra-1564137596324.html
2. 'North Eastern Region Vision 2020', Ministry of Development of North Eastern Region and North Eastern Council, May 2008, p. 208.
3. National Family Health Survey 4, 2015–16.
4. https://censusindia.gov.in/vital_statistics/SRS_Bulletins/MMR%20Bulletin%202016-18.pdf
5. National Family Health Survey 4, 2015–16.
6. https://censusindia.gov.in/vital_statistics/SRS_Bulletins/SRS%20Bulletin_2018.pdf
7. National Family Health Survey 4, 2015–16.
8. 'India: Health of the Nation's States', ICMR, Department of Health Research, Ministry of Health and Family Welfare, Government of India, November 2017.
9. 'Healthy States, Progressive India: Health Index', NITI Aayog, The World Bank, Ministry of Health and Family Welfare, June 2019.
10. https://www.orfonline.org/expert-speak/covid19-the-state-of-health-care-facilities-in-indias-north-east-63889/
11. 'Rural Health Statistics 2018-19', Ministry of Health and Family Welfare, Government of India, 2019.
12. https://nhm.assam.gov.in/schemes/ppp-with-tea-garden-hospitals
13. http://www.rrcnes.gov.in/study_report/PPP%20Evaluation%20Report%20Meghalaya_2018.pdf
14. https://health.economictimes.indiatimes.com/news/industry/ppp-has-the-potential-to-resolve-the-prevailing-disparity-in-healthcare-in-the-ne-dr-n-c-borah/46905080
15. Interaction with the author on 4 August 2020.

16. http://www.cmmanipur.gov.in/shija-hospital-to-set-up-first-ever-healthcity-in-manipur/
17. 'The Health City', in *Borderland City in New India: Frontier to Gateway* by Duncan McDui-Ra (Amsterdam: Amsterdam University Press, 2016), p. 146.
18. https://www.business-standard.com/article/news-ians/japan-seeks-15-000-nurses-from-manipur-116052600612_1.html
19. Title of a book on cancer by oncologist Siddhartha Mukherjee.
20. http://cancerindia.org.in/mizoram-indias-cancer-capital/
21. 'A Report on Cancer Burden in North Eastern States of India', National Centre for Disease Informatics and Research, Indian Council for Medical Research, Bengaluru, 2017.
22. Sharma, Jagannath Dev, et al., 'Cancer: Scenario and Relationship of different geographical areas of the globe with special reference to North East-India', *Asian Pacific Journal of Cancer Prevention*, vol. 15 (2014), pp. 3721–3729.
23. Interaction with the author on 16 August 2020.
24. Interaction with the author on 22 August 2020.
25. https://www.newindianexpress.com/nation/2019/oct/12/mizoram-records-nine-hiv-positive-cases-every-day-2046580.html
26. 'India HIV Estimation 2017', Technical Report, National Aids Control Organization, ICMR, Ministry of Health and Family Welfare, Government of India.
27. Singh, Ningthoujam Koiremba and William Nunes, 'Drug Trafficking and Narco-terrorism as Security Threats: A Study of India's North-east', *India Quarterly*, vol. 69, no. 1 (2013), pp. 65–82, Indian Council of World Affairs, Sage Publications.
28. Interaction with the author on 21 August 2020.
29. Interaction with the author on 12 January 2021.

THE BETTER HALF OF THE NORTHEAST

1. Brara, Vijaylakshmi, 'Culture and Indigeneity: Women in Northeast India', *Explorations*, ISS e-journal, vol. 1, no. 1 (April 2017), pp. 72–90.
2. Mukhim, Patricia, *Waiting for an Equal World: Gender in India's Northeast* (Shillong: Matrin Luther Christian University Press, 2019), pp. 6–30.
3. Email response to the author, dated 10 September 2020.
4. Das, Ira, 'Status of Women: North Eastern Region of India versus India', *International Journal of Scientific and Research Publications*, vol. 3, no. 1 (January 2013).
5. Nath, Debarashi Prasad, 'Assam's Tale of Witch-hunting and Indigeneity,' *Economic & Political Weekly*, vol. xllx, no. 37 (13 September 2014).
6. Interaction with the author on 5 September 2020.
7. Raimedhi, Indrani, *My Half of the Sky: 12 Life Stories of Courage* (New Delhi: Sage Publishers, 2015), pp. 44–56.
8. Conversation with the author on 2 October 2020.
9. Interaction with the author on 4 October 2020.
10. Interaction with the author on 17 October 2020.
11. Quoted in 'Breaking Gender Barriers', by Patricia Mukhim, *The Telegraph,* North East, 6 April 2004, p. 6.
12. Email response to a questionnaire sent by the author on 10 September 2020.
13. https://www.thehindu.com/opinion/op-ed/Pride-as-well-as-prejudice/article17242990.ece
14. https://indianexpress.com/article/opinion/columns/nagaland-violence-kohima-protest-against-women-reservation-4511227/
15. 'Economic Connotations', *Nagaland Page*, 13 January 2017.
16. https://indianexpress.com/article/gender/the-myth-of-the-empowered-naga-woman-why-naga-women-are-demanding-a-chair-at-the-tribal-assembly-4994021/

17. Interaction with the author on 29 August 2020.
18. https://www.telegraphindia.com/north-east/number-battle-won-but-not-the-gender-war-women-underrepresented-in-candidate-list-despite-outnumbering-male-voters/cid/1543467
19. https://scroll.in/article/871738/north-east-politics-the-three-assembly-elections-underline-the-marginalisation-of-women
20. https://www.sentinelassam.com/north-east-india-news/arunachal-news/three-women-legislators-elected-for-arunachal-assembly/
21. https://www.bbc.com/news/world-asia-india-39179515
22. Imphal Free Press, 22 August 2015.
23. Ao, Temsula, *These Hills Called Home: Stories from a War Zone* (New Delhi: Zubaan and Penguin Books, 2006), pp. 23–33.
24. https://timesofindia.indiatimes.com/city/kohima/meet-the-naga-women-warriors-for-life/articleshow/71464234.cms
25. https://www.telegraphindia.com/north-east/nagaland-the-unheard-voice/cid/1547110
26. Interaction with the author on 2 October 2020.
27. Handloom Census 2019-20, Ministry of Textiles, Government of India, pp. 72–76.
28. Interaction with the author on 2 October 2020.
29. https://www.newindianexpress.com/good-news/2020/aug/29/du-student-now-arunachal-pradeshs-michelin-star-2189661.html
30. https://wow.outlookbusiness.com/lakhimi-baruah/

THE GOVERNANCE CHALLENGE

1. Stuligross, David, 'Autonomous Councils in Northeast India: Theory and Practice', *Alternatives: Global, Local and Political*, vol. 24, no. 4, Oct–Dec 1999, pp. 497–525.
2. https://www.outlookindia.com/newsscroll/arunachal-assembly-resolution-for-inclusion-of-state-in-sixth-schedule/1924266

3. https://www.firstpost.com/india/union-cabinet-approves-amendment-in-sixth-schedule-to-strengthen-10-north-east-autonomous-councils-5951561.html
4. Upadhyay, Archana, 'Governance and Human Security Issues in Northeast India', in *Rethinking Economic Development in Northeast India*, ed. Deepak K. Mishra and Archana Upadhyay (New York: Routledge, 2019), pp. 379–402.
5. Pandey, R.S., *Communitisation: The Third Way of Governance* (New Delhi: Concept Publishing Company, 2010).
6. Upadhyay, Archana, 'Governance and Human Security Issues in Northeast India', in *Rethinking Economic Development in Northeast India*, ed. Deepak K. Mishra and Archana Upadhyay (New York: Routledge, 2019), p. 391.
7. Nongkynrih, A.K., 'Privatisation of Communal Land of the Tribes of North East India: A Sociological Viewpoint', in *Land, People and Politics: Contest over Tribal Land in Northeast India*, ed. Walter Fernandes and Sanjay Barbora (Guwahati: Northeast Social Research Centre, 2009).
8. State Finances: A Study of Budgets 2019–20, RBI, pp. 28–30.
9. https://www.telegraphindia.com/india/rs-242-crore-peace-bonus-for-mizoram/cid/910539
10. https://www.himalmag.com/peace-dividend-in-mizoram/
11. https://indianexpress.com/article/india/r-n-ravi-letter-law-and-order-nscim-indo-naga-talks-6482062/
12. Yumnam, Amar, 'Critiquing the development intervention', in *Northeast India: A Reader*, ed. Bhagat Oinam and Dhiren A. Sadokpam (New York: Routledge, 2018).
13. Thakur, Shalakha and Rajesh Venugopal, 'Parallel governance and political order in contested territory: Evidence from the Indo-Naga ceasefire', *Asian Security*, vol. 15, no. 3 (2018), p. 7.
14. Baruah, Sanjib, *In the Name of the Nation: India and Its Northeast* (California: Stanford University Press, 2020), pp. 106–111.

15. https://www.ndtv.com/india-news/in-nagaland-everyone-pays-taxes-to-the-rebels-1205353
16. Thakur, Shalakha and Rajesh Venugopal, 'Parallel governance and political order in contested territory: Evidence from the Indo-Naga ceasefire', *Asian Security*, ISSN 1479-9855 (In Press).
17. https://economictimes.indiatimes.com/news/politics-and-nation/tamil-nadu-tops-good-governance-index-among-big-states-maharashtra-and-karnataka-get-second-third-slot/articleshow/72978601.cms?from=mdr
18. https://timesofindia.indiatimes.com/india/reduce-poll-expenses-cap-mizo-netas-to-ec/articleshow/66945908.cms
19. https://thewire.in/politics/a-church-backed-initiative-sets-an-example-in-mizoram-elections
20. https://www.hindustantimes.com/india-news/need-a-separate-cadre-time-zone-for-arunachal-cm-pema-khandu/story-WqPKglNXEq0V4zgHbBhs1K.html
21. https://www.narendramodi.in/pm-modi-at-inauguration-of-65th-plenary-session-of-north-east-council-483603
22. Singh, Thingnam Kishan, 'Understanding Underdevelopment', in *Northeast India: A Reader*, ed. Bhagat Oinam and Dhiren A. Sadokpam (New York: Routledge, 2018), p. 431.
23. Ahmad, Raiful and Prasenjit Biswas, *Political Economy of Underdevelopment of North-East India* (New Delhi: Akanksha Publishing House, 2004), p. 56.
24. Sharma, Sushil Kumar, 'Dynamics of Bandhs and Blockades in Northeast India: A Study of Manipur and the Way Ahead', Manekshaw Paper, no. 48 (New Delhi: Centre for Land Warfare Studies, 2014).
25. Gupta, Susmita Sen, 'Ethnicity and Development: A Civil Society Perspective from North-East India', *Journal of Social and Political Sciences*, vol. 1, no. 2 (2018), pp. 297–305.
26. https://indianexpress.com/article/north-east-india/meghalaya/meghalaya-khasi-student-outfit-puts-up-posters-targeting-bengalis-6825776/

CHANGE WITH CONTINUITY

1. Appiah, Kwame Anthony, *The Lies that Bind: Rethinking Identity* (London: Profile Books, 2019), p. 133.
2. https://indianexpress.com/article/india/himanta-biswa-sarma-nrc-caa-no-longer-the-discourse-issue-now-is-conflict-of-cultures-this-claim-of-miya-identity-7061653/
3. Baruah, Sanjib, *In the Name of the Nation: India and Its Northeast* (California: Stanford University Press, 2020), p. 53.
4. https://www.newindianexpress.com/nation/2019/dec/15/how-much-burden-can-we-take-asks-tripura-royal-scion-pradyot-deb-barman-after-challenging-citizenshi-2076545.html
5. https://thediplomat.com/2021/02/ripple-effects-of-myanmar-coup-felt-in-indias-northeast/
6. Hazarika, Sanjoy, *Strangers No More: New Narratives from India's Northeast* (New Delhi: Aleph Book Company, 2018), p. 163.
7. https://frontline.thehindu.com/the-nation/article30800941.ece
8. Interaction with the author on 19 January 2021.
9. Interaction with the author on 19 January 2021.
10. https://www.republicworld.com/india-news/general-news/nscn-k-chief-niki-sumi-joins-naga-peace-talks-state-govt-calls-for-finality-in-2021.html
11. Interaction with the author on 19 January 2021.
12. Interaction with the author on 20 January 2021.
13. Interaction with the author on 20 January 2021.
14. Chadha Vivek, ed., *Armed Forces Special Powers Act: The Debate* (New Delhi: Institute for Defence Study and Analyses, 2013), p. 12.
15. Hazarika, Sanjoy, *Strangers No More: New Narratives from India's Northeast* (New Delhi: Aleph Book Company, 2018), p. 5.
16. Ibid., pp. 1–34.
17. Interaction with the author on 13 January 2021.
18. Interaction with the author on 19 January 2021.

19. Interaction with the author on 13 January 2021.
20. India State of Forest Report, 2019.
21. https://www.thehindu.com/news/national/other-states/meghalayas-rat-hole-traps/article25973337.ece
22. Karlsson, B.G., *Unruly Hills: A Political Ecology of India's Northeast* (New Delhi: Orient BlackSwan, 2011), pp. 1–14.

Index

abductions, 19
Abe, Shinzo, 43
Abraham, John, 73
Accredited Social Health Activist (ASHA), 111, 118
Act East policy, xvi, xx–xxi, 29, 35, 37–38, 43–45, 71, 155
activists, 19, 51, 53, 137, 158
Ada (Ardour), Nabokov, 78
Advantage Assam Summit, 38
Affected Citizens of Teesta (ACT), 56
agri-preneurs, 97, *see also* entrepreneurship
Ahuja, Shyam, 95
airports, 25, 61, 149; in Dibrugarh, 25; Donyi-Polo, 27; in Itanagar, 29; Nyingchi Mainling, 25; Pakyong, 29
Aizawl, xiv–xv, 23, 33–34, 36, 64, 95–96, 106, 108, 110, 125, 129; IAF bombing of, 15
Aizawl Football Club, 106
Akbar Hydari Agreement, 157
All Assam Students Union (AASU), 17, 53
Ambani, Nita, 113
Ambedkar, Bhimrao, 3
American Baptists, in Assam valley, xvii
Anglo–Burmese hostilities, xviii
anti-dam movement, 53, *see also* large dam projects
Ao, Temsula, 137
Armed Forces Special Powers Act (AFSPA 1958), xx, 20, 136, 158–159
Arunachal Pradesh, xv–xvi, 24–25, 27, 35, 41, 50–52, 61–62, 66, 70–71, 73, 80–81, 84–87, 112–113, 116–120, 122–123, 132–133, 142–143, 147–148; Dambuk, 80–82; Eaglenest sanctuary in, 66; as

'Hidden Land,' xv; Itanagar, xxii, 24–25, 29–30, 52, 61, 80, 99, 120, 138; Kamlang Wildlife Sanctuary, 54; Khamtis of, xvi; Khandu on, 50; Lower Dibang Valley, 84; Mechuka in, 25; Modi on, 52; Namsai's Sangken festival, 71; panchayati raj institutions, 143; Pangsau Pass, 41; Pasighat, 27, 48; recruitment 'scam', 152; Sela Pass, 30, 63; Tawang, xvi, 5, 30, 55, 59, 61–63, 112; Ziro Valley, 27, 70, 81–82, 97
Arunachal Pradesh Agriculture Marketing Board, 81
Arunachal Pradesh Land Settlement and Records Amendment Act, 2018, 144
Ashley, Laura, 95
Asian Cycling Championship in 2022, 111
Asian Development Bank's (ADB), 37
Asom Gana Parishad (AGP), 18–19
Assam, xvi–xviii, xx–xxi, 5, 7, 12–17, 19–20, 27–30, 48, 61–62, 73, 96–97, 100–101, 115–119, 123–125, 131, 154–155; agitation in, 18; Guwahati, 25, 29–31, 37, 39, 58, 61, 80, 85–86, 96, 100, 124; Kaziranga, 64, 67–68; Nellie massacre, 18; Tinsukia in, 41
Assam Accord, 18–19
Assam Cancer Care Foundation, 124
Assamese, 14–15, 19, 84, 96
Assam Rifles, 5, 28, 35, 136
Assam Witch Hunting (Prohibition, Prevention and Protection) Act, 2015, 131
Association of Southeast Asian Nations (ASEAN), 33, 38–39, 45
Atal Amrit Abhiyan, 124
Athena Projects Private Limited, 57
Athreya, Ramana, 66–67
Automovill, 102
autonomous district councils, 3, 14, 141
autonomy, 16, 141–142, 154
Avasthe, Ravikant, 77
Axomiya, 154
Axone, 90
Ayushman Bharat Yojana, 124
Azu, Taw, 133

bamboo, 34, 64, 67, 70–72, 80, 85, 90, 93, 120; flowering—'Mautam', 14; shoots, 90, 98–99
Bangkok, 29, 121
Bangladesh, xix, 12, 15, 18, 29–31, 37, 39, 42–44, 56, 80,

101, 145, 154–156; migrants, 154
Bangladesh-China-India-Myanmar (BCIM), 41
Baptist Christianity, 20
Bardoloi, meeting Peggy, 85
Barman, Pradyot Deb, 155
Baruah, Lakhimi, 138
Baruah, Sanjib, 16, 20–21, 48
Basamlu, Krisiko, 82
Basar, Liter, 138
Battle of Kohima, xviii
Belho, Richard, 93
Bengali Hindus, 15
Bengali-origin Muslim, 154
Bhartiya Kisan Sangh, 86
Bhupen Hazarika Setu, 27
Bhutan, xvi, 29, 63, 66, 73, 75, 101, 156
Bhutia, Bhaichung, 108
Bhutia, Karma, 83
biodiversity, 65, 162
Bista, Laxmi Prasad, 77
Bodoland Accord, 156, *see also* tribes
Bogibeel bridge, 27
Bohag Bihu celebration, 70
Border Guards Bangladesh, 34
borderlands, xv, 27, 127, 155
Border Roads Organization, 29
Border Security Force (BSF), 34
Bordoloi, Gopinath, 2, 7
Bordoloi, Samir, 84–85
Bordoloi's organization, Society for Promotion of Rural Economy & Agricultural Development, North East (SPREAD-NE), 86
Bose, Subhas Chandra, xviii
Brahmaputra Board Act, 50
Brahmaputra Valley Film Festival, 100
British administration, xvi, xx, 1–3, 31, 34, 78, 105, 140
Broken Landscape, Miller, 162
Bui, Nixon, 97
Bujarbaruah, 87
Bum La, 63
Byrsat, Vijay, 97–98

Cachar Cancer Hospital and Research Centre, 123
Cambodia, 43, 71
Cane Concept, 95
Central Agricultural University, Imphal, 86
Central Water and Power Commission, 56
Chakmas, as foreigners, 14
Chamling, Pawan Kumar, 75–76, 78
Changkija, Monalisa, 49, 135, 158
Chanu, Mirabai, 110
Chapchar Kut celebration, 70–71
Chaudhari, Rohini Kumar, 3
Chengdu, 25
Chennaiyin Football Club, 107
Chhetri, Arjun, 78–79

Chhetri, Rewaj, 99
Chhetri, Sunil, 108
chicken's neck, xix, 30, 39;
  corridor, 42
Chief Minister's Free Diagnostic
  Services Programme, Assam,
  119
China, xvi, xix, 5, 25, 33,
  37–38, 41, 43, 46–48, 58,
  97; commissioning Zangmu,
  58; Guangzhou, 25, 138;
  incursion, 9, 28, 145;
  Kunming, 40–42; skirmishes
  with, 42; Tsona Dzong, xvi;
  Yunnan in, 41; Zangnan, 5
Chingmak, Reverend, 126
'chinki' racial slur, xx, 90
Chin National Army, 155
Chin refugees, 155
Chintan, 52
Chittagong Hills, 16
Chongqing, 25, 41
Chopra, Ajay, 80
Chopra, Priyanka, 96, 103
Christian missionaries, xvii, 11
Cinderella province, 5
Citizenship Ammendment Law,
  155
civil society, 151, 158–159;
  organizations, 134, 150
Communal fires, 2
community forests, 142
connectivity, 9, 12, 22–23, 26–28,
  31–32, 37, 39, 44–45, 65; air,
  29; national highway network,
  29; rural, 28
conservation, 54, 65, 69
Constitution of India, 8, 14,
  141–142, 157; Article 371
  special provisions under, 141;
  73rd Amendment, 142–143;
  sixth schedule of, 3, 141–142
'Coolies' from the Chhotanagpur-
  Santhal territory, xvii
cooperative federalism, 43
corruption, xx–xxi, 20, 22, 51, 81,
  142, 147–148, 152
Coutinho, Desmond, 136
Covid-19 pandemic, 46, 65, 71,
  74, 87, 89, 93, 99–100, 110,
  118, 131
cultivation: jhum, 132; kiwi 97;
  palm oil, 84
culture, xvi, 3, 7, 32, 34, 45,
  69, 71, 135, 153, 155, 157,
  160–161
customary law, 3, 131–134,
  139–141, 143

Daly, Brian, 163
Das, Hima 'Dhing Express', 111
Das, Mridu, 102
Dature, Miuli, 84
Demwe hydroelectric project, 54
dependency syndrome, 144
Devi, Kunjarani, 110
Dhawan, Prince, 83
Dibang Valley, 53

Dibrugarh, 5, 24–25, 80, 85, 119, 124
Dibru-Saikhowa National Park, 54
Dimapur, 26, 93, 95, 160
disturbed area, 20, 136, 158
Donyi-Polo airport, 27
Doulo, Neichute, 157
Doyang Hydro Electric Project, 68
Dutta, Aparajita, 68
Dutta, Sanjukta, 96

earthquake/tremors, 5, 24, 49, 52, 155
Easternization, xxii
EastMojo, 100
East Pakistan. *See* Bangladesh
economic: blockades, 151; infrastructure, 43; liberalization, 50
ecotourism initiatives, 69, *see also* tourism
E-governance, 147–148
Electronic-National Agricultural Market (E-NAM), 87
Elwin, Verrier, 6, 8–9, 11–13, 159, 163
entrepreneurship, 97, 99, 102, 145–146, 149
Etalin hydropower project, 54, *see also* hydropower projects
Ethnic chic, 95
ethnicity, 16, 28, 34, 45, 151, 153, 155; and conflicts, 140, 145
exports, 37, 43–45, 95
extortion, xx, 19, 37, 146, 157

Fabindia, 95
factions, 20, 146, 156–158
famine, 14, 156
Farmer Producer Company (FPC), 81–83, 87
farmers, xxi, 40, 48, 76–78, 80–87, 98, 150
festival, 69–70, 80
fish, 22, 99, 149, 163
fisheries, 150
flash floods, 26, 49
A Fly on the Wheel, Lewin, 34
folklore, 36, 48, 56, 70
foreigners, xxii, 14, 69, 152
Forest Advisory Committee, 53–54
forest-based industry, 22
forest land, 53–54, 144, 162; destruction of, 12
Free Movement Regime, 35
Free Trade Agreement, 39, *see also* trade

Ganden Namgyal Lhatse monastery, 62
Gandhi, Indira, 17–18
Gandhi, Rajiv, 18
Gandhi Sewak Sangh, 8
Gaon burhas (village headman), 142
Garos of Meghalaya, xvi
Garo Students' Union, 151

Geographical Information System (GIS), 148
Gere, Richard, 63
Ghurye, G.S., 13
Glamorizing farming, 86
Godrej Agrovet, 84
Gogoi, Akhil, 53
governments, elected 162
Government of the People's Republic of Nagaland (GPRN), 20, 146
Gowda, Deve, 24
Gradualism, 12
Greater Mekong Sub-Regional Economic Cooperation Program of China, 43
green revolution, 75, 85
Guwahati Neurological Research Centre (GNRC), 120
Gyatso, Lama Lobsang (Anna Lama), 55

Handloom and handicraft, 69, 94, 96, 101, 138
Haralu, Bano, 68
Hauzel, Hoihnu, 132, 137–138
Hazarika, Anurita, 131
Hazarika, Bhupen, 48
Hazarika, Sanjoy, xxi, 32, 115, 128, 159
Hazarika, Tanushree, 100
healthcare, xvii, 26, 115–116, 118–120, 128, 143; cancer care facilities, 124–125; HIV/AIDS, 117, 125–127, *see also* Covid-19 pandemic
Heirloom Naga, 95
Hekani, 92
herbs, 85
heroin (number 4), 126, *see also* opium
Hmar, Lalnghinglova (Tetea), 105
Hmarzote, Lalremsiami, 108–110
Hornbill Nest Adoption Program (HNAP), 68
human rights activists, 158
Hydari, Akbar, 4, 7
hydropower project, xxi, 50–51, 53, 55, 57–58, 149, 162; on Kameng river, 55

I Am Property , Padu, 132
Idu Mishmi tribe, 53
Ima Keithel, all-women market, Imphal, 129
immigrants, 15–16, 145
Immigrants (Expulsion from Assam) Act, 1950, 2
Imperilled Frontiers, Rustomji, 59
Impulse NGO Network in Meghalaya, 94
India–Japan cooperation on development of India's North Eastern Region, 43
India-Myanmar-Thailand trilateral highway, 40
Indian Air Force, 15
Indian Army, xiv, 15, 19, 64, 136

Indian border trade with Myanmar and Bangladesh, 40
Indian Council of Agricultural Research (ICAR), 77, 80
Indian Frontier Administrative Service (IFAS), 8
Indian National Army, xviii
Indian Railways, 30
India's Got Talent, 101
Indo-Bangladesh Protocol on Inland Water Transit and Trade, 31
Indo-Myanmar land border, 37
Indo-Pakistan war, 1965, 16
industrial development programme, 51
influx, 17, 33, 55; of outsiders, fear over, 30
Inner Line, xviii
Insolvency and Bankruptcy Code, 57
insurgency, 22, 26, 65, 104, 114, 125–127, 146, 156
insurgent groups, xiv, xix, 4, 15, 20, 33, 42, 45, 156
Integrated Check Posts, 37, 42, 45
International Fund for Agricultural Development (IFAD), 98
Irrawaddy basin, xix
isolationism, xviii–xix, 3, 8–9, 27, 31, 74, 153
Issac Muivah (IM), 20
I-Tute, 99
Iyer, Pico, 74
Jaintia Students' Union, 151
Jakhalu, Hekani, 91
Jamir, Alemtemshi, 69
Jamir, S.C., 69, 157, 160
Jamir, Toshimenla, 137
Jamsenpa, Anshu, 112
Japan International Cooperation Agency, 43
Japan's Free and Open Indo Pacific Strategy, 43
Jenkins, H.L., xvi
Jio, 160
Justice Jeevan Reddy Committee, 159

Kaladan Multi-Modal Transit Transport Project (KMTTP), 39–40
Kamakhya or Solomon temple in Aizawl, 64
Kangla Fort, 137; women protest at, 136
Kannan, Ravi, 123–124
Kapoor, Karishma, 96
Karmakar, Dipa, 112
Karuna Trust, 120
Kaul, T.N., 7–8
Khan, Salman, 73
Khandu, Dorjee, 50, 52
Khandu, Pema, 30, 59, 73, 147–148
Kharbhih, Hasina, 94
Khasi Students' Union, 151–152
Khathing, Bob, Maj., 5

Khelo India, 110, 113
Khongsai, Kiran, 105
Khundongbam, Palin, 120–121
kidnappings, 19, 157
Kikon, Dolly, 91, 135
Kilo Kilonser, 146
King, George, 78
Kingdom Ward, F., 49
kiwi wine—Naara-Aaba, 97
Kolkata, 30, 39, 42, 79, 82, 122
Kom, Mary, 103–104
Konoklata Mahila Cooperative Bank, 138
Konwar, Pranjal, 101
Konyaks, 70, 154
K-pop, xxii
Krishak Mukti Sangram Samiti (KMSS), 53
Kuki-Chin refugees, xix
Kunming and Yangon expressway, 40

L., Charlee, 96
Laldenga, 15
Lalpekhlua, Jeje, 107, 159
Lalrinnunga, Jeremy, 110
Lalthlennawia, Charlee, 95
Lalzirliani, 135
Lama, Dalai, 55, 63
Lama, Bon, 64
Lanco Teesta Hydro Power Limited, 57
land: alienation, 15; allotment, 141, 143; monetization of, 162; ownership, 3, 11, 143–145
Land Border Crossing Agreement, 121
Land Customs Stations, 36, 42
Land Port Authority of India, 42
landslide, 26, 49, 56
Lao PDR, 43
large dam projects, 59; Kaptai, 16; Klingensmith on, 59
the Last Song, Ao, 137
Lepcha, Gyatso, 56
Lepchas, 56, 66
Lewin, Thangliena Tom, 34
Lhasa, 5, 25, 63; Chinese 'Liberation' Army capturing, 5
Lilienthal, David E., 47
Loder, Gyati, 81
Longchari, Akum, 158
Longfellow, Henry Wadsworth, 88
Look East policy, 38
Lovelace, Richard, 1
Lushai Hill District (village council) Act, 1953, 142

MacNeil, 19
MADessentials, 98
Madhav, Ram, 38
Majaw, Dasumarlin, 98
Mandela, Nelson, xxii
Manekshaw, Sam, Gen., 15
Manipur, xix, 20, 28, 36, 58, 85–86, 101–105, 107–108, 110–111, 118–119, 121–122,

125, 128, 145–146, 158–159; Imphal, 33, 37, 40, 92, 100, 110, 113, 120–121, 129, 132, 136; Moreh, 37, 42, 44–45, 126, 155; Pung Cholom, 71; Ukhrul, 146
Manipur State Hill People's Regulation Act 1947, 142
Manipur Village Authorities (in Hill Areas) Act, 1956, 142
Manorama, Thangjam, rape and killing of, 136, 159
Maoism, 20
Márquez, Gabriel García, xiii, xvii
Mary Kom, 103
Mayudia Pass, 27
McCully, Patrick, 59
Mc Duie-Ra, Duncan, 91
McMahon Line, 64
Medilan Ambulance Service, 100
Meetei, Dayananda Pibarel, 100
Meghalaya, xvii, xix, 16–17, 22, 65, 91, 94, 97–98, 101, 118, 120, 130–131, 142–143; Khasi-Jaintia Hills, xvii; rat hole mining in, 162; Student unions of, 30; Umroi in, 29
Meira Paibis, women vigilante group, 136
Mercy of Tetseo Sisters, 134
migration, 45, 89, 94, 155; illegal Muslim, 2
militants, 24, 137
Mills, James, xviii
Mios, 'Ka ma che' or 'I divorce you' and, 133
Miya culture, 154
Mizo: cable television, 106, 159; consciousness, 156; footballers, 107; insurgency, 156; principle of 'tlawmngaihna', 161; rebellion, 14
Mizo Accord, 15, 19, 156
Mizo Hmeichhe Insuihkhawm Pawl (MHIP), 133, 135
Mizo Marriage, Divorce and Inheritance of Property Act, 2014, 133
Mizo National Front (MNF), 156; Operation Jericho of, 15
Mizoram, xiv–xv, xix–xx, 16, 30, 36, 57, 65–66, 91–92, 105–109, 118–119, 121–123, 125–126, 135, 147–148, 150–151, 154–155; Bara Bazaar of Aizawl, xiv, 14, 129; Siaha, 23; statehood of, 15; Zokhawthar, 35
Mizoram Football Association, 105
Mizoram People's Forum (MPF), 147
Mizoram Premier League (MPL), 106
Mizos, xiv, xvi, 15–16, 30, 36, 92–93, 133, 150, 156, 160–161
Mizo Zirlai Pawl (MZP), 151
Modi, Narendra, 27, 29, 37, 58, 125, 149; on Arunachal

Pradesh, 52; Framework Agreement by, 4
Modi, Zilpha, 90
Mon-Yul corridor, xvi
Moreh to Mae Sot in Thailand, trilateral highway, 39
The Morung Express, 158
Muivah, Thuingaleng, (Ato Kilonser), 146
Mukherjee, Pranab, 38
Mukhim, Patricia, 130–131
Mukhopadyay, Gautam, 44
Munshi, K.M., 3
Muslim infiltrators, 18
Myanmar (earlier Burma), xvi, xviii–xix, 23–24, 27, 30, 33, 35–37, 39–41, 43–46, 121, 125–128, 155; coup in 2021, xix; Mandalay, 33, 36–37, 40, 121; Muse trade zone, 40, 42; Namphalong market in, 37
Myint, U Win, 40

Nabokov, Vladimir, 78
Naga: identity, 70; imbroglio, 158; Independence Day, 146; movement, 3–4; nationalism, 20; politics, 157; reconciliation, 158; woman, 135
Naga Hills-Tuensang Area, 4
Nagaland, xix–xx, 28–30, 35, 65, 68–70, 79, 81, 85–86, 116–119, 125–127, 136–137, 141–142, 145–147, 156, 158–159; Kohima, xviii, 4, 26, 33, 69, 93, 130, 156, 160; Longwa in, 35; Tuensang in, 29, 126
Nagaland Village and Area Council Act, 1978, 142
Nagalim, 20
Naga Mothers' Association (NMA), 134
Naga Mothers' Association, motto of, 137, *see also* Meira Paibis, women vigilante group
Naga National Council, nine-point agreement with, 4
Nagas, xviii, 3–4, 19, 69, 108, 134–135, 146, 157–158, 160; Changkija on, 158; of Khonoma village, 4
'Nagas are not Indians', 4
Narasimha Rao, P.V., 38
National Board for Wildlife (NBWL), 54
National Democratic Front of Boroland (NDFB), 155
National Environmental Policy, 51
National Green Tribunal (NGT), 53–54, 163
National Green Tribunal (NGT) Act, 2010, 51
National Highway and Infrastructure Development Corporation, 29
National Hydro Electric Power Corporation (NHPC), 53–55, 57; MoA with Assam, 53

National Institute of Advanced Mountaineering and Allied Sports in Arunachal Pradesh, 71
National Institute of Mountaineering and Allied Sports in Dirang, 112
National Socialist Council of Nagaland (NSCN), 4, 20, 145–146, 156
National Socialist Council of Nagaland Isak-Muivah (NSCN(IM)), 137, 145–146, 156–157
National Socialist Council of Nagaland-K (NSCN(K)), 157
NE Holiday, 99
Nehru, Jawaharlal, xx, 1, 4–6, 8, 12–13; Panchsheel, 9–10
Nehru–Elwin approach, 10
Nehru–Liaquat Pact, 31
Nepal, 75, 77
nepotism, 22, 81, 152
Neroca Football club, 105
NE Taxi, 99
'New Deal for Tribal India' report, Elwin, 11
NITI Aayog, 58, 117, 149
Nixonbui Vodka, 97
non-indigenous population, xvii
Non-Lapsable Central Pool of Resources, 21
Northbourne, Lord, 75
'The Northeast', xvi, 97
Northeast, 'special category states' of, 21, 144
North East Areas (Reorganization) Act, 1971, 16
North Eastern Council (NEC), 16–17, 148–150
North Eastern Development Finance Institution (NEDFI), 102
North Eastern Electric Power Corporation Limited (NEEPCO), 55, 58
North Eastern Railways, 30
North Eastern Region (NER), 43
North-East Frontier Agency (NEFA), 5–6, 8–9, 16; earthquake at, 5
Northeast India, xv–xvi, xix–xxii, 20–22, 29–32, 38–39, 41–46, 49–50, 57–59, 64–65, 72–74, 77–79, 84–87, 91–93, 96–100, 107–119, 122–123, 128–131, 137–140, 143–156, 158–164
North East Water Management Authority (NEWMA), 58
Nuranang, battle of, 63
Nyishis, 67, 133; Nyokum of, 70

Obama, Barack, 101
Operation Bajrang, 19, 85
Operation Rhino, 19
opium, xvi, 35
oranges, 82, 163; mandarin, 80; Nagpur, 81

organic revolution, 75–76, 83, 87, *see also* Sikkim Organic Mission

Pachuau, Lalhlimpuii, 156
Padmasambhava, Guru, 64
Padu, Karry, 132
Paite, Khemtang, 105
Pakke hornbill conservation initiative, 67
Pakke Tiger Reserve, 67
Paljor, Karma, 100
Palling, Okit, 81
Pame, Armstrong, 28, 79
Panchsheel, 7
Pangsau Pass, 41
Pangti, Nagaland, 68–69
The Pangti Story, 69
Pantling, Robert, 78
Partition, xix, 12, 15–16, 24, 34, 37
Patkar, Medha, 51
peace bonus, 22, 145
People's Liberation Army (PLA), 20, 63–64, 136
People's Resurgence and Justice Alliance (PRAJA), 136
People's Revolutionary Party of Kangleipak (PREPAK), 20
Petrapole Integrated Check Post (WB), 39
Phizo, Angami Zapu, 3–4, 156; for 'Naga central government', 4
Pindi–Peking axis, 4
plebiscite, 4
political bandhs, 151, *see also* 'vai' (pejorative phrase for 'the outsider') bandh
polygamy, 132
Porcine Reproductive and Respiratory Syndrome (PRRS), 36
protests, 28, 53–55, 136–137, 151–152, 155, 158
Public Institutions and Services Act, 2002, 143

Rabha, Birubala, 131
rail links/networks, 27, 30, 40
Rajkumar, Wangcha, assassination of, 24
Ramakrishna Mission, 8–9, 120
Ramesh, Jairam, 51
Rashtriya Swayamsevak Sangh (RSS), 18, 86
Ravi, R.N., 145
Rawat, Jaswant Singh, 63
Rebecca, Mizo singer, 34
rebellion, xx, 16, 156
reconciliation, xxii, 155–156, 158
Regional Foreign Trade Authority, 42
Regional Institute of Medical Sciences (RIMS), 121
Reid, Robert, xviii
Reid Coupland Plan, xviii
resource allocation, 21
Richmond, William, 101

Rih Dil Lake, 36
Rime, Gumpe, 105
Rinpoche, Thegtse, 55
Rio, Neiphiu, 134
Rita, Tage, 97
rivers, 5, 24, 27, 30, 34–35, 48–50, 56, 58, 61, 63, 143; bamboo rafts over, 34; Barak, 27, 58; Brahmaputra, 27, 47–49, 52, 54, 56, 58, 61, 89; Kaladan, 30; Kameng, 55; Karnaphulli, 30, 34; Kushiara, 58; Lohit, 48, 54, 83; Luit, 48; Meghana, 58; Subansiri, 52, 81; Surma, 58; Teesta, 48, 56; Tiau, 35
Rojit Singh, Y., 111
Ronaldo Singh, L., 111
Royte, Robert Rommawia, 106–107
Ruchi Soya, 84
Rustomji, Nari, 8–9, 11, 13, 17, 59–60

Sadar Hills District Demand Committee (SHDCC), 151
Sangsiama, Lalrinngheti, 160–161
Sangthankima, 127
Santayana, George, 62
Sarkar, Manik, 26
Sarma, Himanta Biswa, 125, 154
Sarvodaya Samaj, 8
Schendel, Willem van, xvi
Scottish Giants Rangers Football Club, 108
Sethuraman, Lakshman, 125
settlement frontier logic, 16
Shakdher, Sham Lal, 17
Sharma, R.K., 111
Sharma, Sunder, 99
Shillong Accord of 1975, 19
Shillong Chamber Choir, 101
Shubhra Devi, Hanjabam, 98–99
Siddiqui, Nawazuddin, 73
Sikkim, 56–57, 64–66, 71, 75–77, 81, 86–87, 99, 101, 116–117, 119, 123; Dzongu reserve, 66; as organic state, 75–76; Pakyong in, 29; Rumtek monastery of , 64; Siliguiri in, 77; Tso Lhamo lake, 56
Sikkim Organic Mission, 76
Sikkim Organic Policy, 76
Silchar, xiv, 14, 123–124, 151
Silenced Rivers, McCully, 59
Singapore, 29, 37, 78
Singh, Balmiki Prasad, 16
Singh, Manmohan, 28, 53, 159
Singh, Niranjan, 92, 102
Singh, Okram Ibobi, 136
Singh, Renedy, 105
Skill India, 94
Smoky Falls Tribe Coffee, 98
spices, 76–77, 79–80, 98, *see also* herbs
Sports Authority of India (SAI), 108, 111

spousal violence, 131
S.S. Khaplang (K), 20
Strangers of the Mist by Hazarika, xxi
Sumi, Niki, 157
Surrendered ULFA (SULFA), 19
Suu Kyi, Aung San, 40
Swaraj, Sushma, 45
Swasth Assam, 124
Sylhet, 15
Syngkhong Rympei Thymmai (SRT), 130

Tabu, 96
Talukdar, Prashant, 102
Tamenglong, 79–80
Tapi, Tane, 67–68
Tata Football Academy (TFA), 105
Tata Trusts, 108, 124–125, 127
Tayeng, Oken, 71
Tea Board of India, 82
tea plantations, xviii; *see also* tourism
tea tribes, 72, 131, *see also* tribes
technology, xxii, 99, 120, 153, 159
Teesta-IV project, 56
Teesta-V project, 56
Teesta-VI project, 57
Teesta Urja Limited, 56
Thailand, xvi, 39, 42–43, 68, 71, 78, 125
Thangsing, Chinkholal, 128
3F, 84
Thutak Nunpuitu Team (TNT), 127–128
Tibet, xvi, 25, 29, 47, 49, 63, 75
Tibetans, 64
Tipaimukh multipurpose hydroelectric dam project, 58
Toal, Colin, 108
Tokyo Olympics, 110, 112
tourism, 26, 66–69, 72–73, 92; policy, 66, 73; rural, 71, 143; tea, 72–73
tourists, 23, 27, 62, 64–65, 67–68, 70, 152
trade, xxi, 8, 26, 30, 33, 35, 37, 39, 43–44, 138, 152; barter, 37, 44; formal, 37, 39, 43; infrastructure planning, 42
Trans-Arunachal highway, 29
trans-Asian railway project, 30
transparency, 142, 147–148, 152
tribalism, 154
tribes, 3, 6–13, 15, 18, 61, 69–70, 96, 104, 132, 135, 161; Angamis, 70, 154; Aos, 154; Bodos, 19, 131, 154; Bugun, 66; of central India, 11; Chakmas, 16, 34, 154; hill, xvii–xviii, 2, 15, 140, 154, 161; Hmars, 58, 154; identity pf, 104, 143; Nyishis, 67, 133; rights of, 10, 16, 51, 142; Tangkhuls, 154; Yobin, 28

Tripura, xix, 2, 15–16, 18, 26, 30, 107, 112, 116, 121, 125; Agartala, 30, 42, 112, 150; politics in, 154; riots of 1980, 18
Tuirial Hydro Electric Project in Mizoram, 57

UDAAN International, 29
Unbreakable, 104
United Liberation Front of Assam (ULFA), 19, 61, 85–86, 155
United National Liberation Fund (UNLF), 155
Unlawful Activities (Prevention) Act, 1967, 159
Unruly Hills, Karlsson, 163
U-Nu, 4
Uprising, 8888, 38

Vadhera, R.P., 92
'vai' (pejorative phrase for 'the outsider') bandh, xv
Vajpayee, Atal Bihari, 38, 50
Vietnam, xvi, 24, 43, 125
vigilante activism, 150
Vijayanagar, 27–28
village councils, 140, 142–143
violence, 20–21, 47, 89, 148, 151, 157; in Assam, 19, 155; in Manipur, 128; in Mizoram, 15; in Nagaland, 126
violent unrest, xx
Vision 2020, 28

Wakro Organic Green Tea, 82–83
Wanchoo Committee, 22
war 1965, 24
Wells, H.G., 78
Welsh-Calvinists, xvii
'Why We Travel', Iyer, 74
Winchester, Mary, kidnapping of, 34
women, xx–xxi, 72, 94, 96, 102, 109, 116, 119, 122–123, 125, 129–133, 137–139; Apatani women, 70; candidate of Nagaland, 136; in Mioram, xiv, 135; in politics, 130, 134, 136
World Bank Innovation Challenge, 115
World Commission of Dams, 51
World Weightlifting Championships at Anaheim, 110

Xi Jinping, 40

Young Mizo Association (YMA), xiv–xv, 14, 123, 150–151, 160–161
youth/youngsters, 28, 31, 35, 91, 93, 99–100, 104, 107, 111–112, 114, 159–160, 163; of rural, 32, 89, 94, 106, 161; educated, 93, 97; urban-educated, 32

YouthNet, 91
Youth Olympic Games in 2019, 110
Yunnan, annual trade across, 40–41

Zeliang, Jesmina, 94–96
Zeliangrong Nagas, 58
Zinta, Preity, 96
Zomia, xvi, 1
Zoramthanga, Pu, xix, 21, 107, 145, 156
Zoremsanga, Zico, 106

About the Author

Ashish Kundra is an Indian Administrative Service Officer of the 1996 batch from the Arunachal Pradesh, Goa, Mizoram Union Territory cadre. Over the last twenty-six years, he has served in various leadership roles in the governments of Chandigarh, Mizoram, Arunachal Pradesh, Daman, Dadra Nagar Haveli and New Delhi. He has also worked with the Union Minister of Commerce and Industry as his Private Secretary. Currently, he is working with the Delhi government as Principal Secretary, Transport, and is driving the transition to electric mobility in the national capital. He served in the Northeast for eight years, which was the source of inspiration for this book. An electronics engineer by training from IIT-BHU, Ashish also writes opinion pieces in national dailies on Northeast India.

30 Years *of*

HarperCollins *Publishers* India

At HarperCollins, we believe in telling the best stories and finding the widest possible readership for our books in every format possible. We started publishing 30 years ago; a great deal has changed since then, but what has remained constant is the passion with which our authors write their books, the love with which readers receive them, and the sheer joy and excitement that we as publishers feel in being a part of the publishing process.

Over the years, we've had the pleasure of publishing some of the finest writing from the subcontinent and around the world, and some of the biggest bestsellers in India's publishing history. Our books and authors have won a phenomenal range of awards, and we ourselves have been named Publisher of the Year the greatest number of times. But nothing has meant more to us than the fact that millions of people have read the books we published, and somewhere, a book of ours might have made a difference.

As we step into our fourth decade, we go back to that one word – a word which has been a driving force for us all these years.

Read.

